Introduction to Computer Data Representation

Peter Fenwick
The University of Auckland (Retired)
New Zealand

CONTENTS

Foreword

It is my great pleasure to recommend this excellent book written by my friend and colleague, Professor Peter Fenwick. During the eleven years I have known him, we have had many a discussion, often touching on topics covered here. Though this is the closest we have come to a collaboration I have little doubt that had we met earlier in our careers we would have collaborated extensively.

A major contribution of this book is to bring a historical perspective to many topics that are so widely accepted that it might not be obvious there were choices to be made. The binary representation of numbers was so obvious even in the 1940s that Burks, Goldstine and von Neumann are said to have "adopted it seemingly without discussion". But Burks *et al* considered floating point representation, then argued against supporting it. Long ago I heard it claimed that von Neumann believed any mathematician "worth his salt" should be able to specify floating point computations using only integers. In any case, floating point only came into its own in the 1980s, with the broad acceptance of the IEEE standards. Professor Fenwick shows great insight into why it took decades to get right something as basic as the representation of numbers.

A second important contribution is discussion of the introduction of redundancy to increase reliability in the presence of errors: check sums and variable-length (universal) codes. While simple check sums are frequently discussed, I know of no comparable source for a general discussion of Universal codes, an important but somewhat obscure subject.

I agree with Professor Fenwick's quote, that "everybody thinks they know" about these topics, but there are big holes, even today. Surely most of us have superficial knowledge that fails us when we really need to work through the details. This book covers a huge range of material, thoroughly and concisely. I have taught a good bit of the material, but I learned much, even in areas where I claim some expertise. The book displays a deep understanding of the many and varied requirements for digital representation of information, from the obvious integers and floating point, to Zeckendorf representations and Gray codes; from 2's complement to logarithmic arithmetic; from Elias and Levenstein codes to Rice and Golomb codes and on to Ternary Comma and Fibonacci codes.

In addition to the plethora of ways to represent numbers, it also covers representation of characters and strings. While the book will serve very well as a reference, it is also fascinating reading. Many pages are devoted to obscure topics, interesting largely because of their place in history, but outside the domain of a classic textbook on computer organization or architecture. These are perhaps the most important sections, precisely because they had to be understood and discarded to get us where we are now.

This book definitely does not qualify for the subtitle, "Data Representation for Dummies". While it quickly surveys common forms of representation, the pace and breadth will bewilder the true novice. On occasions, it uses terms unfamiliar (at least to an American), requiring another source. Appropriately, Professor Fenwick acknowledges the role of Wikipedia, which covers rather more topics than his book, but certainly not as coherently.

The author has a wry, if somewhat subtle, sense of humour which often surfaces unexpectedly: it's a bit of a stretch, but of course the description and figure regarding Gray codes include a "grey area"!

Discussion of the roles and interaction of precision, accuracy and range is superb. Floating point representation is highly precise, so why is it dangerous for use in financial calculations? Professor Fenwick points out something that had not occurred to me: a "quite ordinary calculator" is capable of more precise arithmetic than a 32-bit [IEEE single-precision] floating point computation. That explains why the calculator "app" on my iPad has both less range, and less precision, than the HP calculator I bought 35 years ago!

A topic rarely covered so clearly is "unwarranted precision", the process of using a precise mathematical operation to apparently increase accuracy (significant digits) of a number. Professor Fenwick points out confusion over precision created by the fact that the speed of light is so close to 300,000,000 metres per second—and the fact that scientific notation provides information about the accuracy of a value (pp. 106-107). I especially liked his discussion of the sins of the popular press, for example, by apparently increasing precision in the process of converting units: an altitude "10,000 feet"—accurate to, say, ±100 metres—becomes the apparently more precise, but inaccurate, "3 048 metres". It is unfortunate that the general level of this book is beyond comprehension for most journalists!

In short, this is a fascinating book that will appeal to many because of its authoritative exploration of how we represent information. But it will also serve as a reference for those requiring—or simply enjoying—the ability to choose efficient representations that lead to accurate results. It's a good read, and a great book to keep handy.

James R. Goodman, *United States of America*
Fellow IEEE, Fellow ACM, 2013 Eckert-Mauchly Award

PREFACE

This book arose from lectures on data representation given to first year Computer Science students at the University of Auckland. But then it grew as I realised that ever-more material seemed relevant, useful, or just interesting. To a large extent it reflects my own journey through computing from about 1964–2004, starting from logic design, through computer hardware, computer arithmetic and data communications into, finally, data compression. Thus the computers that I reference are largely those with which I have at least passing experience. (There are of course many others that I have not encountered, but few of these are mentioned.) And the footnotes and asides often come from personal experience; many are distant recollections which I cannot now attribute.

A comment made by one person who read this book was "This is an area that everybody thinks they know, but really nobody really knows very well". While most elementary Computer Science books certainly describe some data representation (usually restricted to current "best practice"), and other books give great detail of specialised topics such as floating point, there seems to be a great gap in the middle. It is this gap, giving reasonable coverage of most data types from first principles, that I hope this book supplies.

It deals mostly with data at the architectural level, with no mention of the trees, lists etc as normally covered in Data Structures courses. The main exception here is the description of text strings – characters are of little interest in isolation; strings are the usual entity to be manipulated and are often regarded as a data primitive. It also includes a comprehensive coverage of variable-length integer representations and of checksums, both topics which seem to have little overall coverage in the general literature.

Peter Fenwick
The University of Auckland, New Zealand (retired) email : pmbjfw@gmail.com

Acknowledgements

The book was started while I was employed at the University of Auckland, but with no explicit support.

I acknowledge the assistance from Brian Hicks and Murray Johns who, many years ago, introduced me to computers, and some of whose insights are still present in this book. Bob Doran, Amos Omondi and Brian Carpenter read early drafts and suggested valuable extra topics. Assistance was also received from Prof F.P. Brooks, Dr R.F. Rice and Jørgen Ibsen. Special thanks go to Jim Goodman who provided many useful comments while preparing the Foreword. And last but not least Brenda, who has endured many years (probably far too many!) of "The Book".

Conflicts of Interest

There are no conflicts of interest.

Introduction and Overview

The Background

"My first computer", in 1964, was an IBM 1620 with all of 20 000 decimal digits (10k characters) of $20\mu s$ memory and a Floating Multiply time of 10ms (yes, 10 milliseconds. A division took 50ms and you could see it on the panel lights.). By contrast, a modest current desktop computer might be larger/faster by perhaps 1 million times. (The 1620 had no external storage, but a computer which replaced it in 1967 had a 1 Mbyte disk cartridge, which has perhaps a similar relation to modern storage capacities.) While in those early computers time was important (after all you could, usually, just wait longer), a very real problem was memory. All too often the algorithm or data structure was decided more by memory efficiency than by computational speed. (And memory was expensive, say 10s of cents per byte in 1960s currency, or several dollars in 2013, so you seldom had much available.)

Thus it was often essential to know just how data was actually held, especially if there was a lot of it[1]. "Good" programmers were keenly aware of the detailed structure of records and other data structures. These matters really "hit home" to me in the late 1990s, when I was teaching an introductory Computer Science course and had to change from Pascal to Java. The details of data storage and representation just vanished into the mysteries of Classes and such, buried under layers of abstraction; I suddenly realised that much of my years (decades?) of hard-won knowledge and skills were largely obsolete.

At about the same time, I also realised that too many books presented data representation as "This the way it is, and nothing else is important". Clearly this is wrong and much can be learnt from why things once-popular

---

[1]The word "data", while strictly the plural of "datum" will be treated here as a singular "noun of multitude", following a widely-accepted usage. The plural form "data are" may be used where the individual components are identifiable and important.

became unwanted and ignored. This book therefore looks at some of these topics, comparing them with current practice. So, mingled among the technical material is assorted history, partly because I find it interesting, partly because I think it should be better known, and partly because much seems to be getting lost. Many chapters start with a brief history in the introduction, followed by a more detailed history at the end or in Chapter 11 (where it is less intrusive).

But a word of warning here. The history as given is really no more than a "best effort". What appears to be a definitive statement by one authority is all too easily contradicted by another, equally reputable, authority. So this text is, I hope, correct in general outline, if not in detail. If you are spurred to further investigation and find conflicts, well, that just seems to be the nature of the subject. The history of science and technology has many examples of inventions or discoveries made before their time and then forgotten, made simultaneously when the time is ripe, or finally attributed to a more influential person. Examples of all of these will be found here.

A complication since this book was started has been the development of Wikipedia. Much of the material here will be found in Wikipedia, often to much greater depth but spread across separate entries. Thus the two are, I hope, complementary rather than competitive; where they differ I can only (against my fond hopes) defer to its collective wisdom. But the material of Wikipedia is so pervasive that I have seldom given explicit reference to it—just assume that it is always there, in the background.

Finally, long decimal numbers and fractions are written "European style" (123 456) rather than "English style" (123,456), but with a point or period (.), rather than a comma(,) to separate integer and fraction. Dates and other 4-digit numbers are written without the separator, as 2013.

And, post-finally, my background makes the language of this book more akin to "British English" than "American English". I have tried my best to remove confusions, but please remember the variously-attributed statement that "Americans and British are two peoples divided by a common language".

The Chapter Contents

I conclude this introduction with a brief description of each of the other chapters.

Chapter 1 gives a general history of numbers and computers.

Chapter 2 introduces binary representations including conversion between number bases, especially binary and decimal. It then proceeds to a very brief introduction to decimal coding, a topic which is expanded upon in Section 11.7. (Parts of this chapter, in particular, reflect the origin of the text as an introductory course. Advanced readers may find the descriptions somewhat laboured.)

Chapter 3 introduces signed representations, mixed base number representations, and some other representations.

Chapter 4 deals with basic arithmetic (addition and subtraction), bits and their manipulation (logical operations, shifts and field operations). General arithmetic is deferred until Chapter 5.

Chapter 5 gives an overview of computer arithmetic, describing methods of performing and accelerating addition, multiplication and division.

Chapter 6 describes floating-point representations, covering the basic requirements and emphasising the IEEE 754 standard, but with discussion also of other important representations. Examples illustrate requirements for range, precision and rounding.

Chapter 7 is a brief description of logarithmic number representations, a representation which is different and sometimes useful as in signal processing.

Chapter 8 describes characters, briefly giving their historical development (EBCDIC and ASCII) and text strings. It continues to MIME encodings and Unicode (with UTF-8 and UTF-7). There is brief mention of character coding as required for Internet Internationalized Domain Names. A more complete coverage of character history is given later in Section 11.6.

Chapter 9 reflects my own interest in variable-length codes for the integers. In general these representations allow frequent values to be held in few bits, and are "self-delimiting" needing no auxiliary information to show their boundaries in a bit stream. There are few comprehensive accounts of these representations.

(This chapter is a revision of an earlier publication [87, Chap 3], and is reproduced here by permission of Elsevier.)

Chapter 10 is a discussion of checksums and simpler error-control codes. As with Chapter 9, the original material is scattered far and wide and

I think it deserves to be collected. While perhaps removed from the general emphasis of the book, it is an important topic.

Chapter 11 This is essentially a collection of miscellaneous topics which expand on material given in the preceding chapters. Some are history (see the above comments), others are important points which seem to be seldom discussed, while others are, well, interesting. The following is a list of the section numbers within the chapter.

11.1 A history of numbers.

11.2 Why use bits, 0 or 1?

11.3 What makes a "good" number representation?

11.4 The origin of "bit", "byte" and "word".

11.5 What do we *really* mean by "kilobyte", "Megabyte", *etc*?

11.6 A history of character codes

11.7 More on codes for decimal numbers

11.8 Variations on Roman numbers.

11.9 Scaling invariance.

Chapter 12 An overview of what has been said and its possible relationship to future computing.

Chapter 1

Numbers and Computers

Abstract: We start with the basic ideas of "numbers" and "counting" and how the concepts and requirements differ with different levels of technical and administrative sophistication. This is followed by a brief summary of the development of calculating devices, to the structure of the "von Neumann" computer. Finally, we introduce the requirements of a computer, the importance of memory and an overview of data storage within that memory.

Keywords: Concept of "number", development of calculation, Babbage analytical engine, Babbage Difference Engine, Colossus, ENIAC, von Neumann, underlying technology, data in memory.

1.1   Numbers

The concept of number, or of counting, appears to be inherent in human nature, and is arguably present even in some animals. Most societies were able to specify and count up to a few hundred objects, with number systems that were often descriptive rather than computational. While there was often a clear concept of quantities such as "ten", "hundred" and "thousand", (and few people needed much beyond that) the representation of values in most literate societies was ill-suited to calculation[1]. An excellent example is found in Roman

---

[1]It is said that in one "primitive" society an early European visitor reported "they even have words for thousands and millions!" A later, more numerate, visitor reported that these "large numbers" were actually increasingly rude words, as the original respondent grew ever-more annoyed with the pointless questions.

numbers, with quite different symbols for "five tens", "five hundreds" and "five thousands". Computation with representations such as these is decidedly non-trivial. More information on the history of number representation is given in Section **11.1**.

A very few societies developed number systems which allowed precise description of very large values. Such number systems arose mainly for religious reasons, such as among the Hindus and Maya, or where societies such as the Chinese or Egyptians administered large populations. The ability to combine or manipulate numbers to give precise results (what we would now call "arithmetic") is much rarer than counting or enumeration. Arithmetic, beyond the simple addition of small numbers, developed only in high civilisations which needed good land measurements, prediction of astronomical events such as solstices or eclipses, accounting for commerce, or for taxation.

With most numbering systems, computation of any complexity was a considerable skill, the preserve of an elite. To illustrate the difficulty of "classical" arithmetic even in the 15th and 16th centuries, Ifrah [61] gives the following anecdote.

> A wealthy German merchant, seeking to provide his son with a good business education, consulted a learned man as to which European institution offered the best training. "If you want him to be able to cope with addition and subtraction," the expert replied, "then any French or German university will do. But if you are intent on your son going on to multiplication and division—assuming that he has sufficient gifts—then you will have to send him to Italy."

Even though decimal numbers were introduced into Europe in the 13th century, it took 200–300 years for them to be accepted. Much of this delay has been ascribed to the numerate clerks seeking to retain their skilled and privileged positions (with arcane secrets), much as occurred with the craft guilds.

Aids to computation were therefore important, one of the best being the abacus, or its variants such as the soroban. The abacus has the great advantage that its pictorial view of the number is largely independent of local representational idiosyncrasies. It demands only a decimal representation (but it is not difficult to use an abacus for octal arithmetic). The abacus is still an important calculating device; where data entry times predominate (as in sequences of additions and subtractions) it is competitive in speed with electronic calculators.

1.2   Calculating Machines

Machines for performing simple arithmetic appeared in the 17th century; the first was designed by Wilhelm Schickard about 1623, but its details have only recently been rediscovered [88, p182]. Pascal in 1642 described a calculator which could add and subtract, while Leibnitz in 1683 had one (based on Schickard's design) which could also multiply and divide. But the ideas were far beyond the available technology and commercial calculators did not appear until late in the 19th century. Many of the principles had been developed by Babbage in the 1820s with, first his Difference Engine, and later the Analytical Engine[2]. A calculator based on Babbage's ideas was produced in 1855 by Scheutz, in Stockholm. If the Difference Engine anticipated the practical mechanical calculator, the Analytical Engine anticipated the stored-program computer.

The late 19th century saw the development of cash registers and similar devices, leading ultimately to the accounting machines of 50 years later. Another important development at this time was the use of punched cards by Hermann Hollerith in processing the 1886 United States census. Punched cards had then been in use for a century in controlling Jacquard looms; Hollerith used them instead as data storage[3].

During the first quarter of the 20th century then the possibility of using machines for computation and other data processing was becoming established. Adding machines and cash registers were accepted and ever-more complex accounting and tabulating machines were being developed. The idea of automatic control of computation had been around for a century, even if it had been largely forgotten. Within the period of about 1920–1945 several other developments occurred, many apparently unrelated but all leading in some way to successful electronic computers. The list here is not exhaustive, but is intended rather as a brief outline of developments relating to electronic computation. An excellent collection of early papers relating to computers has been assembled by Randell [82].

---

[2]It has been observed that when Babbage started work on his calculating machines the most complex machinery on most British Royal Navy ships (apart from the chronometer) was the anchor windlass. His workshop had accordingly to develop precision tools and metal working machines just to build his designs. The resulting workshop machinery and practice was the real immediate benefit of his work.

[3]The use of programmed/programmable devices may be far, far older. There are reports that in the 1st century BC, automata in Alexandria used a drum with pegs. The drum was wound with a cord which alternated its direction by wrapping around suitable pegs so that a constant pull on the cord translated into alternating rotations of the drum. Combining several such devices could give quite complex movements.

- As referred to above, commercial card processing equipment developed complex computation facilities and associated card reading, writing and printing equipment. Comrie for example was able to take commercial equipment and build with it a "computing laboratory" in which each machine performed simple predetermined operations. Information was transferred (by people) between machines according to predetermined rules to achieve quite complex operations.

- Automatic telephone exchanges provided reliable logical operations, which were often very complex. For example, in an Ericsson telephone exchange of 1929 an incoming call was passed to one of a pool of "registers". The chosen register accepted the dialled digits and stored them while controlling a complex electromechanical switch and searching for a suitable path towards the called number; this switch worked in a base-500 number system. When the call was established, the register unit disconnected and became available for another call, leaving the call maintenance and disconnection to a relatively simple relay set. There are clear parallels to many modern computer-controlled switching systems with centralised control and distributed switching.

- In 1936 Turing produced his theoretical paper on the principles of computability and postulated a universal computing machine [104].

- In 1936 Konrad Zuse patented his Z-1 computer [113] which, while mechanical, was nevertheless capable of automatic computation.

- In 1938 Atanasoff and Berry at the University of Iowa started work on an electronic calculator for the solution of linear equations. It was not, in modern terms, a computer as it had no conditional execution, but has a firm (though debatable) place in the history of computing. There are reports that this computer was used for code-breaking from 1942.

- Also in 1938, Shannon took the mathematics of logic developed by Boole a hundred years earlier and applied it to the design of telephone exchanges and similar large logical devices [89].

- The early 1940s saw the development of some significant relay computers such as those at the Bell System Laboratories and at Harvard University. These machines introduced techniques such as remote access by teleprinter, error-detecting circuitry, floating-point arithmetic and conditional execution.

- From the 1920s electronic devices had been used as high speed counters to 10s of thousands of counts per second in nuclear physics laboratories.

- The development of electronic high definition television in the 1930s spurred the further development of pulse techniques and of the wide bandwidth amplifiers which were later needed for radar and computers.

- The maturity of radar in the 1940s combined pulse and wideband electronics in devices of unprecedented complexity. By the end of the Second World War the ideas of "microsecond pulses" and even "megaHertz clocks" (then actually "megacycle clocks") were familiar to many people outside research laboratories.

- The ability of radar to detect ever faster aircraft led to a need for anti-aircraft guns to have predictors which could aim a shell at where the aircraft, travelling at hundreds of feet per second, might be 10 to 20 seconds after the shell was fired. The combination of the three dimensional aircraft track and shell ballistics quickly outgrew the simple but ingenious electromechanical predictors, and workers such as Rajchman saw the need for electronic computation.

- Simple theory relates the range of a cannon to its muzzle velocity and angle of elevation. More complete theory requires allowance for air resistance, shell spin, latitude and bearing (for Coriolis forces) and even barrel wear. The computation of artillery firing tables was an enormous task and one that led directly to the ENIAC computer, completed in 1945. ENIAC used plug-boards for instructions, and stored data in 20 "accumulators" each holding 10 decimal digits with 10 flip-flops per digit. The accumulators were also arithmetic elements. It was not programmable in the "von Neumann" sense.

- Cryptanalysis of German and Japanese codes was a major factor in deciding the outcome of the Second World War. Cryptanalytical machinery was initially electromechanical, but the British series of "Colossus" [42] machines (to break the German Lorenz cipher, and *not* the Enigma ciphers, and operating from 1943) were electronic and clearly presaged computers. The later versions of Colossus used pipelining and similar techniques decades before they appeared in general computers.

- The Manchester Mark I computer ran the first computer program, calculating Mersenne primes on the night of 16/17 June 1949, running without error for 9 hours.

1.3 Computers

By 1945 many developments had converged and the development of electronic computers was almost inevitable. If those people normally associated with the "invention" of the computer had not done so, others surely would have succeeded and not long afterwards. In many respects ENIAC (Electronic Numerical Integrator and Calculator, often recognised as the first electronic computer, though not really programmable, but see "Colossus" above) was as much a psychological triumph as an engineering masterpiece. At a time when very few devices had even 18 vacuum tubes (or valves), ENIAC had nearly 18 000! It took enormous faith to even consider that that many devices might work reliably together[4]. Many of the thoughts from the early ENIAC design were collected in a report by Burks, Goldstine and von Neumann [17] which laid out the principles which have been followed by most subsequent computers and were at the time intended as proposals towards the EDVAC computer. The "von Neumann" computer from this report is characterised by several separate functional units, as shown in Figure **1.1**.

1. An arithmetic or computation unit, which accepts numbers, manipulates them according to the accepted rules of arithmetic and delivers the result for later use.

2. A control unit which interprets "instructions" for data manipulation and transfer. Most instructions combine an "operation" (what should be done) with one or more operands (what the operation should be applied to).

3. A "memory" (or "store") which holds both data and instructions as patterns of bits for use by both the arithmetic unit and the control unit.

4. Devices for reading external data into the computer ("input") and presenting data from the computer ("output"). Suggested devices included keyboards, devices for punched cards and paper tape, magnetic tape and cathode-ray tube displays.

Except for the store, holding both instructions and data, this reflects the internal structure of ENIAC.

---

[4]As several tubes failed every time ENIAC was turned on, the whole machine was turned off as little as possible. ENIAC providentially provided excellent case studies in vacuum tube failure modes.

Figure 1.1: The Units of the von Neumann Computer.

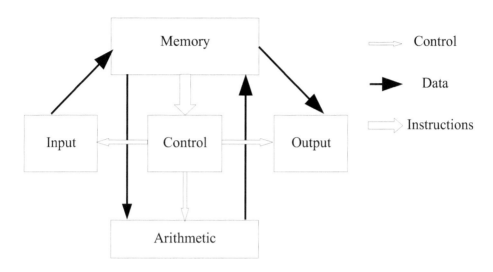

To a large extent though the von Neumann computer was shaped by the development of "random access storage" of a reasonable size and cost. ENIAC stored data in twin-triode flip-flops; at 100 bits per number, 5–10 Watts per bit and probably \$10 per bit (in 1940s currency) storage was a rare and expensive resource. The Burks report proposed a data storage or "memory" based on "Selectron" cathode ray storage devices, with 40 tubes each able to store 4096 bits of information, to a total of about 160 000 bits.

It was realised that with each of the 4096 40-bit words in memory being either data or instructions there was really no distinction between data and instructions. A "word" in memory was data if interpreted by the arithmetic unit and instructions if interpreted by the control unit. The important result was that a word could be first manipulated as data and then executed as an instruction. With appropriate programming discipline, the computer could use present data conditions to modify its future actions, as described in the next section.

Many lessons were learnt from ENIAC, so many that it established a firm computing precedent of being obsolete long before it was completed. The Burks, Goldstine, von Neumann report is fascinating reading. In between numerous diversions into engineering and implementation details, it looks ahead to much modern computing, including magnetic storage and graphical displays, anticipating many (even most) aspects of modern computers.

Unfortunately, although there is no doubt as to the putative authors of this report, there is considerable doubt concerning the provenance of its ideas. These problems are described by McCartney [72] and Stern [92]. They arose largely because the report was written as an internal working document and lacked the references and attribution of ideas which are assumed in the scientific literature. While the concepts may be accurate, the lack of attribution implies that the authors developed them, singly or in concert. However, many of the ideas were apparently beyond the expertise of the authors. In particular, Eckert claimed that he himself developed the idea of a stored program computer in 1944 while developing a delay line memory for radar applications; this claim is supported by eyewitnesses but not acknowledged by Burks *et al.* Although the term "von Neumann computer" is apparently an egregious misnomer, its use is sanctified by custom and is accepted here.

1.4   What Makes a Computer?

Although a computer has been often regarded as a glorified calculator, it can clearly do much more than a calculator. What really distinguishes the two? Here it is asserted that a device is *computer* if it has both of the following attributes, and is a *calculator* if it lacks either or both.

Data-dependent instruction sequence. This is the traditional mark of a computer – "If it has an *if* statement it must be a computer". Recognition of the need for conditional execution is usually attributed to Ada Augusta, Countess Lovelace, in connection with Babbage's Analytical Engine. She is also credited with the invention of the programmed loop (which *must* include a conditional branch)[5]. Note that although most programmed calculators are computers by this criterion, they fail by the second one.

Data-dependent data selection. While in a formal sense, data dependent instruction sequencing is all that is needed, its deficiencies become all too apparent even in a simple example such as summing the positive members of a sequence of values or taking the product of two matrices. Data-dependent data selection allows existing values to determine, not

---

[5]The designers of one of the first very fast computers had designed very efficient arithmetic hardware which assumed no conditional branching. When the design was almost complete the engineers were aghast to discover that most loops are closed by a conditional branch ...

the choice of subsequent operations as above, but the actual data to be used in those calculations. It is most obviously seen in array subscripts, as in `array[subsc]` and similar constructs on which so much of modern computing depends. It is less obviously seen in subroutine mechanisms and pointers, which are equally at the heart of modern computing.

In the simplest and most obvious method instructions are genuinely treated as data, with addresses and even operations subject to manipulation. Although such use is at least deprecated in modern computers if not actually forbidden, instruction modification was widely used in some early computers. The same effect is now achieved by techniques such as index registers and indirect addressing which leave the instructions inviolate in memory.

1.5   Development of Memory

The importance of storage or memory capacity to computers has been mentioned above, in connection with the development of EDVAC and later computers from ENIAC; the availability of much larger and much less expensive data storage meant that completely new concepts (such as the stored program) could be introduced. This trend has continued with main storage capacities increasing from a few kilobytes (delay and CRT memories until mid 1950s), to megabytes (magnetic core memories (1955–1980) and now to gigabytes (semiconductor memories, from about 1970). The trend in main storage capacities has been paralleled by increases in the sizes of disk and similar "backing" or "mass" storage devices, with disk capacity often being 100–1000 times the capacity of the main store.

Data storage was once a *very* rare and expensive resource which had to be husbanded very carefully. Algorithms and programming techniques often emphasised economy of space rather than execution speed. This situation has now changed completely; memory is often regarded as a resource of negligible cost and limitless capacity, with programming techniques changing accordingly.

This trend is indeed one of the incentives behind the writing of this book; it used to be that programmers were of necessity very much aware of how and where data is held in the computer. With current trends such as Object-Oriented programming, the hardware data may be several levels of abstraction removed from what the programmer manipulates. While this might be not an altogether bad thing, there are times when programmers should be aware of how information is really held to recognise limitations of data representations and perhaps avoid especially inefficient techniques.

1.6   Data in Memory

Data in most computers is organised, or considered, in a hierarchy of different-sized aggregates—bits, bytes and words and sometimes other units such as "short words" or "long words". While any one of these units may be used as the addressable entity, most modern computers address to an 8-bit byte. A short history of these terms is given in Section **11.4**.

bit A bit, short for "binary digit" is the fundamental unit of data storage in all modern computers, and leads naturally to using a binary number system. Section **11.2** discusses reasons for using bits.

A single bit can represent the *numerical* values 0 and 1. It can also represent the *logical* values FALSE and TRUE, conventionally written also as 0 and 1. These aspects are also discussed in Section **11.2**.

byte While the term "byte" now always means a unit of 8 bits, it originally meant any contiguous group of bits within a word, equivalent to a "field" of bits.

IBM adopted a uniform 8-bit byte for their 7030 (Stretch) computer and retained that usage for the System/360 in 1964. The widespread adoption of the S/360 computers led to the general acceptance of an 8-bit byte.

word A "word" is conventionally some larger unit of data storage and in many older computers is the unit of addressing. Other than that a word is an aggregate of bits (and more recently of bytes), there is no agreement on the size of a word. Sizes from representative computers known to the author are given in Table **1.1**. (There are certainly other word lengths, but the list is limited to computers with which the author has at least a passing acquaintance.)

There is a wide variation of "word" sizes; a word is precisely what the machine designer says it is (shades of Humpty-Dumpty in Alice in Wonderland!).

In current usage a "word" often means the unit of internal data transfer between memory and CPU; it therefore becomes a reflection of the hardware implementation rather than the programmer-visible architecture.

Table 1.1: Word Lengths of Some Computers

word size (bits)	computers
12	PDP-8
16	most mini computers
18	PDP-7, PDP-9
24	ICL 1900
32	IBM S/360, most RISC computers
36	Univac 1108, IBM 7090, DEC-10
39	Elliot 503, 803
48	Burroughs B6700, ICL Atlas, CDC 3600
60	CDC 6600
64	Cray

nibble A collection of 4 bits is sometimes called a "nibble". Data General apparently introduced the term for their Nova computer in 1968, where 16-bit words were processed in units of 4 bits.

The "Memory" of a computer is now usually a numbered set of "bytes". (Older computers were usually addressed by words or very occasionally by bits, as in the IBM Stretch or Burroughs B1700.) For a "1 Gigabyte" memory the numbers, or "addresses", range from 0 to about 1 000 000 000 (actually 1 073 741 823). Each address identifies one unique byte out of the 1 billion (or whatever is the memory size).

A very important point (it is difficult to over-emphasise it) is that a pattern of bits in memory is just a pattern of bits—no more and no less—with no intrinsic meaning at all. Its meaning depends entirely on how we (the programmer) or the computer interprets it. Thus a group of 32 bits may be

- four 8-bit characters
- one 32-bit integer
- one 32-bit instruction
- one 32-bit address
- two 16-bit integers
- one 16 bit integer, one 8-bit integer, and one 8-bit character, *etc* ...

The meaning depends entirely on its use by the computer, a concept which is at the heart of the von Neumann computer model.

Send Orders for Reprints to reprints@benthamscience.net

Chapter 2

Binary and Other Representations

Abstract: The initial idea of "number" leads quickly to the need to *represent* numbers and then *manipulate* numbers. We emphasise the representation as the terms of polynomial in some *base* and especially "binary numbers" (to base 2) and "decimal numbers" (to base 10). This leads into conversion between bases and the representation of fractions in binary.

Keywords: Polynomial Representation, Binary, octal and hexadecimal representations, base conversion by arithmetic, base conversion by table lookup.

2.1   Introduction

As computers are obviously meant to "compute" or, in popular terms, to work with numbers, there equally obviously must be some way of representing numbers within the computer. This chapter deals with the representation of numbers, in some sense paralleling the development of European mathematics. It starts with the positive integers (the "natural" numbers) and then proceeds to the "less natural" negative numbers and fractions.[1] The computer equivalents of the "irrational" real numbers will be deferred until Chapter **6**.

---

[1]Strictly the fractions are always of the form $N/2^i$, with a value between 0 and 1.

Chapter **11** has several sections related to this chapter including the history of numbers (Section **11.1**), reasons for using binary (Section **11.2**), and various other topics.

In dealing with numbers it is important to distinguish between the *value* or the measure of its quantity and the *representation* of the value. In customary usage the value and its representation are often confused, especially as we normally use decimal numbers for both, but the difference will become apparent when we give both the *value* (usually in decimal, for *us*) and its *representation* (often binary, for the *computer*)[2]. The distinction between the value and the representation is especially marked with Roman numbers.

A "useful" representation usually consists of a string of digits, with an associated base, written as $ddd\ldots dd_b$; the base b is usually omitted if it is 10. As almost all representations are equivalent to regarding these visible digits as coefficients of some (implicit) polynomial, it is appropriate to start by considering general polynomial representations.

2.2   Polynomial Number Representation

With a base b, we will usually represent values as a sequence of digits, for example $(d_{n-1}, d_{n-2}, \ldots, d_1, d_0)$. The number is then written as $ddd\ldots dd_b$, with b usually omitted if $b = 10$. A value N with base b and n digits is given by

$$N = d_{n-1}b^{n-1} + d_{n-2}b^{n-2} + \ldots + d_1 b + d_0$$

The value is represented by a polynomial in the base, with the digits of the visible representation being the coefficients of the polynomial. Each coefficient d_i is in the range $0 \leq d_i < b$, but note that the powers increase from *right to left* for integers, the opposite from the normal left to right increase for a power series.

The two simplest, and basic, cases of decimal and binary are conveniently treated together to emphasise their essential similarity. Extensions to any other base should be obvious, but are seldom needed.

---

[2]The term "binary number" will often be used as a technical equivalent to the more correct "binary representation of the number", following accepted, though careless, practise. Likewise for "decimal numbers" and some other representations that will be introduced.

2.2.1   Decimal and Binary Representations

This section initially assumes arithmetic in base 10 because we are familiar with it; it will be seen later as the current example of an *arithmetic base.*

Decimal representations If the number base is 10, things aren't very interesting. A decimal number such as 56 432 just means, working in decimal

$$5 \times 10^4 + 6 \times 10^3 + 4 \times 10^2 + 3 \times 10 + 2.$$

Binary number representations In base 2 though, and doing the arithmetic in our familiar base 10, the value 10101_2 is

$$1 \times 2^4 + 0 \times 2^3 + 1 \times 2^2 + 0 \times 2^1 + 1 \times 2^0 = 16 + 4 + 1 = 21$$

Table 2.1: Small Powers of 2

	Binary (to 13 bits)	Decimal		Decimal
2^0	...0 0000 0000 0001	1	2^{12}	4096
2^1	...0 0000 0000 0010	2	2^{13}	8192
2^2	...0 0000 0000 0100	4	2^{14}	16 384
2^3	...0 0000 0000 1000	8	2^{15}	32 768
2^4	...0 0000 0001 0000	16	2^{16}	65 536
2^5	...0 0000 0010 0000	32	2^{17}	131 072
2^6	...0 0000 0100 0000	64	2^{18}	262 144
2^7	...0 0000 1000 0000	128	2^{19}	524 288
2^8	...0 0001 0000 0000	256	2^{20}	1 048 576
2^9	...0 0010 0000 0000	512	2^{21}	2 097 152
2^{10}	...0 0100 0000 0000	1024	2^{22}	4 194 304
2^{11}	...0 1000 0000 0000	2048	2^{23}	8 388 608

So to convert a binary number to decimal we can write, in decimal, the values of the powers of 2 corresponding to 1s in the binary representation and add these powers together—the obvious evaluation of the polynomial. To do that, we need the powers of 2, as in Table **2.1**. These should be learnt, certainly up to $2^8 = 256$ and preferably up to $2^{16} = 65\,536$.

2.2.2 Octal and Hexadecimal Integers

While values can be written and used in any convenient base, bases of 8 and 16 have a very special relationship with binary[3]. Because $8 = 2^3$, bits can be collected in threes and each group regarded as a single base-8 or octal digit. Similarly, because $16 = 2^4$, groups of 4 bits can be combined to form base-16 or hexadecimal digits (*not* "hexidecimal").

Octal values lie in the range $0-7$ and may be represented by the conventional decimal digits. Hexadecimal values have the range $0-15$; while values up to 9 can be represented by the corresponding decimal digits, we need other "digits" for the values from 10 to 15. By general convention these values or bit combinations are represented by the six letters 'A' ... 'F'. Many systems allow the lower-case letters 'a' ... 'f' as alternative digits.[4] Equivalences between binary, octal and hexadecimal are shown in Table **2.2**.

Table 2.2: Binary to Octal and Hexadecimal.

octal		hexadecimal		hexadecimal	
bits	digit	bits	digit	bits	digit
000	0	0000	0	1000	8
001	1	0001	1	1001	9
010	2	0010	2	1010	A
011	3	0011	3	1011	B
100	4	0100	4	1100	C
101	5	0101	5	1101	D
110	6	0110	6	1110	E
111	7	0111	7	1111	F

Octal and hexadecimal are often thought of as just ways of rewriting binary, and the conversion is normally done by inspection. When octal digits are being converted to binary, they must be always written out as 3 bits, with leading zeros added to complete a group of three if necessary. Similarly a hexadecimal digit always yields 4 bits, with binary values "padded out" to a multiple of 4 bits if necessary. The binary value $10\,1101\,0011\,0100_2$ expands to $0010\,1101\,0011\,0100_2$ and is written in hexadecimal as $2D34_{16}$.

---

[3]The Merriam-Webster dictionary©2013 states that the term "octal" was first used in 1948 and "hexadecimal" in 1954. But the ideas of base 8 numbers, and even the term octal may be far, far, older. (See Wikipedia entries for *Octal* and *Hexadecimal*).

[4]The author has seen other systems, such as U...Z instead of A...F.

Using hexadecimal (or octal) eases the problem that pure binary numbers have so many digits that they are often difficult to handle. For example

$$123\,456\,789 = 0111010110111100110100010101_2 = 75bcd15_{16}$$

The hexadecimal representation is much easier to think about than the equivalent binary. (Sequences of more than 7 or 8 digits or other unrelated objects are usually very difficult for people to remember.)

Octal, and especially hexadecimal, representations are almost always used for values where the bit configuration is more important than the numerical value.

When converting binary integers to hexadecimal, start at the right and count off groups of 4 bits, filling out with high-order zeros as needed. (For octal, count in groups of 3 bits from the right.)

For example, with the "fill" bits shown as leading subscripts –
hex 1010111010110 $\rightarrow$ $_{000}$1 0101 1101 0110 = 1 5 D 6, and
oct 1010111010110 $\rightarrow$ $_{00}$1 010 111 010 110 = 1 2 7 2 6

If converting between octal and hexadecimal (or vice versa) it is usually best to expand out to binary as an intermediate value, with 4 octal digits always corresponding to 3 hexadecimal digits and then re-group these intermediate bits. Here is an example of an octal to hexadecimal conversion –

Octal	5			6			4			5		
Convert to binary	1	0	1	1	1	0	1	0	0	1	0	1
regroup bits	1	0	1	1	1	0	1	0	0	1	0	1
Hexadecimal	B			A			5					

All of the algorithms given here for base conversion may use octal or hexadecimal to reduce the amount of arithmetic, with the result then converted to binary if needed. (Octal conversion is often more convenient for manual calculation, simply because people are more familiar with the 8-times table than with the 16-times table.)

To convert 237 to binary, using octal arithmetic

$$
\begin{array}{r}
8)237 \quad + 5 \text{ rem} \\
\overline{8)29} \quad + 5 \text{ rem} \\
\overline{8)3} \quad + 3 \text{ rem} \\
\overline{0}
\end{array}
$$

The octal representation is 355_8 which in binary gives 11 101 101

To convert 237 to binary, using hexadecimal arithmetic

$$
\begin{array}{ll}
16\overline{)237} & + \ 13 \ \text{rem} = \text{D}_{16} \\
\quad 16\overline{)14} & + \ 14 \ \text{rem} = \text{E}_{16} \\
\qquad 0 &
\end{array}
$$

The hexadecimal representation is ED_{16} which in binary gives 1110 1101 (the same bits as before, but divided differently).

In Java and C hexadecimal constants are denoted by a leading "0x", so that 0xcafe (or 0xCAFE) corresponds to the bits 1100 1010 1111 1110. The hexadecimal digits themselves may use either upper-case or lower-case letters.

2.3   Converting Integers Between Bases

In converting between bases we must perform arithmetic in some base, which it is convenient to call the *arithmetic* base. When doing manual or personal calculation the arithmetic base is usually 10. With computers, working close to the hardware, the arithmetic base is usually 2 but, when working on computers in a high-level language which does not really support binary arithmetic, it may be more convenient to retain 10 as the arithmetic base—it is after all the way we usually think. The material to follow essentially expands and formalises the methods given earlier in section **2.2**.

2.3.1   Conversion Into the Arithmetic Base

There are two ways of converting into the arithmetic base, based on the two different ways of evaluating the polynomial. The first assumes that we know the powers of the base. We multiply each of the powers by its appropriate digit and add the values, as was done earlier –

$$1 \times 2^4 + 0 \times 2^3 + 1 \times 2^2 + 0 \times 2^1 + 1 = 16 + 4 + 1 = 21$$

But if a polynomial is to be evaluated on a computer the recommended technique is to factorise it in a way which minimises the total amount of arithmetic and eliminates the need to raise the variable (here the base) to many different powers.

$$\ldots + ax^4 + bx^3 + cx^2 + dx + e = ((((\ldots a)x + b)x + c)x + d)x + e$$

The usual conversion algorithm implements this polynomial evaluation. The number here would appear as the digit string *abcde*. Assume a "value so far" (V), which is initially set to 0. Working from the left-most (most significant) digit, multiply V by the base and add in the next digit, repeating until all the digits have been processed; V is then the converted value.

Figure 2.1: Conversions with Decimal Arithmetic

$$\text{Binary digits} = 1_7\ 1_6\ 1_5\ 0_4\ \ 1_3\ 1_2\ 0_1\ 1_0$$

Binary to decimal	Decimal to binary
$2 \times 0 + 1_7\ \ = 1$	$2\ )\overline{237}\ \ \ + 1$ rem
$2 \times 1 + 1_6\ \ = 3$	$2\ )\overline{118}\ \ \ + 0$ rem
$2 \times 3 + 1_5\ \ = 7$	$2\ )\overline{59}\ \ \ + 1$ rem
$2 \times 7 + 0_4\ \ = 14$	$2\ )\overline{29}\ \ \ + 1$ rem
$2 \times 14 + 1_3\ = 29$	$2\ )\overline{14}\ \ \ + 0$ rem
$2 \times 29 + 1_2\ = 59$	$2\ )\overline{7}\ \ \ + 1$ rem
$2 \times 59 + 0_1\ = 118$	$2\ )\overline{3}\ \ \ + 1$ rem
$2 \times 118 + 1_0\ = 237$	$2\ )\overline{1}\ \ \ + 1$ rem
Binary to decimal	Decimal to binary

To convert 1110 1101 to decimal, using the first method, we have $1 \times 128 + 1 \times 64 + 1 \times 32 + 1 \times 8 + 1 \times 4 + 1 = 237$. Figure **2.1** shows conversions of 237 between binary and decimal, using decimal arithmetic. The digits are written with subscripts to identify the individual bits as they enter the calculation.

2.3.2   To Convert From the Arithmetic Base.

This conversion simply reverses the operations of the second method. At each stage of that conversion we can write $V_{n+1} = V_n b + d_n$, where b is the base and d_n is the corresponding digit. Dividing V_{n+1} by b yields as quotient (V_n) and as remainder (d_n).

The conversion algorithm from the arithmetic base is then –

- Set the working value V to the value to convert.
- Calculate $d = V \bmod base$ and then $V = V \div base$ (integer division)
- Repeat above steps until $V = 0$.

The successive values of d are the digits in order, from least-significant (right most) to most-significant (left most)[5].

---

[5]If converting between two bases, *neither* of which is the arithmetic base, it is simplest to use the arithmetic base as an intermediate stage.

Table 2.3: Hexadecimal to Decimal Conversion Table.

	X	X0	X00	X000	X 0000	X0 0000
0	0	0	0	0	0	0
1	1	16	256	4 096	65 536	1 048 576
2	2	32	512	8 192	131 072	2 097 152
3	3	48	768	12 288	196 608	3 145 728
4	4	64	1024	16 384	262 144	4 194 304
5	5	80	1280	20 480	327 680	5 242 880
6	6	96	1536	24 576	393 216	6 291 456
7	7	112	1792	28 672	458 752	7 340 032
8	8	128	2048	32 768	524 288	8 388 608
9	9	144	2304	36 864	589 824	9 437 184
A	10	160	2560	40 960	655 360	10 485 760
B	11	176	2816	45 056	720 896	11 534 336
C	12	192	3072	49 152	786 432	12 582 912
D	13	208	3328	53 248	851 968	13 631 488
E	14	224	3584	57 344	917 504	14 680 064
F	15	240	3840	61 440	983 040	15 728 640

The right-hand side of Figure **2.1** shows the conversion of 237 to binary using decimal arithmetic. Collecting the remainders gives 1110 1101 as the result, with first-to-last remainders becoming the bits in succession, right-to-left.

2.3.3   Conversion by Table Lookup

For this method we have a table of the decimal equivalents of selected hexadecimal numbers (or octal, but we will use hexadecimal.). Each table entry, as shown in Table **2.3**, has the decimal value if its "row digit" is substituted for X in its column header.

Thus 400_{16} (row 4, column X00) is 1 024, and $B000_{16}$ is 45 056.

To convert from hexadecimal to decimal, we use the table to get the decimal equivalent of each hexadecimal digit and add up those values. For example $ABCD_{16}$ is $40 960 + 2816 + 192 + 13 = 43 981$.

To convert from decimal to hexadecimal, look for the largest table value which does not exceed the value. Write down its hexadecimal digit and subtract the decimal value. Repeat until the value has been reduced to zero. For

Table 2.4: Decimal to Hexadecimal Conversion Table.

	1	10	100	1000	10 000	100 000
0	00	00	000	0000	0 0000	0 0000
1	01	0A	064	03E8	0 2710	1 86A0
2	02	14	0C8	07D0	0 4E20	3 0D40
3	03	1E	12C	0BB8	0 7530	4 93E0
4	04	28	190	0FA0	0 9C40	6 1A80
5	05	32	1F4	1388	0 C350	7 A120
6	06	3C	258	1770	0 EA60	9 27C0
7	07	46	2BC	1B58	1 1170	A AE60
8	08	50	320	1F40	1 3880	C 3500
9	09	5A	384	2328	1 5F90	D BBA0

example, to convert 45 678 to hexadecimal, we see that the first digit must be B (B000 = 45 056); subtracting this value gives a new value of 622. Repeating the operation gives successive digits of 2 (200=512), 6 and E. Thus 45 678 = B26E$_{16}$.

Table **2.3** uses decimal arithmetic to convert hexadecimal to decimal. A similar table (Table **2.4**) is interrogated with decimal values and gives the corresponding hexadecimal values. The table has columns giving the hexadecimal equivalents of tens, hundreds, thousands, *etc.* (The hexadecimal digits in the table body are grouped in fours for improved readability.) Arithmetic is now done in hexadecimal (or binary). To convert 45 678 to hexadecimal (with hexadecimal arithmetic) with Table **2.4** –

$$
\begin{aligned}
40\,000 &= 09C40 \\
5\,000 &= 01388 \\
600 &= 00258 \\
70 &= 00046 \\
8 &= 00008 \\
\hline
\text{value} &= 0B26E \quad (= 45\,678)
\end{aligned}
$$

2.4   Representing Fractions in Binary

The polynomial representation used for integers can be extended to handle negative powers of the base and therefore values less than 1. (For more discussion on the development and philosophy of fractions, refer to Section **11.1.1**.)

The rules are very similar—each bit corresponds to a power of 2, but now a negative power, and we get the decimal value by adding up the decimal values of these powers. A fractional value F is represented in base b by the polynomial –

$$F = d_1b^{-1} + d_2b^{-2} + d_3b^{-3} + d_4b^{-4} + \ldots$$

and is written as

$$F = 0.d_1d_2d_3d_4\ldots$$

(In this section the "point", decimal or binary, will be shown as ".".) While integers can be always represented exactly in binary, few decimal fractions have an exact binary representation. The binary representations of three decimal values, two simple in decimal, and one complex are –

$$
\begin{aligned}
0.1010_{10} &= 0.0001\ 1001\ 1001\ 1001\ 1001\ 1001\ldots \\
0.0110_{10} &= 0.0000\ 0010\ 1000\ 1111\ 0101\ 1100\ldots \\
1/\sqrt{2}_{10} &= 0.1011\ 0101\ 0000\ 0100\ 1111\ 0011\ldots
\end{aligned}
$$

There is little obvious difference between 0.0110 and $1/\sqrt{2}$ even though one is a rational decimal and one an irrational number; both are seemingly random collections of bits.

While it may be useful to remember the first few negative powers of 2, they are generally less important than the positive powers.

n	2^n	n	2^n
0	1	-7	0.007 812 5
-1	0.5	-8	0.003 906 25
-2	0.25	-9	0.001 953 125
-3	0.125	-10	0.000 976 562 5
-4	0.0625	-11	0.000 488 281 25
-5	0.0312 5	-12	0.000 244 140 625
-6	0.0156 25	-13	0.000 122 070 312 5

2.4.1   Converting Fractions Between Bases

When converting fractions between bases we clearly have the two combinations binary→decimal and decimal→binary. Furthermore, each conversion may be done with either decimal or binary arithmetic. Because few computers now use decimal arithmetic we omit the decimal option. But should that be necessary the extensions should be obvious.

Underlying the conversions is of course the polynomial representation parallelling that for integers. A fractional value F is represented by the polynomial –

$$F = d_1 b^{-1} + d_2 b^{-2} + d_3 b^{-3} + d_4 b^{-4} + \dots$$

If the fraction is multiplied by the base, we get

$$
\begin{aligned}
F &= d_1 b^0 . d_2 b^{-1} + d_3 b^{-2} + d_4 b^{-3} + \dots \\
&= d_1.d_2 d_3 d_4 \dots \quad \text{in conventional form}
\end{aligned}
$$

which has the most-significant digit now in the units position and, more importantly, in its "natural" representation. The integral part of the product can be removed as the digit and then set to zero. Repeating these steps (multiplying by b and removing the integral part) obtains successive digits of the base b representation, from the more significant to the less significant digits.

Thus, to convert a binary fraction to decimal, on a binary computer, repeatedly multiply by 1010_2, collecting the integral parts each time as the successive decimal digits. To convert a decimal fraction to binary with decimal arithmetic, successively multiply by 2, removing integral parts as the binary digits. Alternatively, multiply by 8 or 16 to generate 3 or 4 bits at each step.

Take $0.00101 (= 2^{-3} + 2^{-5} = 0.125 + 0.03125 = 0.156\,25)$. (To multiply x by 1010, add x shifted left 1 and x shifted left 3.)

$$
\begin{aligned}
0.00101 \times 1010 &= 0001.10010 \quad &\text{int} = 1 \\
0.10010 \times 1010 &= 0101.10100 \quad &\text{int} = 5 \\
0.10100 \times 1010 &= 0110.01000 \quad &\text{int} = 6 \\
0.01000 \times 1010 &= 0010.10000 \quad &\text{int} = 2 \\
0.10000 \times 1010 &= 0101.00000 \quad &\text{int} = 5
\end{aligned}
$$

Stop when the fraction becomes zero.

Collecting digits, we get $0.156\,25$ as the decimal fraction equivalent to 0.00101.

2.4.2 Extending Binary Fractions

Irrespective of the sign, binary fractions always extend to longer precision by adding zeros to the right. When converting binary fractions to hexadecimal or octal they should be extended on the right with as many zeros as are needed to complete the octal or hexadecimal digit.

2.5   Decimal Coding

There are times when it is desirable to keep all values in decimal, such as where values are read and written extensively with little intervening calculation, or where precise decimal arithmetic is essential without the possibility of decimal rounding errors. Thus most calculators, cash registers and so on use decimal coding and arithmetic. Almost all decimal applications now use a simple "BCD" coding in which four bits represent the digits $0 \ldots 9$ with the binary codes { 0000, 0001, ..., 1000, 1001 }. The six unused codes may be used for signs or special delimiters. Some other representations have been important and these (and others) are described in Section **11.7**.

Send Orders for Reprints to reprints@benthamscience.net

Chapter 3

Signed, and Other, Representations

Abstract: Although the "natural" integers 1,2,3,...) are adequate for many, everyday, purposes they do not handle concepts such as debts; the representation must extended to handle negative values. This chapter therefore introduces the three conventional forms of signed binary representation (sign and magnitude, ones complement and two complement). Finally, it describes some other important number representations, especially mixed base (for non-metric measures), but also the more-specialised redundant codings, Gray codes and Zeckendorf representations.

Keywords: Signed Binary, Ones Complement, Twos Complement, Sign and Magnitude, Biased, Sign extension, Fibonacci Numbers, Zeckendorf representation, Gray codes, redundant codes.

3.1   Negative Integers

Although positive integers (the "natural" numbers) are important, they are inadequate for practical arithmetic (in modern usage). To allow negative values as well we require a signed number representation.

The three important representations for signed binary numbers all represent positive integers as for unsigned integers and most reserve the most-significant bit as the sign bit ($0 \Rightarrow$ +ve, and $1 \Rightarrow$ -ve).

An important operation is that of complementing a value, or changing its sign. In normal notation, the complement of $+3$ is -3, and of -46 is $+46$; we can complement a positive value (to get a negative value) or a negative value (getting a positive value).

We often say "twos (or ones) complement a value". This means "change the sign of the value's representation according to twos (or ones) complement rules" (given later). If the original value was positive it will end up negative; if it was negative the result will be positive (usually).

As a closing comment to this introduction, note that signed number representations are closely connected with the operations of binary arithmetic described in Chapter **4**. In particular, signed numbers and subtraction are intimately linked; each is really a precursor to the other. Here we choose to defer the operations until after signed numbers have been described.

3.1.1   Sign and Magnitude

This form corresponds to the conventional way of representing signed decimal numbers (with the prefixes '+' and '−'). Only the sign bit changes when complementing the number. In 8 bits, $+5$ is 00000101, and –5 is 10000101, with '0' indicating positive and '1' negative values. Sign and magnitude representation is now used only in the significands of floating-point numbers and is otherwise unimportant.

3.1.2   Ones Complement

To complement a value of either sign, change *all* the bits, $0 \rightarrow 1$ and $1 \rightarrow 0$. So 00000101 ($+5$) becomes 11111010; recomplementing obviously recovers the original 00000101.

From the description of the complementing method it is obvious that if any number and its ones complement are added, each and every digit position will be adding one 0 and one 1, with no carries at any stage. Any number and its complement then add to the number $111\ldots111$, which acts as the *arithmetic* zero.

With numbers of N bits, $x + (-x) \equiv 2^N - 1$.

Ones complement has two representations for zero; $+0 = 000\ldots000$ (the *numeric zero* and $-0 = 111\ldots111$ (the *arithmetic* zero, from above), but every value can be complemented. It was once an important number representation, but is now seldom used.

3.1.3   Twos Complement

In many early computers numbers were regarded as fractions rather than integers. With fractions $x + (-x) \to 2.000\ldots$ (and hence the name twos complement). Note that the $2.0\ldots$ overflows the fraction, extending beyond the sign bit.

With numbers now usually regarded as integers, the complementation is reinterpreted so that if x is any number represented in twos complement to N bits, then with unsigned addition $x + (-x) \to 2^N$, again overflowing past the sign bit. With fixed-length precision to N bits, the result is always truncated to N bits, or reduced modulo 2^N, forcing $2^N \to 0$. For example, to 8 bits, $+5$ is 00000101 and -5 is 11111011; adding the two gives

$$00000101 + 11111011 \to 100000000 = 256 = 2^8.$$

More importantly, as a number and its ones complement always sum to $2^N - 1$ and if the same number and its twos complement sum to 2^N then clearly we get the twos complement by adding 1 to the ones complement. Thus, if $+5$ is 00000101_{both}, then -5 is 11111010_{ones}, and complementing -5 gives 00000101_{twos}.

Values represented in twos complement are added just as if they were simple unsigned quantities. There is only one representation for zero, but the most negative number has no complement. With 16 bits the range is $-65\,536 \leq V \leq 65\,535$ and with 32 bits $-4\,294\,967\,296 \leq V \leq 4\,294\,967\,295$.

There are two rules for complementing twos complement numbers –

Parallel complementing Take the ones complement and add 1, as stated above.

Serial complementing Working from the right, copy all trailing 0s and the least-significant 1, and then ones complement all more-significant bits. Consider a binary number which ends in some 0s, with a preceding 1, as $\ldots x1000$. Ones complementing turns this value into $\ldots y0111$. Adding a 1 recomplements all trailing 1s turning them back to 0s; the 0 (which was the least significant 1) absorbs the carry and reverts to a 1. Bits to the left of that are not affected by the addition.

3.1.4   Biased, or Excess

In this representation a "bias" is added to the value so that all legitimate values appear, after adjustment, as positive, unsigned, integers. This unsigned integer is used as the representation of the value. The bias is usually about half of the number range; for 8-bit representations it is either 127 or 128. Excess representations are used mainly for the exponents of floating-point numbers as in Section **6.3**.

In the special case that an N-bit number has a bias of 2^{N-1}, the sign bit has the meanings $1 \Rightarrow +\text{ve}$ and $0 \Rightarrow -\text{ve}$.

3.2   Sign Extension

A positive or unsigned integer is always extended by prefixing it with zeros. (As in decimal, 1234 is identical to 00 001 234, but we usually suppress leading zeros.)

Just as positive numbers extend to the left with 0 bits, so do negative numbers extend to the left with 1 bits (except for sign and magnitude). The operation of sign extension is important if we have say a signed 8-bit or 16-bit value and must extend it to a 32-bit signed value. The sign bit of the old value is "propagated through" the unused bits of the new value.

For example, 8-bit to 16-bit extensions are

$$0011\ 0101 \quad \rightarrow \quad 0000\ 0000\ 0011\ 0101$$
$$\text{and} \quad 1101\ 1001 \quad \rightarrow \quad 1111\ 1111\ 1101\ 1001$$

A longer value can be converted to a shorter value by discarding the high-order or left-hand bits, *provided that the discarded bits are all equal to the sign bit of the new, shorter, value.*

Fractions extend in all cases by just appending 0s to the right.

Sign and magnitude numbers are extended by inserting 0s between the sign bit and the following digit. They are contracted by deleting bits after the sign bit, checking that the deleted bits are all zero.

3.3   Summary of Signed Binary Numbers

- To extend a number (ones or twos complement) to a greater precision fill the extra bits with the sign bit; for a sign and magnitude number insert the necessary number of zeros just after the sign bit.

- To complement (change the sign of) a sign & magnitude number, change the sign bit to 0 (+ve result) or 1 (–ve result)

- To complement a ones complement number, change all the bits, $0 \rightarrow 1$ and $1 \rightarrow 0$ (the logical NOT operation).

- To complement a twos complement number, take the ones complement and then add 1, OR starting from the rightmost bit, copy all 0 bits and the rightmost 1; then complement all the more significant bits.

3.4   Use of Signed Representations, *etc*

Although all of the signed binary representations have been important at some time in the history of computing some are now restricted to quite specialised uses.

Sign and Magnitude is now used only in the significands (or fractions or mantissæ) of floating-point numbers. Floating-point arithmetic emphasises fast arithmetic; multiplication and division are somewhat easier with unsigned operands.

Ones Complement was once a very important internal representation for integers and fractions, but now survives only in some computers which must perpetuate aspects of old designs. Another area where ones complement addition is important is in checksumming transmitted data and verifying correct transmission. Ones complement checksums are used in the TCP/IP protocol suite (Section **10.5.1**); this may well be now the only area where many people will ever meet ones complement, but probably without realising it.

Twos Complement This is used for virtually all integers in modern computers and will not be discussed further. (Or at least tacitly assumed everywhere!)

Biased This is used in the exponents of most floating-point number representations.

3.5 Other Number Representations

Until now we have dealt only with "standard" binary or decimal representations. But others, which are useful in specialised situations (or are merely interesting) include

Redundant codings These are important mainly in computer arithmetic.

Mixed base These include times and angles (minutes, seconds, *etc*) non-metric weights and measures, and pounds Sterling (old style English currency).

Zeckendorf These are an interesting example of numbers where the base is not an integer. They find practical application in variable-length codes.

Gray Codes These codes are important in analogue–digital conversion to guard against the situation where physical reading cannot ensure that all the bits of a binary value actually change at the same time. In the Gray codes, successive values always differ in only one bit.

3.5.1 Redundant Codings

The representations used so far have all required $0 \le d < base$ for each digit d. If this requirement is relaxed, or we allow a digit to be held in two or more components, we obtain various "redundant" codings, in which a value can be represented in more than one way. These codings are seldom if ever used in data storage, but can be very useful when performing arithmetic; they are then buried in the middle of arithmetic units. They will be discussed in more detail in Chapter **5** on arithmetic but it is appropriate to mention them here.

-1, 0 +1 As the cost of a multiplication often increases with the number of 1s in the multiplier, a ternary coding with digit weights of $\{-1, 0, +1\}$ is often used in multipliers to reduce the number of non-zero digits in the representation. The recoding relies on the fact that a string or run of 1s can be written in the form $2^n - 2^m$, where the most significant bit of the run corresponds to 2^{n-1} and the least significant bit to 2^m. The basic rule is modified for an isolated 1 and for a single 0 within a run of 1s. The following example reduces the number of non-0s from 7 to 4

original bits	0	0	1	1	1	0	0	1	1	1	1	0
recoded bits	0	+1	0	0	-1	0	+1	0	0	0	-1	0

Carry-save Again in multiplication, the cost of multiplication depends on the time to complete an addition, and that depends on the time to propagate the carry through the adder. In the "carry-save" adder, carries-out do not connect directly to the next carry-in (as described in section **4.3**) but are instead saved with a left shift of 1 place. Each digit is then held as two bits, whose sum will be correct after incoming carries are included.

Augend	0	0	1	0	1	1
Addend	0	1	1	1	0	1
carry sum	$\begin{pmatrix} 0 \\ 0 \end{pmatrix}$	$\begin{pmatrix} 1 \\ 1 \end{pmatrix}$	$\begin{pmatrix} 0 \\ 1 \end{pmatrix}$	$\begin{pmatrix} 0 \\ 1 \end{pmatrix}$	$\begin{pmatrix} 1 \\ 1 \end{pmatrix}$	$\begin{pmatrix} 0 \\ 0 \end{pmatrix}$

(The carry-save adder actually adds *three* bits at each stage, one being the saved carry from the previous cycle.) The principles of carry-save addition will be explained in section **4.3**; for now it is enough to recognise that this redundant number representation exists.

3.5.2   Mixed Base Numbers

Until now we have used only numbers based on a polynomial representation. But there are many other representations, as described by Fraenkel [39], some of them quite unusual and probably impractical.

The more familiar representations, and the only ones that will be used here, represent an integer N as the scalar product[1] $N = \mathbf{d}.\mathbf{w}$, where N is the *digit vector* (the visible digits of the representation) and $\mathbf{w}$ is a *weight vector*. To conform with normal conventions for displaying number representations these vectors are written in the order

$$\ldots w_i, w_{i-1}, \ldots, w_2, w_1, w_0$$

The weight vector is in turn derived from a *base vector* $\mathbf{b}$ by

$$w_k = \prod_{i=0}^{k-1} b_i$$

---

[1]For readers less familiar with mathematics, the *scalar product* is obtained by multiplying corresponding elements of two vectors and adding those products. For example, given the two vectors {2, 3, 4} and {9, 8, 7}, their scalar product is $2 \times 9 + 3 \times 8 + 4 \times 7 = 70$.

Table 3.1: Examples of Mixed-Base Number Systems.

Time	days	hours 24	minutes 60	seconds 60
Angles	revolutions	degrees 360	minutes 60	seconds 60
Distance	miles	yards 1760	feet 3	inches 12
Weight	tons	cwt 20	pounds 112	ounces 16
Sterling currency	pounds	shillings 20	pence 12	

with the k-th weight being the product of all *less-significant* base terms. In the conventional *uniform base* number systems such as binary or decimal the weights are powers of the base (..., 16, 8, 4, 2, 1 in binary, and ... 1 000, 100, 10, 1 in decimal). Thus $b_i = b$ for all i and $w_k = b^k$, where the constant b is the base of the number system. So a number such as $40 = 1 \times 2^5 + 1 \times 2^3$ has the binary (base 2) representation 101000.

Sometimes numbers use a mixture of bases. There used to be many more before the adoption of decimal money and metric measurements, because traditional weights and measures are full of strange relations between units. Now only time and angles are important (except that some countries do still perversely use non-decimal distances and weights).

Some examples are shown in the Table **3.1**. In all cases the unit has its base below. The base vector is $\mathbf{b} = \{24, 60, 60\}$ for time, or $\mathbf{b} = \{360, 60, 60\}$ for angles. The "digits" are usually written as decimal integers, so that hours are in the range $0 \ldots 23$, and minutes $0 \ldots 59$. The corresponding weight vectors are, respectively, $\mathbf{w} = \{86\,400, 3600, 60, 1\}$ (for time; 86 400 seconds in a day) and $\mathbf{w} = \{1\,296\,000, 3600, 60, 1\}$ (for angles; 1 296 000 seconds in a revolution).

Addition is done from right to left, at each stage reducing the result by the corresponding component of the base vector, shown immediately below the unit name. The "reduction" is actually a division by the base element, producing a quotient (as the carry into the next digit) and a remainder (as the current digit). Thus the pence total is divided by 12 to give the shillings carry, and the remainder is the pence result.

For example, if an angle of 24 degrees, 35 minutes and 25 seconds is written as $24° \, 35' \, 25''$, and we want to add

$$
\begin{array}{rrrr}
& 83° & 42' & 54'' \\
+ & 75° & 23' & 58'' \\
+ & 66° & 45' & 32'' \\
+ & 84° & 23' & 12'' \\
+ & 75° & 56' & 11'' \\
\hline
& 386° & 11' & 47''
\end{array}
$$

- First add the seconds, for a total of $167''$. Divide 167 by 60, for a remainder of 47 (which is the seconds result) and quotient of 2 (which carries into the minutes).

- Adding the minutes, with carry-in of $2'$, gives 191 minutes $= 3° \, 11'$. Save the $11'$ as the minutes sum and carry the $3°$ to the next (degrees).

- Now add the degrees to give a total of $386°$, or $360°$ (1 revolution) $+ \, 26°$.

- The sum is then either $386° \, 11' \, 47''$, or (reducing to whole revolutions) $26° \, 11' \, 47''$.

While some early British computers did provide hardware for Pounds Sterling addition, the general recommendation is to convert mixed-base values into multiples of the smallest unit for all arithmetic.

3.5.3   Zeckendorf (Fibonacci) Representations

An interesting number representation which is useful in variable-length coding (Section **9.12**) is based on Fibonacci numbers. These numbers were proposed by Fibonacci (Leonardo of Pisa, c1170–1250) in response to the following problem —

> A pair of newly born rabbits is placed in a cage (a *large* cage!). This pair, and all later pairs, produce one further pair every month starting at their second month. How many pairs will there be after each month, assuming no deaths?

If there are F_n pairs at the start of the nth month and F_{n+1} at the start of the next $(n+1)$th month, then at the start of the following month $(n+2)$, the

F_n rabbits will breed, adding to those present at the start of month $(n + 1)$, to give a total of $F_{n+2} = F_n + F_{n+1}$ pairs. Each number is therefore the sum of its two predecessors, as shown in Table **3.2**.

Table 3.2: The First Fibonacci Numbers

n	1	2	3	4	5	6	7	8	9	10	11	12	13	14	15
F_n	1	1	2	3	5	8	13	21	34	55	89	144	233	377	610

A standard result of Fibonacci number theory is that

$$\lim_{n \to \infty} \frac{F_{n+1}}{F_n} = \frac{\sqrt{5}+1}{2} = \phi \approx 1.618\,033\,988\,749\,895\ldots \quad \text{(the ``Golden Section'')}$$

In 1972 Zeckendorf [112] showed that the Fibonacci numbers can be used as the basis of an integer number representation. In the above notation, the weight vector **w** is the Fibonacci numbers $\{\ldots, F_4, F_3, F_2\}$, writing in reverse order and omitting F_1.

To form this *Zeckendorf representation* $\mathcal{Z}(N)$, take the integer N, subtract from it the largest $F_i \leq N$, set $d_i = 1$ in the representation, and repeat until N is zero.

The Zeckendorf representation has no two adjacent 1s. If any number did have two adjacent 1s, they are immediately equivalent to the next most-significant bit by the rules for generating Fibonacci numbers. ($\ldots 00110 \ldots \rightarrow \ldots 01000 \ldots$). This property is important for addition and subtraction, and later when we consider variable length codes of the integers. For example $45 = 34 + 8 + 3$, with its representation $\mathcal{Z}(45) = 10010100$. Again $10 = 8 + 2$ and $\mathcal{Z}(10) = 10010$. Some representative Zeckendorf representations, with the weights heading the columns of digits, are given in Table **3.3**.

Table 3.3: Some Zeckendorf Representations.

N	Summed values	Weights and digits									
		89	55	34	21	13	8	5	3	2	1
1	1	0	0	0	0	0	0	0	0	0	1
10	8+2	0	0	0	0	0	1	0	0	1	0
100	89+8+2+1	1	0	0	0	0	1	0	0	1	1
123	89+34	1	0	1	0	0	0	0	0	0	0
140	89+34+13+3+1	1	0	1	0	1	0	0	1	0	1

All of the normal arithmetic operations are possible on Zeckendorf representations, as discussed by Fenwick [35]. Some unusual features are –

1. Addition and subtraction have *two* carries, one going one place to the left as in normal binary arithmetic, and one *two* places to the right.

2. It is sometimes necessary to extend the sum to the right by 1 or 2 places, both with a weight of 1 and then "sweep" these added 1s to the left into the normal F_2 position.

3. If we assume that a 1 in the most-significant bit denotes a negative number, there are are about 1.62 times as many positive values as negative values. If F_N is the sign bit, a negative number must start with the bits 10... and have F_{N-2} possible values. A positive number must start with 0... and has F_{N-1} values.

4. With a negative number having a sign fill of 101010..., the sign pattern can interact with the numeric bits in two different ways. There are then *two* representations for each negative value. Some examples are shown in the following table.

N	$\mathcal{Z}(N)$	$F(8)$ comp	$F(9)$ comp	$F(10)$ comp	$F(11)$ comp
6	1001	100010	1001010	10100010	101001010
7	1010	100001	1001001	10100001	101001001
8	10000	100000	1001000	10100000	101001000

With an almost constant ratio between successive Fibonacci numbers, the Fibonacci number system and the Zeckendorf representation form a polynomial number system with base $b = \phi \approx 1.618\,033\,989\ldots$. (As the digits of the visible digit vector must be integers less than the base the Zeckendorf digits are necessarily 0 and 1.)

3.5.4   Some Metric Curiosities

Alert readers may have noticed that the Zeckendorf base (1.618...) is very close to the number of kilometres in 1 mile (1.609...)[2]. Therefore, if we write a distance in miles as a Zeckendorf integer and shift the bit-pattern one to the left, we get the distance in kilometres! (And vice-versa.) Except for small values the result is correct to with ±1 for distances to 100 miles.

---

[2]This observation is apparently due to Richard Hamming.

And ... a left shift of 2 places multiplies by 2.618 (3% different from 2.54 cm/inch) and 3 places by 4.236 (11% less than 3.785 litres per U.S. gallon, and 7% less than 4.546 litres per imperial gallon).... .

3.5.5   Gray Codes

What is now known as "the Gray Code" was devised to solve a particular problem in analogue-digital conversion; there are many other codes with similar properties, but this one has a special construction method and is associated with the name of its inventor. Frank Gray was an engineer at Bell System Laboratories in the 1930s and 1940s where he worked extensively on television, producing few papers but many patents. He is reported to have developed, in the 1930s, the techniques which were adopted for NTSC television in 1953. Here we give only a very brief introduction to Gray codes, as they are peripheral to most data within computers.

The problem which led to the Gray code was that of digitising an analogue waveform; even at telephone speeds this needs 8 000 samples per second and with modern methods requires component accuracies of 0.1% or better. In the middle 1940s, any resistors more accurate than $\pm 20\%$ were probably inductive and unsuitable for anything other than DC operation. Flip-flops were limited to 100 kHz or less, occupied 10s of cubic centimetres and consumed several Watts of power. Solutions which would be natural now were then quite infeasible.

Gray's solution was to deflect the beam vertically in a cathode ray tube according to the analogue signal and then sweep it horizontally across a suitable mask to give a sequence of pulses which encoded the vertical deflection. A binary-code mask, with two scan lines, is shown in the left side of Figure **3.1**, along with a central graticule giving the nominal position of each coded value. The black scan line is correctly registered and codes 1010_2 or 10_{10}. But in practice there is always some doubt about the transitions; one or more sensors (switches, photocells, *etc*) may be misaligned, or they may switch at different physical positions or levels. We can show this uncertainty as the grey 'line' in Figure **3.1**, meaning that *any* of the bits can switch at *any* position as long as the grey area includes the transition. Here the grey area is actually either 11 or 12, but decodes as a binary '1???' (8–15); three bits are doubtful and could be read either way. The problem is that several bits change around this value and if some are read as the 'upper' value and some corresponding to the 'lower' value the actual value is indeterminate.

The general problem is that of "bit skew". If several bits are handled in parallel it is usually necessary to sample them all at some known time (for parallel transmission over wires) or at some known position (for position encoding). A bit may be sampled just as it is changing; it may be either 0 or 1 and with a normal binary code the decoded value may be wildly in error.

Gray's solution is ensure that at most one bit changes in any transition between two adjacent values; the mask at the right of Figure **3.1** with copies of the same scan lines follows this principle.

Here the grey line delivers either '1110' (11) or '1010' (12), which is an error of no more than 1 unit and the best that can be done. Even though similar problems arise from manufacturing problems or other poor alignment the Gray code always guarantees a value within 1 unit of the correct value.

Figure 3.1: Gray Code

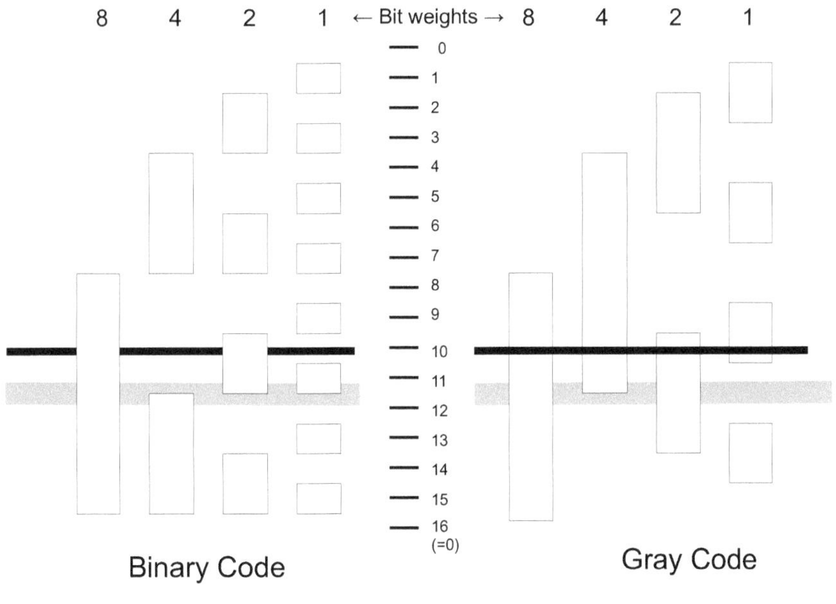

Gray codes are useful in any situation where a condition is represented by several bits and those bits must be sampled with minimum ambiguity. Thus they are useful in communications systems where a given "state transition" (amplitude, phase, or both together) conveys several bits. Encoding states as a Gray code gives at most a single bit-error; single errors are much easier to correct than multi-bit errors. In general any system where parallel data is transferred between systems with asynchronous clocks may benefit by using a Gray code.

Extensive descriptions of Gray codes, their properties, their use in arithmetic, and relation to other codes are in Wikipedia [47] and Doran [23]. Doran gives a comprehensive description of the Gray Code, its mathematics and applications. Some idea of the breadth of Gray Codes may be judged by his nearly 80 citations. Gray's description of a method for constructing his codes is stated by Doran as one of the best explanations given. The description here follows that outline.

The generation of the Gray Code is shown in Figure **3.2**, starting from an empty ("null") code and developing first the obvious codes for 0 and 1. Verbally –

1. Take the existing values (always 2^n values) and write them in the *reverse* order in the next 2^n positions. This corresponds to a *reflection* of the previous set of values; note the arrows connecting the extremes of each table to its successor.

2. Prefix the first group of 2^n codes with '0' and the second, reflected, group with '1'.

3. Repeat the first two steps until the code has expanded to the desired size.

Figure 3.2: Construction of a Gray Code

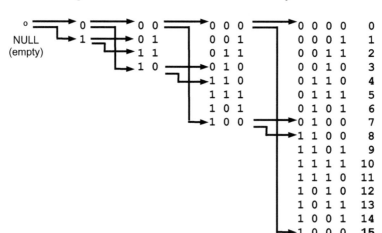

Taking the codewords in order, the bits have a consistent pattern, numbering the rightmost bit n

bit n　　　　0011001100110011001100110011...　groups of 2 bits
bit $n-1$　0000111100001111000011111...　groups of 4 bits
bit $n-2$　0000000011111111000000000...　groups of 8 bits

The reflection of prior codewords into the upper half of the newer code leads to the name "reflected binary" as a frequent synonym for the Gray code. It follows from the construction that adjacent codewords differ in exactly one place; the Gray Code is an example of a Hamming *distance-1 code*.

Figure 3.3: Gray Code—Direct Analogue to Decimal Conversion

```
int pow2[]={1, 2, 4, 8, 16, 32, 64, 128, 256, 512};

void GrayDtoD(int N, int V, int bit[])  // convert bin. integer
{
    int Gray, i;
    Gray = V ^ (V >> 1);          // convert to Gray integer
    for (i = N-1; i >= 0; i--)    // extract bits
        bit[i] = (Gray >> i) & 1;
} // end GrayDtoD

void grayAtoD(int N, int V, int bit[])  // convert value
{
    int i, V1;
    V1 = V;                        // copy the input value
    for (i = N-1; i >= 0; i--)     // scan MSB -> LSB
    {
        V1 = V1*2;                 // double the range
        if (V1 >= pow2[N])         // test which half
        {
            bit[i] = 1;            // upper -- bit = 1
            V1 = pow2[N+1] - 1 - V1;  // reflect upper to low
        }
        else                       // lower half
            bit[i] = 0;            // bit = 0
    }
} // end grayAtoD
```

3.5.6 Converting to Gray Code

A fast method of converting binary to Gray is to invert each bit if the next more-significant bit of the input value is 1. Thus if the bit vectors **B** and **G** denote the binary and Gray representations of some value, then $g_i = b_i \oplus b_{i+1}$ Converting 13_{10},

$$
\begin{aligned}
\mathbf{B} &= \{1,1,0,1\} \\
\mathbf{G} &= \{1,1,0,1\} \oplus \{0,1,1,0\} \\
&= \{1,0,1,1\}
\end{aligned}
$$

(The inverse conversion, Gray-to-binary, requires a serial scan because each Gray-bit depends on its more-significant binary-bit. It is therefore necessary to scan serially from more- to less-significant bits.

Figure **3.3** gives two algorithms for converting a value to Gray code. Both accept a codeword length (N) and a value (V), delivering the bits in an array.

- The first "digital to digital" is a direct implementation of the Exclusive-Or algorithm above, assuming a binary integer; most of the code just unpacks the bits.

- The second "analogue to digital" algorithm mirrors the construction of the full Gray code and assumes a "value", which need not be in binary. It is convenient to normalise the whole operation to a range $\{0 \ldots 2^{n+1} - 1\}$. At each step we double the value and test it against 2^n. If in the lower-value half we just develop a 0 bit; if in the upper we generate a 1 and then reflect the value into the lower half[3]. Doubling *before* the test is needed to handle a 1-bit code. This routine works with non-binary representations; floating-point may need a rounding-up (add 0.5) to avoid dithering around zero.

---

[3]This description uses "upper" and "lower" to refer to *values*; on diagrams the positions may be reversed.

Send Orders for Reprints to reprints@benthamscience.net

Chapter 4

Basic Arithmetic and Logic

Abstract: Given that quantities may be represented as bit patterns within the computer, how may these patterns be manipulated to achieve useful results? We look first at the "basic" operations of addition and subtraction in the various binary number representations, extending to addition of multiple-precision values and decimal addition. Then we examine the logical operations, where the bits are "bits", with no numerical significance. Operations here include AND, OR, NOT, XOR, shifting of various types, bit-field operations and, finally, parity.

Keywords: Binary addition of signed values, subtraction by complement addition, multiple precision addition, decimal addition, logical operations, shift operations, bit-field operations, parity.

4.1   Introduction.

"What are the fundamental operations of computer arithmetic?". The quick answer is "addition and subtraction", but that is clearly not true because

- Many early minicomputers such as the PDP-8 and HP-2116 worked quite successfully with addition and complement as the only arithmetic operations. (In both computers the complement and increment—for 2's complement operation—were combined in a single "micro-coded" instruction.) Subtraction was done by complementing and adding, as discussed later in this chapter, and multiplication and division were realised by programmed combinations of complementing and addition.

- One very early computer had subtraction as its only arithmetic operation and addition relied on $x + y = x - (0 - y)$. (Addition is unsuitable as the sole operation because of its symmetry or, mathematically, commutativity.)

- As an unrealistic extreme, we need no more than "add 1" and "subtract 1" as shown below (and with suitable comparisons).

```
while (y > 0)    // simple addition x + y
  { x++; y-- }

while (y > 0)    // simple subtraction x - y
  { x--; y-- }
```

- Some computers using ones complement arithmetic had *subtraction* as the fundamental arithmetic operation, with addition performed as subtraction of the complement. (The user never realised it, but that was how the hardware worked—Section **4.6.2**.)

4.2 Addition

Even though it might not be one of the most fundamental operations, addition is the most obvious of the simple operations and it is convenient to start with it.

The rules for adding numbers are very similar in all number bases, provided that we can add pairs of digits (or triples, to allow for carries). To introduce addition, consider a simple decimal addition, as shown in Figure **4.1**.

Figure 4.1: Example of Decimal Addition

augend		7	4	9	2	3	0
addend		8	7	9	3	8	8
carries	1	1	1	0	1	0	0
sum	1	6	2	8	6	1	8

The values to be added are known as the "augend" (that which is augmented) and the "addend" (that which is added), producing a "sum" and intermediate "carries" which link adjacent digits of the addition. (Because of the essential symmetry of addition, we can use the term "addend" for both inputs. Where however the operation is one of repeatedly adding the next value into a "running total", the terms here are more appropriate.) The carry digits are shown here as smaller (to emphasise their different nature, as internal values rather than inputs or results) and are displaced to the right (to emphasise that they link between columns.)

Points to note from this example are –

- Addition proceeds from right (least-significant digit) to the left (more-significant digits).

- For each digit position, add the corresponding input digits and the "carry-in" which was produced as the "carry-out" from the digit immediately to the right. This gives an intermediate sum, whose units digit becomes the sum digit for this position and whose tens digit becomes the "carry-out" to be used as the carry-in to the next digit.

- There is a carry-out from the most-significant position or digit. The handling of this carry depends on the context of the addition.
  ○ If the sum may expand beyond the precision of the inputs, the carry can simply appear as another digit to the left of those in the inputs.
  ○ If the maximum number of digits or precision is limited (as is usually the case in computers) and the inputs already fill the permitted digits, the sum cannot be represented accurately and we have an "overflow", discussed in Section **4.5**.

In handling the intermediate sum, it is worth noting that the "splitting" operation is really a division by the number base, with the remainder becoming the current sum digit and the quotient the carry-out. When the base of the arithmetic is the same as the base of the number representation the division is equivalent to splitting the intermediate sum.

If we are adding two numbers x and y in base b, with the digits

$$\begin{aligned}
\text{add} \quad & \{x_n \ x_{n-1} \ \dots \ x_1 \ x_0\} \\
\text{and} \quad & \{y_n \ y_{n-1} \ \dots \ y_1 \ y_0\} \\
\text{for the sum} \quad & \{z_n \ z_{n-1} \ \dots \ z_1 \ z_0\}
\end{aligned}$$

we can hold each of the sets of digits in an integer array and add them with the program of Figure **4.2**. The operation follows exactly from the description above, but with the division replaced by a test and optional correction, which is appropriate in simple cases.

Addition is very seldom performed this way in real computers; the code is meant to show the fundamental operations underlying general addition. Code

Figure 4.2: Code to Add Two Numbers in Any Base

```
// The "numbers" are in integer arrays, one digit per integer
// The addend and augend are in x[ ] and y[ ], the sum in z[ ].

carry = 0;
for (i = 0; i < N; i++)        // right to left scan
    {
    z[i] = x[i] + y[i] + carry; // the add
    if (z[i] >= base)          // digit overflow!!
        {
        carry = 1;             // carry to next stage
        z[i] -= base;          // correct overflow
        }
    else
        carry = 0;             // no carry to next stage
    }
```

like this may be appropriate though when performing arithmetic to very large precisions. For example, the author has some programs which calculate the value of π to 100 000 or more places and use base 10 000 arithmetic (with 32 bit integers, or 10^8 with 64 bit floating-point), with precisely the above code for addition.

4.3   Binary Addition.

In principle, binary addition may be performed by the code of Figure **4.2** with *base* = 2, or by procedures analogous to familiar decimal addition. In fact, it is better to define binary addition by an addition table. (And of course implemented in the fastest-possible hardware.) Figure **4.3** shows all possible values of the three inputs to a binary addition and the corresponding Sum and Carry-out. It also shows an alternative approach to the Sum and Carry-out, based on the number of inputs which are 1.

Add (0110 1111 0101 1001 + 0010 0000 1011 0011)

Take augend	0110	1111	0101	1001
and the addend	0010	0000	1011	0011
with the carries	1101	1111	1110	0110
then add, to get answer	1001	0000	0000	1100

Check that the answer is $(28\,505 + 8371) = 36\,876$

Figure 4.3: Binary Addition Table

Add-end	Aug-end	Carry In	Carry Out	Sum		Sum inputs	Sum inputs ≥ 2	Sum inputs 1 or 3
0	0	0	0	0		0	0	0
0	0	1	0	1		1	0	1
0	1	0	0	1		1	0	1
0	1	1	1	0		2	1	0
1	0	0	0	1		1	0	1
1	0	1	1	0		2	1	0
1	1	0	1	0		2	1	0
1	1	1	1	1		3	1	1

Each carry digit is shifted left by one place from where it is generated, to be added in with the next-significant digits. See the "carry propagation" through most of the middle 8 bits.

- For each position, proceeding right to left, we add the digits and the incoming carry.

- If the sum is not less than the base, enter a 1 as the carry-in to the next position to the left and subtract the base from the sum; enter the difference as the sum digit.

4.4   Subtraction.

Subtraction is superficially similar to addition. We work in the same direction (right to left), but now must borrow if the subtraction "cannot be done" rather than carry if the addition overflows.

Before examining binary subtraction it is best to consider decimal subtraction in some detail, and especially the action of the "borrow". ("Borrowing" is an aspect which is seldom well-explained.) Remember always that any generated digit d of the difference must be such that $0 \leq d < 10$.

As an example, take $416 - 263$.

- The first subtraction, of the units digits, is $6 - 3 = 3$ with no problem. The next, tens digit, subtraction yields $1 - 6 = -5$, which is outside the valid range.

- To correct this "overdraw", add 10 (the number base) to the tens digit of the minuend and compensate by subtracting 1 from the hundreds digit of the minuend. (Both correspond to an adjustment of 1 in the hundreds digit and have no overall effect.) Alternatively, we may compensate by *adding* 1 to the hundreds digit of the subtrahend; the difference is one of pedagogical style or practical convenience rather than of substance.

- The tens digit subtraction is now $11 - 6 = 5$, which is a valid result.

- With the borrow of 1, the hundreds digit subtraction is no longer $4 - 2$ but $(4 - 1) - 2 = 3 - 2 = 1$.

The difference is then 153.

As for addition, the simple program of Figure **4.4** can describe the subtraction $x - y$. The subtraction is generalised to base b and the digits again held in integer arrays, corresponding to the polynomials –

$$\begin{aligned} \text{from} \quad & \{x_n \ x_{n-1} \ \cdots \ x_1 \ x_0\} \\ \text{subtract} \quad & \{y_n \ y_{n-1} \ \cdots \ y_1 \ y_0\} \\ \text{for the difference} \quad & \{z_n \ z_{n-1} \ \cdots \ z_1 \ z_0\} \end{aligned}$$

Figure 4.4: Code to Subtract Two Numbers in Any Base

```
// The "numbers" are in integer arrays, one digit per integer
// The minuend and subtrahend are in x[ ] and y[ ],
//    and the difference in z[ ].

borrow = 0;
for (i = 0; i < n; i++)
    {
    z[i] = x[i] - y[i] - borrow;
    if (z[i] < 0)
        {
        borrow = 1;
        z[i] = z[i] + base;
        }
    else
        borrow = 0;
    }
```

The values in subtraction have specific names, but note that they are no longer symmetric. Using X, Y and Z as in Figure **4.4**, the names are –

- X   is the *minuend* (that which is diminished)
- Y   is the *subtrahend* (that which is subtracted)
- Z   (the result) is the *difference*

The actions in binary subtraction are identical apart from the change of base; if the subtraction "won't go", add the base (10_2) to the minuend digit and decrement the next most-significant minuend digit by 1 (or increment the next subtrahend digit).

Again we can use a subtraction table, or we can just use our familiar decimal subtraction with appropriate changes. Starting from the right (least significant) digit, subtract each pair of digits. If the result is less than zero, add on the base to the result and generate a "borrow" to include in the next subtraction to the left.

The subtraction table in Figure **4.5** contains two additional columns relating the results to some obvious arithmetic functions, in the spirit of the addition table in Figure **4.3**. The borrow is now a 1 if the intermediate D is negative (as might be expected), while the final difference is 1 if D is odd (which is exactly as for addition, if the borrow is equivalent to a carry). (A better way of binary subtraction is given later!)

Figure 4.5: Binary Subtraction Table

Input Values			Results			Alternatives		
Minu-end	Sub-trahend	Borrow In B_{in}	Borrow Out B_{out}	Diff		X-Y-B$_{in}$ = D	D < 0	D *odd*
0	0	0	0	0		0	0	0
0	0	1	1	1		-1	1	1
0	1	0	1	1		-1	1	1
0	1	1	1	0		-2	1	0
1	0	0	0	1		1	0	1
1	0	1	0	0		0	0	0
1	1	0	0	0		0	0	0
1	1	1	1	1		-1	1	1

Subtract (0110 1111 0101 1001 - 0010 0000 1011 0011)

$$
\begin{array}{rcccc}
\text{Take minuend} & 0110 & 1111 & 0101 & 1001 \\
\text{and the subtrahend} & 0010 & 0000 & 1011 & 0011 \\
\text{with the borrows} & 0000 & 0001 & 0100 & 1100 \\
\hline
\text{subtract, to get answer} & 0100 & 1110 & 1010 & 0110 \\
\end{array}
$$

Check that the answer is (28 505 - 8371) = 20 134 Each borrow digit is shifted left by one place from where it is generated, to be subtracted from the next-significant minuend digit.

4.5 Overflow

An overflow strictly refers to a result which has no valid representation. As computers always represent integers to some small number of bits, say 32 or 64, only a limited range of values can be represented. If two large positive values are added the result may exceed the maximum value, leading to an *overflow*. Overflows can also occur when adding two large negative values, but never when adding numbers of opposite sign.

An overflow shows itself as a number of the wrong apparent sign. For example, with 4 bits and twos complement, the range is $-8 \leq V \leq 7$.

$$
\begin{array}{r}
\text{Adding } 6 + 7 \text{ gives} \quad\quad 0110 \\
+ \quad 0111 \\
\hline
1101 \\
\end{array}
$$

The result (13) is outside the valid range and appears as a negative sum of two positive values.

Similarly, $-6 + -7$ gives an apparently positive result –

$$
\begin{array}{l}
1010 \\
+1001 \\
\hline
10011 \quad = 0011 \text{ after truncation to 4 bits} \\
\end{array}
$$

Both results would be correct with more digits available. In general an overflow may be detected as a result of unexpected sign (+ve + +ve → –ve, or –ve + –ve → +ve).

A better way to detect overflow is to look at the carries into and out of the sign bit. If these are not equal, there is an overflow. (This method works for subtraction by addition of the complement, as described later.)

When adding N-bit twos complement numbers, always discard the carry out of the sign bit (truncate the result at N bits).

4.6   Signed Addition and Subtraction

The earlier rules given for addition and subtraction really apply only to unsigned (positive) numbers, although negative values have been mentioned at times. When we have genuinely signed numbers, the rules depend on the representation.

Assume N-bit numbers, where N is large enough to represent all the values concerned without overflow. We will use $\mathcal{X}, \mathcal{Y}, \mathcal{Z}$ to denote the current signed representation of the positive values $X, Y, Z = X + Y$ and handle subtractions as complement additions. Remember that positive values are represented in "natural form" in all cases.

4.6.1   Sign and Magnitude

Sign and magnitude numbers are usually converted to one of the other representations and the result converted back if necessary. This means that sign and magnitude addition and subtraction is relatively complex and is one good reason for avoiding this representation.

4.6.2   Ones Complement

If $X < 0$, then $\mathcal{X} = 2^N - 1 - X$ and similarly for $\mathcal{Y}$ and $\mathcal{Z}$. There are now five cases to consider –

1. $X > 0$, $Y > 0 \rightarrow Z > 0$. (+ve + +ve $\rightarrow$ +ve)
   These values are all in "natural" unsigned binary with no adjustments involved or need to consider any aspects of signed representations. It is therefore a conventional unsigned addition.

2. $X < 0, Y < 0 \rightarrow Z < 0$. (-ve + -ve → -ve)
   Expanding the sum as represented

   $$\mathcal{X} + \mathcal{Y} = (2^N - 1 - X) + (2^N - 1 - Y) = (2 \times 2^N) - (X + Y) - 2$$

   But as $\mathcal{Z} = 2^N - 1 - Z = 2^N - 1 - (X + Y)$, the result is too large by $2^N - 1$. The 2^N does not matter because it is a single bit beyond those represented and can be dropped, but that still leaves a deficit of 1.

3. $X < 0, Y > 0 \rightarrow Z < 0$. (-ve + +ve → -ve)
   Expanding the sum gives

   $$\mathcal{X} + \mathcal{Y} = (2^N - 1 - X) + Y = 2^N + (Y - X) - 1 = Z + 2^N - 1$$

   which is the correct value for a negative $\mathcal{Z}$.

4. $X < 0, Y > 0 \rightarrow Z > 0$. (-ve + +ve → +ve)
   Expanding the sum gives

   $$\mathcal{X} + \mathcal{Y} = (2^N - 1 - X) + Y = 2^N + X - Y - 1$$

   But the correct representation for the positive Z is $\mathcal{Z}$ is $2^N + (Y - X)$, so there is again a deficit of 1 in the result after dropping the 2^N.

5. $X + Y = 0$. $(-X = Y)$
   This is in some ways the simplest case, because with $Y = (-X)$ we have $\mathcal{X} + \mathcal{Y} = X + 2^N - 1 - X = 2^N - 1$. This result is the $111 \ldots 111$, the negative zero, sometimes called an *arithmetic zero*, because it is the result of signed additions, in contrast to the $000 \ldots 000$ *numeric zero*. The existence of two zeros is a nuisance because tests for zero should recognise these two cases of all 1s and all 0s. (But should $111 \ldots 111$ test as zero if it arises from a *logical* operation, rather than from arithmetic?)

Table 4.1: Signs and Corrections in Ones Complement

case	correction	sign bit	carry out
$+ve + +ve \rightarrow +ve$	0	$0 + 0 \rightarrow 0$	0
$-ve + -ve \rightarrow -ve$	1	$1 + 1 \rightarrow 1$	1
$-ve + +ve \rightarrow -ve$	0	$1 + 0 \rightarrow 1$	0
$-ve + +ve \rightarrow +ve$	1	$1 + 0 \rightarrow 0$	1
$-ve + +ve \rightarrow 0$	0	$1 + 0 \rightarrow 1$	0

There are then two cases with an error of 1 in the least significant bit. All the cases, together with that for positive inputs, are shown in Table **4.1**. A correction is needed if, and only if, there is a carry out of the sign bit. Ones complement addition therefore requires a *wrap-around carry*, (or *end-around carry*) feeding the carry from the sign bit back into the least-significant carry-in.

An interesting solution to the "two zeros" problem with ones complement was used in the Univac 1108, CDC 6600 and similar computers. There the fundamental arithmetic operation was *subtraction*, rather than addition, with $\mathcal{X}+\mathcal{Y}$ implemented as $\mathcal{X}-(-\mathcal{Y})$, relying on the natural property of subtraction to give a $000\ldots000$ result. (When adding $\mathcal{X}+-\mathcal{X}$, each bit position is either $0+1 \rightarrow 1$ or $1+0 \rightarrow 1$, whereas with $\mathcal{X}-\mathcal{X}$, each bit position is either $0-0 \rightarrow 0$ or $1-1 \rightarrow 0$.)

4.6.3 Twos Complement

In twos complement $-\mathcal{X} = 2^N - X$, without further adjustment as is needed for ones complement. The lack of adjustment means that when two values are added, whether positive or negative, the result is always correct as it stands. In other words there is virtually no special treatment needed in addition or subtraction, and that is one good reason using twos complement.

4.6.4 Subtraction by Complement Addition

Computers usually perform subtraction by adding the complement of the subtrahend—use X–Y = X+(–Y). To calculate

$$0100\ 1011\ 0110 - 0011\ 0111\ 1001\ \ (1206_{10} - 889_{10})$$

using twos complement arithmetic.

Take subtrahend	0011 0111 1001
ones complement it	1100 1000 0110
add minuend	0100 1011 0110
with a carry-in for the +1	1
then add, to get answer	1 0001 0011 1101 = 317

The answer has a carry out of the high order bit.

Inspection shows that there is also a carry into the high-order bit. A correct twos complement addition requires that the carry into the sign bit must be equal to the carry out of the sign bit.

4.6.5 A Geometric View of Signed Addition.

A useful alternative view comes from considering the integers as points along a line, as in Figure **4.6**(a). With addition to only N bits, only the portion of the line in Figure **4.6**(b) is relevant; all other points on the line fold or map into the sections shown. The arrows of Figure **4.6**(a) reflect these mappings, with all of the "larger" sections folding back by, firstly 2^{2N} bits, or in general, any even number of sections. In fact, even this figure is redundant, because it shows the regions of the line used for *unsigned* numbers[1] (approximately $0 \ldots 2^N$), and for *unsigned* numbers (approximately $-2^{N-1} \ldots 2^{N-1}$). The two end regions, for large positive and for negative, coincide with the representation of any value in these regions dependent on the assumption of signed or unsigned numbers.

Figure 4.6: Addition with Arithmetic Modulo 2^N.

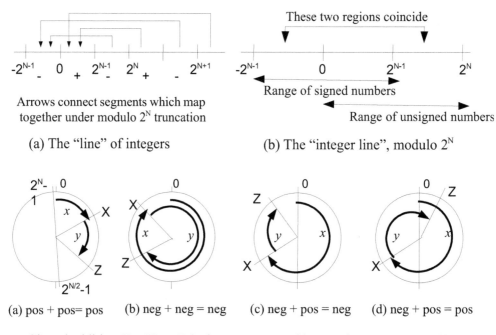

Arrows connect segments which map together under modulo 2^N truncation

(a) The "line" of integers

(b) The "integer line", modulo 2^N

(a) pos + pos= pos   (b) neg + neg = neg   (c) neg + pos = neg   (d) neg + pos = pos

Signed addition X + Y → Z (values represented by rotations – -ve > 180°)

Of more importance, we can now change the line of Figure **4.6**(b) into the circle of Figure **4.6**(c). In the *unsigned* interpretation the largest value $2^N - 1$ is followed by zero (the smallest value). In the *signed* interpretation, the largest value 2^{N-1} is similarly followed by the smallest value -2^{N-1}, but

---

[1]In much of this discussion (but not all) it is convenient to refer to the extreme values as $\pm 2^m$, ignoring the fact that the correct value is often $2^m - 1$

at the diametrically opposite point on the circle from the unsigned case. A value may be represented by a radius vector in this circle. Addition always corresponds to a clockwise movement of the radius vector; the addition of a positive value always gives a movement of less than 180°. A subtraction uses a clockwise motion of more than 180°; substituting for example a clockwise rotation of 300° for an anticlockwise rotation of 60°.

Figure **4.6**(c) shows the addition of two positive values, where X is represented by a rotation angle of θ and Y by ϕ. $X > 0$ corresponds to $\theta < \pi$, while $X < 0$ corresponds to its angle $\theta > \pi$. We continue with further cases, given in the order used earlier in Section **4.6.2**.

1. $X < 0$, $Y < 0 \rightarrow Z < 0$ or $\theta > \pi, \phi > \pi$. Figure **4.6**(d)
   The value X corresponds to a rotation from 0° of θ or about 300° (or an anticlockwise rotation of about 60° corresponding to the negative X). The position is marked by the radial line X. The subtraction of Y corresponds to a further positive rotation of about 300° , giving a final position corresponding the radial line Z.

2. $X < 0$, $Y > 0 \rightarrow Z < 0$ or $\theta > \pi, \phi < \pi$. Figure **4.6**(e).
   The total rotation angle is $\theta + \phi < 360°$, for the negative sum.

3. $X < 0$, $Y > 0 \rightarrow Z > 0$ or $\theta > \pi, \phi < \pi$. Figure **4.6**(f).
   The total rotation angle for the positive sum is now $\theta + \phi > 360°$.

Before proceeding further, remember that the circle has a finite number of steps around it and that each addition of 1 corresponds to a definite angular motion of the radius vector corresponding to the current value. Furthermore, an addition of n corresponds to a clockwise movement of n distinct steps; we can if necessary consider each step individually.

There are two possible discontinuities around the circle of values, one at 0 and one diagonally opposite, and both where the sign bit changes. With twos complement numbers the interval $-2^{N-1} \ldots 2^{N-1} - 1$ maps continuously onto the circle.

With twos complement numbers the region of the integer line around zero maps smoothly to the circle around zero; steps on the one correspond precisely to a like number of steps on the other. Addition is then as described above, with no special actions or corrections apart from the transition between the extreme positive and negative numbers.

The situation is different with ones complement, because of the discontinuity around zero. Whenever the radius vector reaches $111 \ldots 111$, or -0 the next step should be to $000\ldots001$ or $+1$ rather than to $000\ldots001$. At the transition from $111\ldots111$ and only at this step, an addition of 1 gives a carry-out in changing the value to $000\ldots000$. Feeding the carry-out of the adder into the carry-in provides the necessary correction, as was derived earlier by algebra.

Looking at Figure **4.6**, we see that it is only in cases (d) and (f) that the radius vector passes zero, and it is only in these cases that we actually need the correction provided by the end-around carry. (In all other cases the output carry is always zero and no adjustment occurs.)

4.7   Multiple Precision Addition

It often happens that the required number precision exceeds that provided by the hardware operations, especially on computers with short word lengths. To a first approximation, there is nothing special to do because addition is just as already described, but with a number base of say 2^{16} rather than 2.

At one extreme are those computers which make no provision whatsoever for multiple precision addition. These are either old designs, or not quite so old RISC designs such as the MIPS R2000 where multiple precision addition was judged to be insufficiently important to warrant much assistance (probably justified with a reasonable word length to start with). In these computers a complicated series of tests on operands and results is necessary to decide whether there is an emergent carry to propagate to the next stage of the addition.

The emphasis here though is on computers with "Condition Codes", or bits which are set to indicate the nature of the last arithmetic result. Typically, these are a set of bits, labelled Z, N, C, and V, being set to 1 for respectively zero result, negative result, carry-out from last addition, and overflow. The values to be added are usually a set of contiguous bytes or words, addressed initially at the least-significant end.

- One of the simplest implementations is the IBM S/360, with a 2-bit condition code which normally encodes the results 'Zero', 'Negative', 'Positive' and 'Overflow'. For the "Add Logical" instruction the two bits of the Condition Code are redefined to mean zero/not-zero and carry-out/no-carry. A carry-out can be tested by a conditional branch and a 1 added to the next word if needed.

- Next in complexity is the PDP-11, with a full set of condition bits as above. The "Add Carry" instruction nominates a single 16-bit operand and adds 1 to it if the "C" bit is set; the addition may continue to more-significant words if the Add Carry itself sets C (the incremented operand was all 1s). The improvement over the S/360 is that the C bit does not have to be explicitly tested.

Both this and the previous method are awkward for precisions over two words because the carry from the first addition may have to propagate completely before the next two words can be added, giving an N^2 complexity in the number of component words or bytes.

- Finally, computers such as the Motorola 6800 and 68000 and Intel 80x86 have an Add with Carry instruction which adds two values, including the carry-in and providing a carry-out for propagation to the next stage.

  After a normal Add instruction for the least-significant digits, a succession of Adds with Carry will correctly combine the more significant "digits" and handle carry propagation, proceeding to the more-significant parts of the number. Some of these computers provide auto-adjustment addressing modes which facilitate the scan over the number.

Given that addition is a fundamental and well-understood operation, one might assume that correctly setting the condition code (Z, N and V bits) for a multiple-precision would be a trivial exercise. It is trivial, but even so some designers have got it wrong or laboured mightily to succeed[2]. The rules are indeed simple –

The N bit is always set according to the sign bit of the last result, whether from an Add or an Add with Carry.

The V bit is also set from the last result, as for the N bit, but according to whether the carry propagates through the sign bit.

The Z bit is the one which seems to be difficult. The initial Add may set or clear the Z bit; this allows a single-precision addition to work normally and correctly and is also the correct preparation for succeeding Adds with Carry. An Add with Carry may *clear* the Z bit, (for a non-zero result) but may never set it. This *should be* obvious, because any non-zero component causes the whole result to become non-zero. Once a

---

[2]One major manufacturer perhaps committed a "big blue" (Australian and New Zealand idiom for a mistake) in discussing the design of a new 16-bit computer which provided multiple-precision binary addition. They admitted that finding how to correctly set the condition codes took several *man-months* of work!

non-zero component has been detected, no sequence of more-significant 0s can ever over-ride it. The Z bit is often described as a "sticky bit".

4.8 Decimal Addition

Decimal numbers in computers are usually held as variable length strings of BCD digits in some form of sign and magnitude notation. Computers such as the M6800, 68000 and 80x86 provide a decimal-adjust instruction which, applied after a normal binary addition, converts the result to a BCD addition, superficially by adding a 6 to those BCD digits which exceed 9 and propagating carries. This converts a variable-length binary addition into a variable-length decimal addition, with 2 BCD digits per 8-bit byte.

In the IBM System/360 BCD digit strings are addressed at the left-most digit, with the right-most or least-significant digit the sign. The preferred signs are – +ve 1100 (C_{16}) and –ve 1101 (D_{16}). The Burroughs B2500 and B3500 were similar, but with the sign in the most-significant BCD digit. Both computers have the operand length held in the instruction.

Decimal numbers are usually added serially, digit by digit from the least-significant to the most-significant. While some implementations may introduce a degree of internal parallelism by adding say 32 bits or 8 BCD digits in parallel, the operation is still conceptually serial as in the algorithms of Figure **4.2**.

An interesting exception this 'rule' is found in the Burroughs 3500 and re-lated computers with a left-to-right addition, working from the most-significant digit towards the least. As the addition proceeds, the adder notes the position of the last '9' produced as a sum digit and retains that position as long as further 9s are produced. If a carry is generated, all of those pending 9s are converted to 0s and the digit preceding the string incremented to absorb the carry. The generation of a 'non-9' digit, and no carry, allows the string of 9s to be accepted as the correct result. (Note that the 9s belong to the *sum* and that the only possible action of a carry-in of 1 is to change all of the 9s to 0 and increment the preceding digit; the carry can never propagate beyond that preceding digit.)

The method is acceptable for decimal addition because carry propagation is relatively rare and occurs over relatively few digits. In practice, the adder can 'look-ahead' and defer writing the string of 9s until either some other digit is generated (in which case the whole pending string will be written), or a carry is generated (in which case a string of 0s will be written and the preceding digit adjusted), so any penalties are probably small.

There are some important advantages, which justify the method –

1. When reading or writing digit strings it is more natural to address them at the left rather than the right, so the same addressing may be used for arithmetic and input-output.

2. One of the more frequent "addition-type" operations is the comparison of two numbers. Although this is normally thought of as a subtraction followed by examination of the result, it need not be—there is no need to produce the complete difference. If the comparands are examined from left to right and are the same sign, the first position with different digits can resolve the comparison. Any further examination is wasted effort. If the signs differ the comparison resolves immediately.

3. As decimal numbers are usually held in sign-and-magnitude form any "addition-type" operation which gives a negative result must be recomplemented. With a conventional right-to-left addition or subtraction the sign is not known until the most-significant digit (the very last one) has been processed. The result must be traversed twice, the first time to produce it and the second time to correct it. With left-to-right arithmetic, the sign is usually apparent very early in the addition and the remaining arithmetic can be adjusted to absorb the complementing. Only a single traversal is needed, apart from minor backtracking to handle carries.

4.8.1   Decimal Arithmetic by Complementing

Decimal numbers can also be represented in a form equivalent to twos complement, allowing subtraction by adding the complement. In the subtrahend, retain any trailing zeros, tens complement the least-significant non-zero and nines complement all digits to its left. (If the digit y is the 9s complement of the digit x, then $x + y \equiv 9$, and if z is the 10s complement of x, then $x + z \equiv 10$.) A negative number now has leading 9s, or a leading digit of 5 or greater.

For example to calculate $235 - 164$,

- The subtrahend complement is 836 ($1 \rightarrow 8$, $6 \rightarrow 3$ and tens complementing 4 gives 6.)

- add the 836 to the minuend 235 to give $235 + 836 = 1071$.

- Ignoring the carry out gives the correct answer of 71

With trailing zeros take $7435 - 1250$ (and extending with high-order zeros)

- The complement of 1250 is 998 750

- Add 7435 ($007\,435 + 998\,750 \rightarrow 1\,006\,185$)

- Discard the carry-out to give the difference 6185.

To add *two* negative numbers by adding their decimal complements, consider $-4512 + (-1200)$, which gives $995\,488 + 998\,800 = 1\,994\,288$. Discarding the carry gives $994\,288$, which is the complement representation of -5712.

4.8.2 Complementing Revisited

For another look at decimal complementing, take the nines complement of every digit, and add a 1 carry-in. Trailing 0s then revert to 0 and the carry propagates through them. The first complement digit which is not a 9 absorbs the carry; the addition of the 1 from the carry turns it into a tens complement. More-significant digits stay as the nines complement. This is the precise analogue of adding 1 to the binary ones complement.

The complementing of decimal digits helps explain "serial" twos complementing which was described as *working from the right, copy the trailing 0s and the least significant 1, and then ones complement all digits to the left.*

The corresponding decimal rule is—*working from the right, copy the trailing 0s, tens complement the least significant non-zero digit, and then nines complement all digits to the left.*

In binary, the twos complement of a digit is the original digit; the least-significant non-zero digit is not really "copied" but is twos complemented, leaving the original value unchanged.

4.9   Using Bits as Bits.

Although a great deal of effort has gone into designing programming methods which conceal the underlying binary nature and bits of a computer, there are times when we must consider the bits of a word, not as binary digits, but as a collection of logical units. This usually occurs when working close to the hardware, with miscellaneous status or control bits collected into status or control words. Programmers not working directly with hardware devices or within the operating system may seldom if ever use "bit bashing" operations.

These operations also arise when a small data structure is being packed into a word, as is needed in software floating-point (and sometimes in languages such as C which provide bit-field structures). The operations of this section are then needed to extract and insert the component fields of the word. A few languages, such as C, provide direct support for manipulating fields within words but most require the methods described in this section.

Although this section is nominally concerned with bit operations, the discussion of parity (a purely logical operation) develops easily into the much wider area of check digits and checksums, which are covered in Chapter **10**.

4.9.1   Bit Numbering

If we want to work with individual bits, it is necessary to identify those bits within a word (or byte, *etc*). Even this apparently simple task has its complications.

It is usual to write binary numbers with the most significant bit (MSB) to the left and the least-significant bit (LSB) to the right, as is usual for decimal values. It is also usual to number the bits, but there the agreement stops. Several systems have been used, which have been described [14, 62] as "current" (left to right), and "contracurrent" (right to left), together with numbering, usually from 0 or 1.   The four combinations are shown in Figure **4.7** for an 8-bit byte. The extension to words and other long entities is obvious[3].

Current, 0-origin is used in the IBM System 360 and its successors. It comes from regarding the byte (or word) as a logical vector of bits. It

---

[3]The terms "current" and "contracurrent", although wonderfully descriptive, have not entered the general literature. They are closely related to the concepts of "big-endian" and "little-endian" of Section **8.5** and discussed in [19].

may also come from the convention in some of the first computers that a word represented, not an integer, but a fraction where bit i represents a weight of 2^{-i}.

Contracurrent, 0-origin is the form used in most computers, and follows from interpreting bits as polynomial coefficients, or as powers of two.

Contracurrent, 1-origin Numbering the bits from 1 is extremely rare; the author has seen it only in the long-obsolete Prime computers.

Current, 1-origin Yet another convention is used in many data communications standards. Bits of an octet (byte) are written in the order of transmission, with the *least-significant* bit on the left and with the bits numbered from 1 to 8. This can be most confusing—and it is a moot point whether is really *contracurrent, 1-origin*, but written backwards.

Figure 4.7: Systems for Numbering Bits

	Description	Bit Numbers							
		MSB							LSB
1	Current, 0-origin	0	1	2	3	4	5	6	7
2	Contracurrent, 0-origin	7	6	5	4	3	2	1	0
3	Contracurrent, 1-origin	8	7	6	5	4	3	2	1
		LSB							MSB
4	Current, 1-origin	1	2	3	4	5	6	7	8

In most cases the numbering is purely a programming convention and has no bearing on the operation of the computer. The one exception is in computers which have hardware for manipulating bit fields or groups of bits, as described in Section **4.9.8**. These computers have instructions which refer explicitly to bits by their number; the bit numbering is a part of the computer architecture, or programming specification.

4.9.2 Logical Operations

So far we have dealt with "numbers" which for the end results are just convenient collections of bits. But sometimes we must go deeper, to bits which compose the numbers. To handle individual bits we require logical operations, essentially the same logical operations as used to implement the computer in the first place. Most computers provide the basic set of operations – AND,

OR, Exclusive OR and NOT as detailed in Table **4.2**, but we will see some variations. Because logical variables are limited to values of '0' and '1' (or FALSE and TRUE), for functions of a few variables it is possible to define the function by enumerating the result for all possible input values, as in Table **4.2**.

Table 4.2: Basic Logic Operations

Inputs		NOT	AND	OR	EOR	NAND
X	Y	$\neg X$	$X \wedge Y$	$X \vee Y$	$X \oplus Y$	$\neg(X \wedge Y)$
0	0	1	0	0	0	1
0	1	1	0	1	1	1
1	0	0	0	1	1	1
1	1	0	1	1	0	0

Table **4.2** also shows the NAND operation, a combination of NOT and AND. While this is not an important operation in computer programming, it is included as an example of how the simpler operations can combine, in this case to produce one of the most important hardware logic operations.

The operation "OR" is ambiguous in English. It can be a *inclusive OR* in which (A OR B) is true if at least one input is true. It can also be an *exclusive OR* in which (A OR B) is true only if *exactly* one of A and B is true; if *both* are true the result is false. In computer logic the term "OR" is restricted to the *inclusive OR*. The *exclusive OR* is a distinct operation, and is abbreviated to EOR or XOR (the two forms seem to be used about equally).

The symbols for the logical operations are far from standard. There are many conventions apart from that used here and shown in Table **4.3**; some alternative symbols are shown to the right of the table. This table also gives brief textual descriptions of each operation, which may be more convenient than the more formal definitions of Table **4.2**.

Table 4.3: Symbols and Alternatives for Logical Operations

Name		Description	Alternatives
NOT	$\neg$	Inverts its 1-bit argument	$\overline{x}, \sim x$
AND	$\wedge$	Yields 1 (TRUE) if both inputs are 1	$x \& y, x \cdot y$
OR	$\vee$	Yields 1 if either input is true (1)	$x \mid y, x + y$
EOR	$\oplus$	1 if either input $= 1$, but not both	$x \neq y, x \not\equiv y, x \forall y$

4.9.3 Shifting

Just as it is necessary to move words around in conjunction with the arithmetic operations, so is it sometimes necessary to move bits within words. For example, to work on the left-most byte of a 32-bit word it may be necessary to move it to the right by 24 bit positions so that it appears as an 8-bit integer. Having worked on these 8 bits as an integer, they may have to be moved back to the correct position within the word.

Moving bits within a word is usually performed with the "shift" operations, which occur with several variations (and are often combined). In most cases we just assume that the word is a collection of bits with no numeric significance (except perhaps for arithmetic shifts). It may be in a register or in memory, depending on the computer. The shift functions occur with various options, such as direction, quantity shifted, and handling the sign –

left/right The whole pattern of bits is shifted left or right by some distance (or number of bit positions). For example

0000 1101 0110 0000	right 3 →	0000 0001 1010 1100
0000 1101 0110 0000	left 4 →	1101 0110 0000 0000

Simple right and left shifts

shift/rotate The above examples were carefully chosen so that only 0s were "lost" or shifted out. (They also quietly and surreptitiously shifted in 0s, but that is dealt with later.) What should be done with any "lost" 1s? There are two alternatives –

1. allow the disappearing bits to be discarded and completely lost; this is the basis of most *shift* operations.

2. allow the bits to re-enter at the opposite end. These *rotate* operations link the two ends of a word so that it behaves as a circular structure, rather than as the linear structure of the shifts (compare, end-around carry).

0000 1101 0110 1111	shift right 3 →	0000 0001 1010 1101
0000 1101 0110 1111	rotate right 3 →	1110 0001 1010 1101
1110 1101 0110 0000	shift left 4 →	1101 0110 0000 0000
1110 1101 0110 0000	rotate left 4 →	1101 0110 0000 1110

Shifts and rotates

signed/unsigned If a word starting with 1101...is shifted right 2 places, should the result be 001101..., regarding it as unsigned, or should the result be 111101..., regarding the word as signed, and shifting with sign fill? Both are valid interpretations—it just depends on which one we want. The choice must be with the programmer. Most computers provide both a *signed* or *arithmetic* right shift which fills the sign bit into vacated bits and an *unsigned* or *logical* right shift which fills in with 0s on the left.

0000 1101 0110 1111	logical right 3 →	0000 0001 1010 1101
0000 1101 0110 1111	signed right 3 →	0000 0001 1010 1101
1110 1101 0110 0000	logical right 4 →	0000 1110 1101 0110
1110 1101 0110 0000	signed right 4 →	1111 1110 1101 0110

Logical (unsigned) and arithmetic (signed) shifts

There is seldom any distinction with left shifts; most just discard any bits shifted out, without regard to "signed" or "unsigned". Some computers may set an Overflow indicator if the sign changes at any stage during the shift. A few computers do provide an *arithmetic* left shift which retains the sign bit, discarding bits from the place immediately after the sign bit.

carry included/omitted A final option is to link the Carry bit or Carry indicator into the shift. The simplest, for both left shifts and right shifts of any style, is to just save the last of the lost bits in the Carry indicator.

A frequent option with Rotates is to regard the Carry as a 1-bit extension of the basic operand, so that a 16-bit word expands to a 17-bit quantity when rotated.

0000 1101 0110 1111 1	rotate right 3 →	1110 0001 1010 1101 1
0000 1101 0110 1111 0	rotate right 3 →	1100 0001 1010 1101 1
1110 1101 0110 0000 0	rotate left 4 →	1101 0110 0000 0111 0
1110 1101 0110 0000 1	rotate left 4 →	1101 0110 0000 0111 1

Rotates, including carry

If the Carry is used in this way with a rotation of 1 bit it allows a multi-word or multi-byte operand to be shifted left or right by one place, with the Carry linking between words. The first operation (a left shift of the right-most word, or a right shift of the left-most word) may be a normal shift (say logical or arithmetic right) to set the handling of the extreme bit; the following rotates with Carry extend the shift over the whole multi-word operand. (Compare with Add-with-Carry for multiple precision operations.)

4.9.4 Signed Shifts and Division

Extreme caution is required concerning signed or arithmetic shifts[4]. Superficially, the arithmetic shifts correspond to multiplication or division by a power of 2. This interpretation is correct for positive values and for left shifts of negative values, but does not agree with arithmetic conventions for right shifts of negative values. In division we normally assume that $11 \div 4 \to 2$ (+3 rem) and that $-11 \div 4 \to -2$ (-3 rem).

For a positive number, 00001011 right 2 $\to$ 00000010 = 2, but for a negative 11110101 right 2 $\to$ 11111101 = -3, corresponding to $-11 \div 4 \to -3$ (+1 rem).

While we normally assume that a division will truncate towards zero, the arithmetic right shift truncates towards $-\infty$, which is an equally correct but less usual interpretation. Right shifts of negative quantities are seldom suitable replacements for a division by a power of 2.

4.9.5 Programming Bit Operations

We can illustrate the bit operations by showing their implementations in C. (Java is more complex, using Methods associated with the integer-type classes.) The general rule is that logical operations may be applied to "integer type" operands, in other words to `byte`, `short`, `int` and `long` values. The operations are always applied between corresponding bits of the two operands (except for ~ which is unary). Shorter values are extended as necessary with 0s on the left. When bit values are important, integer constants may be written in C with a preceding `0x` for hexadecimal (or `0` for octal).

Hexadecimal		*Decimal*
0x100	$\Longleftrightarrow$	256
0xF4240	$\Longleftrightarrow$	1 000 000
0x0FFFF	$\Longleftrightarrow$	65 535
0x2540BE400L	$\Longleftrightarrow$	10 000 000 000L$(= 10^{10})$

With values shown in binary, the bit-wise operations are –

---

[4]Caution may be needed when "faking" shifts with arithmetic on a computer using 1s complement representation. With 2s complement a multiplication by 256 may be optimised to an arithmetic left shift of 8 bits. The corresponding 1s complement optimisation is a *rotate* left by 8 bits, filling the sign into the lower significance bits. This is all very well, except if the intention is to discard the more-significant bits of the word.

name	Java	example
AND	&	00111 & 01010 → 00010
OR	|	00111 | 01010 → 01111
EOR	ˆ	00111 ˆ 01010 → 01101
NOT	˜	˜ 01010 → 10101

It is essential to re-emphasise that these bit operations apply to "integers" acting as collections of 8 to 64 bits, whereas the Boolean operations apply to single-bit Boolean variables or to results of comparisons. The difference (in C and Java) is in the NOT or negation operators, with the Boolean '!' applying only to a Boolean value, whereas the bit-wise negation ˜ applies to integer-type values.

C provides three shift operators, for "integer type" operands; Java adds a "logical right" (>>>) for zero-fill.

description	symbol	example	result
left	zero fill	<<	0000 1101 << 3 → 0110 1000
signed right	sign fill	>>	1100 1101 >> 3 → 1111 1001

Examples of using these logical operations and shifts are given in the next Section.

4.9.6 Bit Operations—Masking and Shifting.

A computer word is often divided into several fields, or groups of bits, as in floating-point representations. Sometimes we handle the word as a whole; sometimes we must get inside it and work on its internal fields. The fields can be extracted and inserted using the logical operations and suitable *masks* with patterns of 0s and 1s corresponding to the fields or selected bit positions.

Fields may be moved left or right to bring them into the correct alignment. For example, if the left-most byte (8 bits) of a 32-bit word is sometimes used as an integer, it may have to be shifted right by 24 bits before it can be used. Equally, an integer value must be shifted 24 bits to the left before it can be inserted in the left-hand byte of the word.

For example, later we will meet floating-point numbers, where the 32 bits of a single word are divided as –

```
sxxx xxxx xfff ffff ffff ffff ffff ffff
```

where **s** is the sign bit, **xx** ...**xx** is the exponent, and **ff** ...**ff** is the significand, fraction, or mantissa.

With a floating-point value **fp** (more correctly the bits corresponding to that value), we can use the combinations of shifts and hexadecimal masks in Figure **4.8** to manipulate its fields –

Figure 4.8: Manipulating Floating-point Bit Fields

1	fp & 0x7F800000	extracts the exponent
2	(fp & 0x7F800000) >> 23	gets exponent as an integer
3	(fp & >> 23) & 0xFF	gets exponent as an integer
4	fp & 0x80000000	obtains the sign bit
5	(fp & 0x80000000) >> 31	gets sign as 0 or 1
6	fp >> 31	gets sign as 0 or -1
7	(fp >> 31) & 0x1	gets sign as 0 or +1
8	fp >>> 31	gets sign as 0 or +1 (Java, not C)
9	fp & 0x007FFFFF	obtains the significand
10	fp & 0x807FFFFF	clears the exponent
11	fp & 0xFF800000	clears the significand
12	fp & 0x807FFFFF | $(x << 23)$	places x into the exponent
13	fp & 0xFF800000 | sig	places sig into significand

Lines 2 and 3 show two different ways of getting the 8 exponent bits as an integer (in the range $0 \ldots 255$). Line 2 does the mask first to select the bits and then moves the selected bits into the correct alignment, whereas line 3 does the shift first and then masks. The choice is often one of individual preference. Either right shift can be used in lines 2 and 3 because the sign is removed either before or after the shift.

Lines 5 to 8 show four ways of handling the sign bit, with various combinations of masking and shifts, both signed (>>) and unsigned (>>>, Java only). (Line 6, propagating the sign bit through the whole word, needs no masking.)

Line 12 clears the 8 exponent bits to 0 and then sets the exponent to the value x, after shifting x into the correct position, and assuming that the exponent field has been cleared using the code of Line 10. This illustrates the use of an OR to insert values into a field, once the field has been cleared with an AND and a suitable mask. (This code assumes that $x < 256$ so that it fits into the 8 bits of the exponent.) Line 13 similarly shows the insertion of new significand bits, again assuming that they do not overflow the allocated 23 bits.

4.9.7   Variant Logical Operations

The binary (two-operand) logical operations combine in sometimes unexpected ways. Often they need to be reinterpreted in ways other than their fundamental definitions to see their utility.

AND Although AND is in some respects *the* archetypical logic operation, it is nevertheless capable of reinterpretation. Its most frequent use is in extracting bits or bit fields from a word or, equivalently, setting the undesired bits to zero. For this, the AND is used with a logical *mask* or bit vector which is set to 1s where bits are to be retained and to 0s where the bits are to be deleted, suppressed or set to zero. Thus in some respects its fundamental operation is to force selected bits to be set to zero.

Computers such as the DEC PDP-11 and DEC VAX provided instead of the AND a *bit-clear* or BIC operation. The two operations are –

$$
\begin{aligned}
\text{AND} \quad & \text{result} \leftarrow \text{input} \wedge \text{mask} \\
\text{BIC} \quad & \text{result} \leftarrow \text{input} \wedge \neg\text{mask} \\
\text{or} \quad \text{BIC} \quad & \text{result} \leftarrow \text{input} \wedge \overline{\text{mask}}
\end{aligned}
$$

Thus the 1s in the mask specified which bits were to be *cleared*. Note that here, as for any operation with AND, the "bit field" does not have to be contiguous bits. Some examples of non-contiguous bits are included with the examples.

Inclusive OR While the AND is used to force bits to 0 (and often eliminate an unwanted bit field, leaving a wanted one), the OR is used to force bits to a 1 (and often insert a field).

This was one of the reasons why the PDP-11 and VAX computers replaced the AND with a Bit-Clear and renamed the OR as a "Bit-Set" (BIS). If single bits are to be manipulated the same mask can be used to both set or clear the bit.

Exclusive OR, XOR While the AND and OR operations have some fairly obvious uses in bit manipulation, the Exclusive-OR is a much more subtle operation, as illustrated by the following examples. Many Exclusive-OR examples need some lateral thinking or less-obvious approaches to really appreciate what is happening.

1. We have already seen how a bit-field can be extracted from a word using an AND operation; how about obtaining the discarded bits? An obvious technique is to use the statements

$$thebits \leftarrow input \wedge mask$$

and

$$otherbits \leftarrow input \wedge \neg mask$$

using two masks, the original and its complement. A tidier method which needs no extra masks is to Exclusive-OR the extracted field with the original

$$otherbits \leftarrow thebits \oplus input$$

Where bits were suppressed by 0s in the mask any input 1s will be inserted into the result. Where bits were copied through the mask, every 1 in the result is matched by a 1 in the input and the two will cancel in the result.

2. Just as the Exclusive-OR can assist in separating a word into two components as specified by a bit mask, it can also assist in combining the components into a single result.

   This corresponds to Iverson's APL mask operator [62].

$$result \leftarrow /left, mask, right/$$

Wherever *mask* contains a 0 bit, that bit of *result* is copied from *left* and wherever the *mask* bit is a 1, the corresponding bit of *right* is copied[5]. An obvious method is to calculate

$$result \leftarrow (left \wedge \overline{mask}) \vee (right \wedge mask)$$

using complementary masks to prepare the two halves before combining them with a final OR.

A less obvious method, using the Exclusive-OR is

$$result \leftarrow ((right \oplus left) \wedge mask) \oplus left$$

Where a *mask* bit is 0 the whole outer parenthesised expression is 0 and the Exclusive-OR with *left* just copies that bit of *left*. Where the *mask* bit is a 1, then that bit of *right* is Exclusive-ORed twice with *left*; the two EORs cancel and the *right* bit is copied.

---

[5]We assume here that *left*, *mask* and *right* are all bit vectors. In APL *left* and *right* may be vectors of any type.

In summary –

- An AND clears to 0 wherever the mask is 0

- An OR forces to 1 wherever the mask is 1

- An XOR (or EOR) complements a bit wherever the mask is 1

4.9.8   Bit-Field Operations

As an alternative to shifting and masking, some computers specify the actual bits to be moved, using some variation on –

1   Move n bits, starting from bit i in *word1*, to bit j in *word2*.
2   Move the least-significant n bits from *word1*, to bit j in *word2*.
3   Move the n bits, starting from bit i in *word1*, to *word2*.

Computers such as the DEC VAX and Motorola MC68020 include several bit field operations as described above, and also operations for testing, clearing and setting bit fields. They are however accessible only through Assembler code and are therefore difficult for ordinary programmers to appreciate. In any case, they are alternatives to the more conventional logical and shifting operations. A contrast is found in the Burroughs B6700 computer, which has no shift operations at all, relying entirely on field manipulations. The languages, especially B6700 Algol, provide full access to these operations. The examples here are taken directly from a Burroughs Algol Reference Manual [18] and use the syntax of that manual.

The B6700 has a 48-bit word, with bits numbered from 0 on the right (least-significant) and using a unique number representation described in Section **6.1**.

The simplest bit field is the "partial word part", x.`[left-bit:length]` , where x is any word-type value, including an intermediate result from a calculation. This extracts a field as a right-aligned numeric operand. Thus `W.[23:16]` extracts two bytes from the word as a 16-bit value, shifting the field right by 8 bits, and `W.[38:39]` retrieves the rightmost 39 bits of the word.

More complex are the "concatenation" operations, which take a base value and follow it with any number of insertion operations to move bits into the base. B6700 Algol uses "**&**" as the concatenation operator. The result of a concatenation is an arithmetic primary, equivalent to a simple variable or parenthesised expression –

```
base & word1.[left-to:left-from:length]
     & word2.[left-to:left-from:length] ...
```

Any of the components can be arbitrarily complex arithmetic expressions. Bits wrap round into the most-significant bits if `length` exceeds either of the "left-bit" values. The B6700 Algol manual [18] gives the examples of Figure **4.9**, assuming the values X=32 767, Y=1024 and Z=1. (Some are understandable only after reference to the B6700 number format—Section **6.1**.)

Figure 4.9: B6700 Bit Manipulations

operation	result
Y & (2*Z)[11:1:2]	2048
Y & Z[9:0:1] & X[3:13:4]	1551
Z & Y[40:10:2] & Z[45:0:1]	floating-point 1/64
X & Z[47:0:1]	32 767
Y & (2*Z)[11:1:2]+5	2053
Y & (4*Z+1)[9:6:7] & X[14:14:15]	32 767

4.9.9 Combined Logic and Arithmetic

Sometimes it is appropriate to combine logic and numeric operations in the one calculation. Very simple examples are the logical negation ($\neg x$) to form the ones complement, and $1 + \neg x$ to form the twos complement of an integer. (Equally, $-x - 1$ gives the logical negation.)

- Another obvious example involves ANDing a number (2s complement) with $2^N - 1$ to reduce it modulo 2^N. For example X & 0xFFF is equivalent to x % 4096 (or x % 0x1000). ("&" now reverts to its more conventional meaning as AND.)

- A well-known test is $(x \wedge (x - 1))$ is zero if, and only if, x is a power of 2 (explained below).

- More generally, $x \wedge (x - 1)$ removes the least significant 1 bit of x; if $x = 2^n$ its sole bit is removed and the result must be zero. If, for example, $x = 00101100$ (in binary), then $x - 1 = 00101011$, complementing the

least-significant 1 and following 0s. ANDing the two gives $x \wedge (x-1) =$
$00101100 \wedge 00101011 = 00101000$.

This strange operation, with a general x, is needed in traversing a special data structure [32] designed for the efficient management of cumulative probability tables.[6]

- A related operation, needed by the same data structure, is $x \wedge (-x)$, which isolates the least-significant 1 bit, assuming twos complement numbers. (Consider that after twos complementing, the least-significant 1 bit is present in both x and $-x$ and is the only 1 which will "survive" the AND. All other bit positions contain 1 or 2 zeros.)

4.9.10   Parity

An important use of Exclusive OR is in "parity checking" to detect corrupted data, whether in memory, disk storage, or in transmission. In the simplest case, each word has one added "parity" bit, which is set to make the total number of 1s in the word either even (even parity) or odd (odd parity). If a word is found to have the wrong parity when read, then an error must have occurred during reading or transmission. Simple parity is an example of a "Single Error Detecting" (SED) code.

$$
\begin{aligned}
&\text{If the bits of the word are} \quad && x_{n-1}, x_{n-2}, \ldots, x_1, x_0, \\
&\text{for even parity} \quad Pbit_{even} &=& \quad x_{n-1} \oplus x_{n-2} \oplus \ldots \oplus x_0 \\
&\text{and for odd parity} \quad Pbit_{odd} &=& \quad x_{n-1} \oplus x_{n-2} \oplus \ldots \oplus x_0 \oplus 1 \\
&\text{or} &=& \quad \neg(x_{n-1} \oplus x_{n-2} \oplus \ldots \oplus x_0)
\end{aligned}
$$

The "word" for parity checking may be any convenient unit. While it may coincide with whatever the computer interprets as a "word", many computers use separate parity bits for each byte, or some other convenient unit.

More advanced forms of parity and related error control codes are described in Chapter **10**. Some of these techniques use multiple parities, with appropriate inter-relationships, while others extend some of the fundamental ideas of parity in quite different directions.

---

[6]It must be admitted that this structure is now known as a "Fenwick Tree".

Send Orders for Reprints to reprints@benthamscience.net

Chapter 5

Computer Arithmetic

Abstract: This chapter firstly extends the earlier principles of addition to provide faster adders. It then describes the underlying principles of binary multiplication and division, and especially techniques for fast operations.

Keywords: Adders, carry-lookahead adder, carry-skip adder, asynchronous adder, carry-save adder, fast carry-path adder, multipliers, twos-complement multiplication, skipping over 0s and 1s, high radix multiplier, combinational multiplier, restoring division, non-restoring division, SRT division, approximate quotient digit division, additive refinement division.

5.1   Introduction

The fundamentals of signed numbers and addition and subtraction have been given in Chapter **4**. This chapter builds on those basic principles to give a brief overview of the techniques and implementation of computer arithmetic. It is not meant to be comprehensive, but covers the more important arithmetic techniques, at least enough to prepare for further reading. As far as possible it will present the general principles, without discussing the details of hardware logic and implementation (although there are some places where this is not possible and an elementary knowledge of digital logic is assumed).

Goldberg [43] gives a good summary of current arithmetic techniques, with a much more comprehensive treatment given by Omondi [78]. Knuth [66] analyses arithmetic in great detail, devoting the whole of the second volume of "The Art of Computer Programming" to the subject. Many early papers on computer arithmetic are reprinted by Swartzlander [95], while MacSorley [71] gives an excellent overview from a similar period.

Throughout this chapter we will use conventional "0-origin contra-current" indexing (Section **4.9.1**—numbering from 0 on the right) so that, with integers, bit numbers indicate the corresponding power of 2.

5.2 Adders

Addition can be performed serially, bit-by-bit, which is slow and rare in modern computers, or in parallel in which all bits are conceptually added at one time. [A "serial adder" has just one of the "Full Adder" blocks of Figure **5.1**, with a 1-bit register accepting the "carry-out" and providing the "carry-in" for the next cycle. The adder inputs and output are successive digits of the summands and sum; the digits may be 1-bit binary, 4-bit 'nibbles' or 4-bit decimal.]

Figure 5.1: A Parallel Adder

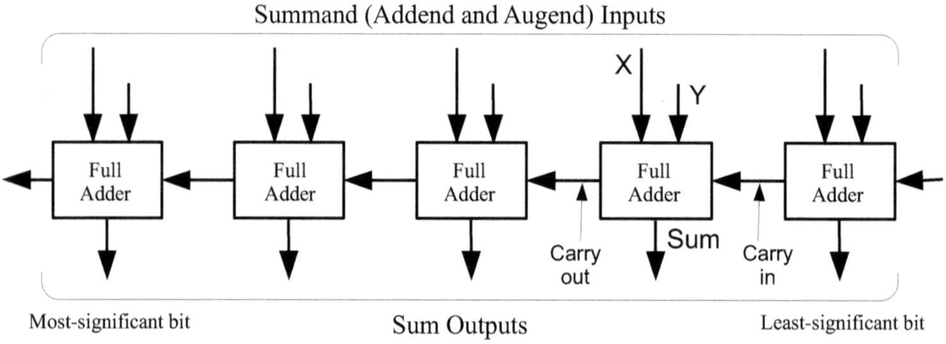

A parallel adder is shown in Figure **5.1**, with one stage annotated to show details of its inputs and outputs. Although it is shown as just an "adder", most adders would also allow inputs to be complemented to facilitate subtraction. (The logic at each stage is often extended to provide the logic functions such as AND, OR, NOT, Exclusive-OR, but that is irrelevant to the present discussion.) The most important point to note in view of the following discussion is the chaining of carries, with the Carry-out of each stage becoming the Carry-in of the stage to its immediate left.

Figure 5.2: Equations for a Binary Adder

$$S \;=\; \begin{cases} (X + Y + C_{in}) \text{ is odd} \\ X \oplus Y \oplus C_{in} \end{cases}$$

$$C_{out} \;=\; \begin{cases} 0 & \text{if } (X = 0) \,\&\, (Y = 0) \\ C_{in} & \text{if } X \neq Y \\ 1 & \text{if } (X = 1) \,\&\, (Y = 1) \end{cases}$$

Equations for each stage are shown in Figure **5.2**, illustrating a "Full Adder"[1] which produces the sum of three input bits. Both the *Sum* (S) and the *Carry* (C) can be expressed in different ways from those shown, but the form here facilitates the discussion to come. Two versions of the *Sum* formula are provided, the top one emphasising the numerical aspect and the bottom one the logical operations. The *Carry* equations are chosen to emphasise that the carry may be *generated* within this stage, independently of the $Carry_{in}$ (top and bottom lines) or that the $Carry_{in}$ may *propagate* (middle line).

Carry propagation is probably the single most important feature of adder design, and especially in "ripple carry" adders such as discussed here. In the worst case, such as $1 + (-1) \rightarrow 0$, the most-significant bits of the sum are not known until the carry has travelled right through the adder. With modern computers having to add 64 or 80 bit values, it is quite impracticable to require the worst-case carry to traverse 64 bits, with probably two logic "stages" for each bit. As the adder is usually on a critical path and largely determines the basic operating speed of a computer, addition needs to be made as fast as possible[2]. And as worst-case carry propagation is a probably rare event, it is clearly sensible to avoid its effects as far as possible.

Methods for accelerating addition include –

1. Detecting and bypassing long carry propagation

2. Detecting that the carry has propagated through the whole adder and the result is stable

---

[1]An older element, the "half adder" takes two inputs X and Y, delivering a "half-sum" $X \oplus Y$ and a "half-carry" $X \wedge Y$; two are required to make a full-adder. It will not be used here.

[2]One rule of thumb is that a computer can operate with a clock period of 10–15 logic gate delays. If the adder, in the critical path, contributes an extra $130 - 160$ gate delays, the clock period might have to increase to say 10 times what would be reasonable otherwise. The need for accelerating additions is obvious.

3. Avoiding slow logic in the carry-path

4. Avoiding carry propagation altogether

In all of this discussion we say rather little about the generation of the sum. The sum digits are all generated in parallel. At worst a sum digit may depend on the Carry-in to that stage, but rather simple logic is then needed to generate the correct sum once the incoming carry is known. Certainly sum-generation delays do not accumulate in the way that carry-propagation delays accumulate and can be ignored (assuming that the design is reasonable anyway).

5.2.1   Carry-skip and Carry-lookahead

Equation **5.1** shows that it is easy to generate a "carry propagate" function for an adder stage (the middle of the three cases). ($C_{out} = C_{in}$ if $X \neq Y$ or, *equivalently* $X \oplus Y$ is true.) The $Carry_{out}$ of a given stage is the OR of a *generated carry* from this stage together with a *propagated carry* from the previous stage. The generate function at stage i is $G_i = X_i \wedge Y_i$ and the propagate function is $P_i = X_i \neq Y_i$ (or $P_i = X_i \oplus Y_i$).

Using the logical operations $\vee$ for the logical-OR and $\wedge$ for the logical-AND (and $\wedge$ associates more strongly that $\vee$), and assuming that the carry-out from stage i is C_i, we have that

$$C_i = G_i \vee P_i \wedge C_{i-1}$$

But as

$$C_{i-1} = G_{i-1} \vee P_{i-1} \wedge C_{i-2}$$

we get the equations shown in Figure **5.3**

Thus the output carry C_i arises from
1. a carry generated in the last stage i (G_i), OR
2. a carry from earlier stages propagating through intervening stages, OR
3. an incoming carry propagating through *all* stages.

These equations define a section of a "carry-Lookahead" adder which guarantees to generate its carry-out with a single AND-OR cascade. The expansion of these equations to larger blocks is obvious, but leads to progressively larger equations and correspondingly greater implementation cost. The logic delays

Figure 5.3: Carry LookAhead Equations

$$
\begin{aligned}
C_i \;=\;& G_i \vee P_i \wedge (G_{i-1} \vee P_{i-1} \wedge C_{i-2}) \\
=\;& (G_i) \vee (P_i \wedge G_{i-1}) \vee (P_i \wedge P_{i-1} \wedge C_{i-2}) \\
=\;& G_i \\
& \vee (P_i \wedge G_{i-1}) \\
& \vee (P_i \wedge P_{i-1} \wedge G_{i-2}) \\
& \vee (P_i \wedge P_{i-1} \wedge P_{i-2} \wedge C_{i-3}) \\
=\;& G_i \\
& \vee (P_i \wedge G_{i-1}) \\
& \vee (P_i \wedge P_{i-1} \wedge G_{i-2}) \\
& \vee (P_i \wedge P_{i-1} \wedge P_{i-2} \wedge G_{i-3}) \\
& \vee (P_i \wedge P_{i-1} \wedge P_{i-2} \wedge P_{i-3} \wedge C_{i-4})
\end{aligned}
$$

also tend to increase as fan-in and fan-out[3] increases—with large blocks the fan-in of the OR which combines the lines of the equations grows, as does the fan-out of the P_i signals.

Large carry-lookahead adders therefore use multiple levels of look-ahead. If, say, an economic or electrical limit is a look-ahead block of 6 bits, then that block can be regarded as a radix-64 adder which generates its own level-2 propagate and generate signals, say P_i^2 and G_i^2. These can be fed into look-ahead logic exactly as used for the simple radix-2 adder. There is slightly more delay in forming and using these higher-level look-ahead and generate functions, but the economics is greatly improved. Lookahead can be applied at three or more levels, using obvious extensions of these techniques.

A simplification of carry-lookahead is to ignore the internal terms in the above equations, to obtain

$$
C_i = G_i \vee (P_i \wedge P_{i-1} \wedge P_{i-2} \wedge P_{i-3} \wedge C_{i-4})
$$

leading to the "carry-skip" adder, so-called because it allows the carry to skip over blocks while making no effort to accelerate propagation within blocks. It is a useful compromise between the simplicity of the ripple-carry adder and the

---

[3]The "fan-in" of a logic circuit is the number of inputs which it receives, and the "fan-out" is the number of circuits which one can drive. In general the delays increase with increasing fan-in and fan-out, and there are physical limits to the fan-out, or driving ability.

complexity of a full look-ahead adder. Analyses show that carry-skip blocks should be of unequal size, with larger blocks in the middle of the adder and smaller blocks near the end [68]. (Grading the block sizes tends to equalise the carry-propagation distances.)

5.2.2 Carry Completion Detection

Although the *maximum* carry propagation distance is about N bits in an N bit adder, the *average* distance is much less than this. Burks, Goldstine and von Neumann [17] report an average carry propagation distance of about $\log_2 N$ for an N-bit adder. Later authors differ in detail but report similar distances of about 5–6 stages for an adder of 32 or 64 bits. In any adder stage, the carry is either known (if it is locally generated) or is unknown (if it depends on propagation and the carry-in is unknown). With carry-complete detection, each stage reports when its Carry-in, and therefore its Sum are known; when all stages report known values the addition as a whole is completed.

The "asynchronous adder", using carry-completion detection, has two parallel carry-paths, one reporting $Carry = 0$ and the other $Carry = 1$. Neither signal is true if the carry is propagating to the current stage and still unknown. Each stage OR-s together its two carry-in signals to give a "result known" signal; these are ANDed over the whole adder and when all stages report a known result the overall Sum is also known.

The asynchronous adder has several disadvantages –

1. The variable cycle time does not fit easily into much modern processor design which relies on fixed timing and predictable activity.

2. The adder requires a resynchronisation from the asynchronous completion signal. Resynchronisation is not easy, and if not done properly can lead to meta-stable states where flip-flops are in a temporarily undefined condition. Reliable synchronisation methods are certainly known, but often need extra decision time and clock cycles, partially destroying the advantage of decreased addition time.

3. There is some doubt as to average carry propagation distance anyway. Note that the maximum propagation occurs when integer values are changing sign; such changes may be quite frequent in loop termination. Thus the carry distance can be determined only from real-world measurements rather than some empirical analyses and may well be skewed to larger values than simple analyses might predict.

4. A lesser problem is that of implementing the very wide AND to decide that all stages have reported completion. The fan-in limitations will probably require a cascade of logic gates, leading to a further (but slight) increase in the addition time.

5.2.3   Fast Carry-Paths

The large potential carry delay of a ripple-carry adder arises because each bit must include two stages or levels of logic in the carry path. The first is an AND to allow or prevent propagation of the incoming carry, (the P_i terms, and the second is an OR to combine that carry with one generated within the current stage (the G_i term). An alternative to minimising the amount of logic to be traversed by a carry redesigns the carry path to avoid conventional logic altogether. Conceptually, the carry path uses on-off switches which allow transmission with negligible delay; a practical design implements a three-way switch as needed by the equations of **5.2**.

This approach originated with Kilburn [64] in the adder designed for the Manchester Atlas computer, the first computer to use virtual memory and one of the first with instruction pipelining and an operating system as an essential component. Atlas used a unique carry-path with saturated, symmetrical, transistors which, although slow to switch on or off, had negligible delay once ON. Although such transistors are no longer available (and were indeed unusual around 1960 when Atlas was designed), the adder is well-suited to modern analogue "transmission gates" which also provide non-logic data transmission and switching with negligible delay [29].

5.2.4   Carry-Save Adders

If the major delay in many adders lies in the carry propagation, an obvious solution is to eliminate the carry propagation. This is done in the carry-save adder, which is appropriate to multipliers or other applications which accumulate a succession of many sums, but need to deliver only the final result.

In its basic form, each stage of the carry-save adder takes its three input bits (addend, augend and carry-in) and delivers two output bits (sum and carry-out) with the carry-out shifted one place to the left into its proper significance. A carry-save adder therefore reduces three inputs to two outputs, which represent the same numerical value as the sum of the original inputs. Although a carry-save adder can be used as a stand-alone entity, the two outputs are often saved in registers for feeding back into the adder when the next summand of the sequence is introduced, as in multiplication.

Carry-save addition usually requires a carry-propagate adder to assimilate carries at the end of the sequence of additions[4]. Examples of carry-save adders are given in Figure **5.4**. The first example shows sequential addition of operands one at a time, while the second shows values being presented four at a time. The extension to more than four inputs is obvious; the hardware just becomes more bulky.

Figure 5.4: Carry Save Adders

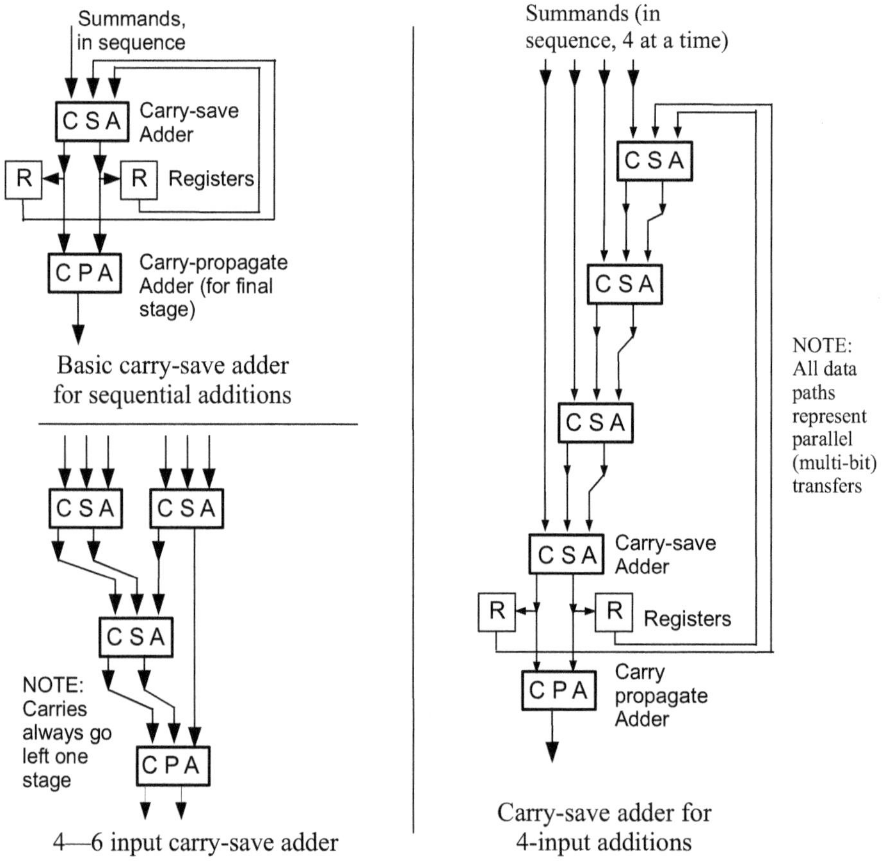

Two points may be noted here –

---

[4]The IBM 1130 computer used an unusual adder which was equivalent to a carry-save adder and simply cycled until the carry register was zero.

1. The carries-out *always* shift left to the next most-significant position between the CSA stages.

2. If all of the inputs are equivalent the adder can be rearranged as shown in the small section at the bottom-left to give one less carry-save adder delay. This leads to the "Wallace-tree" multiplier as discussed later.

5.3   Multiplication

Multiplication is, like addition, a symmetrical operation which yields a *product* from two *factors* known as the *multiplicand* and the *multiplier*. In contrast to addition, where the augend and addend are treated quite symmetrically within the adder, a multiplier[5] usually treats the two factors quite differently.

Multiplication is usually performed as in traditional long multiplication, adding together appropriately shifted (or scaled) multiples of the *multiplicand* under the control of successive digits of the *multiplier*. A binary multiplication is shown in Figure **5.5**. Each row in the multiplication is either all-0 if the corresponding bit of the multiplier is 0, or an appropriately shifted copy of the multiplicand if the multiplier is 1.

It is obvious from Figure **5.5** that the product is *twice* the length of either factor (actually the sum of the lengths, but they are usually the same precision.) With integers the desired result is in the least-significant half; any content in the more significant half implies an overflow. With fractions the least-significant half is usually discarded. The double-length product matches the double-length dividend in division (the inverse operation from multiplication), as seen in Section **5.4**.

Although Figure **5.5** implies that a complete tableau of multiplicand multiples is prepared and then added in a single multi-operand addition, this is not how most multipliers work. The usual procedure is to shift the multiplicand step by step along the product, adding it in at each stage if the corresponding multiplier bit is a 1. (Adding or not adding corresponds to adding the ×1 and ×0 multiples, according to the multiplier bit.) Although multiplication involves the parallel addition of the multiples into the product, these additions are done in sequence as each bit of the multiplier is examined. The number

---

[5]The term "multiplier" is ambiguous, being both one of the factors and the device or functional unit which performs the operation of multiplication. The precise meaning is usually apparent from the context.

of additions then increases with word length N, and the expected execution time is proportional to N for fixed addition time, to $N \log N$ for most adders, or even N^2 for a simple ripple-carry adder.

Figure 5.5: Binary Multiplication (100101×110110)

```
           multiplicand →      1  0  0  1  0  1
↓ multiplier
0 × 2⁰                          0  0  0  0  0  0
1 × 2¹                       1  0  0  1  0  1  .
1 × 2²                    1  0  0  1  0  1  .  .
0 × 2³                 0  0  0  0  0  0  .  .  .
1 × 2⁴              1  0  0  1  0  1  .  .  .  .
1 × 2⁵           1  0  0  1  0  1  .  .  .  .  .
                 ─────────────────────────────────
                 1  1  1  1  1  0  0  1  1  1  0
```

Multiplication is a potentially expensive operation, especially with the long factors which are needed in much numerical computation. A great deal of effort has therefore been put into designing fast multipliers; the multiplier (or multipliers) is a significant component of most processor chips. As the time for a multiplication is dominated by the need to perform a sequence of additions, a faster multiplier requires a faster adder, or fewer additions, or both.

The major techniques, to be examined in later sections, are –

1. Increasing the adder speed with extensive carry look-ahead or similar techniques. Alternatively eliminate carry propagation altogether by using a carry-save adder with carry-assimilation only at the end.

2. Recoding the multiplier (factor) so that strings of 1s need additions only at the ends. This technique is graphically described as "skipping over 0s and 1s" and uses the redundant codings of Section **3.5.1**.

3. Regarding the multiplier (factor) not as a binary number, but as one in base-4, base-8, base-16, *etc.* In other words, examine the multiplier bits in groups of 2, 3, 4, *etc.*

4. Providing a completely combinational multiplier, which accepts the two factors and delivers their product.

5.3.1   Twos Complement Multiplication

All of the discussion here will assume twos complement integers, with unsigned numbers being a special case of twos complement. The N-bit twos complement representation of a negative value $X < 0$ was shown earlier to be equivalent to the *unsigned* value $2^N - |X|$. Alternatively, the bit pattern with *unsigned* value X has the twos complement value $X - 2^N$.

If we have a negative multiplier X and a multiplicand Y of arbitrary sign, the unsigned product of the two is $X \times Y - 2^N \times Y$. (The sign of the multiplicand is irrelevant because it is only added in as the product develops and twos complement addition is independent of the sign.) The simple-minded product is therefore in error by $2^N \times Y$ and $2^N \times Y$ should be added as a correction. In fact, we will find that some multiplication methods are actually in error by precisely this amount; ignoring the error yields the correct twos complement product.

5.3.2   Improving Adder Speeds

All of the techniques of Section **5.2** are relevant here; indeed the need for fast multiplication has been one of the main incentives for developing faster adders. We may assume that some form of accelerated addition underlies all fast multiplication methods.

5.3.3   Skipping Over 0s and 1s

Although this section uses the redundant codings already described in Section **3.5.1**, it is appropriate to repeat that description here, where it is actually used. It is obvious that a string of consecutive zeros $100 \ldots 001$ will produce no additions and can be ignored as far as arithmetic is concerned. If the hardware can detect a string of zeros in the multiplier (factor) *and* can perform a variable-length shift, the multiplier and product may be just shifted by the appropriate amount to skip over the consecutive zeros.

It is less obvious that a string of ones can be treated in a similar way, but note that any string of j ones $011 \ldots 110$ can be written as $2^{i+j} - 2^i$; for example $011100 = 28$ can be written as $2^5 - 2^2 = 32 - 4 = 28$. Any binary number is a sequence of 0-strings alternating with 1-strings; the multiplier (factor) is recoded with a +1 at the rightmost digit of a string of zeros and a −1 at the rightmost of a string of ones, as shown in the "first recoding" of Figure **5.6**.

But this change is hardly satisfactory; the original has 5 ones and needs 5 add/subtract operations, but the recoded version needs 6 operations! The problem arises because an isolated 1 is converted to $(2 - 1)$ (00100 becomes $8 - 4$). The solution is to recognise isolated or singleton ones in the multiplier and encode each as a single addition. This, in the "second recoding" line, gives 4 operations. Similarly, an isolated zero in a string of ones recodes as $-2 + 1$ (adjacent addition and subtractions) and should be replaced a −1 or single subtraction.

Figure 5.6: Recoding of a Binary Multiplier.

original bits	0	0	1	1	1	0	0	1	0	1
first recoding	0	+	0	0	-	0	+	-	+	-
second recoding	0	+	0	0	-	0	0	+	0	+

A negative multiplier has a string of most-significant ones, which will re-code to '−' at the rightmost end in anticipation of a compensating '+' just beyond the leftmost digit of the string. But the multiplication stops before the compensating addition can be performed, leaving the product with a deficit of 2^N times the multiplier. Fortunately this "error" is precisely the correction needed to get the correct twos-complement product from an unsigned multiplication. We conclude that this algorithm works correctly for signed factors in twos-complement representation.

The average shift length is found to be about three, allowing an approximate tripling of the multiplication speed provided that all shift lengths are possible. These improvements apply to floating-point factors; integers are predominantly small values with a long run of significant zeros and can expect a greater increase in speed. Variable shift multiplication has the disadvantage that its execution time is variable and this can cause problems when designing pipelined and overlapped-execution computers.

This algorithm is an extension of the "Booth" algorithm [12] which first showed that recoding could facilitate signed twos-complement multiplication. In its original form it deals with one bit at a time, according to the rules below. (The colon ':' is used as a separator; the bit to its left is the one being examined and the one to its right was the one examined on the previous cycle.

$$\begin{aligned}
\text{multiplier} &= 0{:}0 \quad \text{no arithmetic}\\
&= 0{:}1 \quad \text{ADD multiplicand}\\
&= 1{:}0 \quad \text{SUBTRACT multiplicand}\\
&= 1{:}1 \quad \text{no arithmetic}
\end{aligned}$$

5.3.4   High Radix Multiplication

Another technique for fast multiplication, and one which is generally preferred over variable shifts because of its deterministic performance, considers several multiplier bits at a time; with n bits we get a radix 2^n multiplier.

As high-radix multipliers invariably combine several multiples at each step they are excellent candidates for carry-save adders, as shown in Figure **5.4**.

The simplest case is radix=4, from examining bit-pairs. An obvious implementation requires multiplicand multiples of 0, 1, 2 and 3, corresponding to the four possible values of the current multiplier bit-pair. Although the triple can be pre-calculated and saved, this is not necessary as the triple can be recoded as $(4-1)$. Noting that $+2$ can itself be recoded as $(4-2)$ we get an initial table, where the "C" indicates that a $4\times$ multiple must be added, or an extra $+1$ on the next cycle –

$$\begin{aligned}
\text{multiplier} &= 00 \quad \text{no arithmetic}\\
&= 01 \quad +1\\
&= 10 \quad \text{-2, C}\\
&= 11 \quad \text{-1, C}
\end{aligned}$$

But "C" is clearly set from the most-significant bit of the multiplier pair. All that is needed is to examine the two current multiplier bits and the most significant of the previous pair, giving the full table in Table **5.1**. Note that this improvement requires negligible extra logic over the basic 1-bit multiplier.

It is interesting to compare this table with the rules for variable-shift multiplication. This alternative interpretation is also given in Table **5.1**. We also see that the method works for signed twos-complement numbers, for exactly the same reason as for variable-shifts. A negative number must have a most-significant run of ones with the anticipated addition of 2^N left pending; this "error" is just what is needed to correct for multiplying signed values as though unsigned.

Operation beyond bit-pairs is quite possible, but demands increasingly more hardware and multiples of the multiplicand. For example bit-triples superfi-

Table 5.1: Table for Bit-pair (radix-4) Multiplication

multiplier	multiple	variable-shift comparison
00:0	0	run of zeroes – no action
01:0	+1	isolated 1 – +1
10:0	-2	possible run of ones – -1, with shift
11:0	-1	possible run of ones – -1
00:1	+1	end of run of ones – +1 just past end
01:1	+2	end of run of ones – +1 just past end, with shift
10:1	-1	isolated zero – -1
11:1	0	run of ones – no action

cially demand the multiples {0, 1, 2, 3, 4, 5, 6, 7}. Even multiples can be generated by shifting and others as the 8s-complement with a subsequent add. The multiplicand triple ($\times 3$) cannot now be simulated and must be precalculated or otherwise obtained.

5.3.5   Combinational Multipliers

If we look at the times involved in a fast carry-save adder, we find that much of the time is concerned, not with addition *per se*, but with saving the temporary results in registers and reading from those registers at the next step. We have already seen, in Figure **5.4** how several carry save adders may be combined to add four multiples at once. A logical step is to extend this so that *all* of the additions of the multiplication are performed in one large combinational step, without any saving or storage of intermediate values. This leap (essentially psychological rather than technological) was first presented by Wallace [109], when he described what is now known as the "Wallace tree" multiplier. The idea is certainly older than that, because Richards [84] in 1955 describes a "simultaneous multiplier" with 4 bit factors and clearly anticipates its extension to a "useful size (say, 16 binary digits or larger)". It was however Wallace who clearly presented a multiplier for 39 bits and analysed its performance and economics.

Figure **5.7** shows a Wallace tree for 8 bit factors. Several points must be remembered in considering this diagram –

- The diagram is really an end-on view of a rather complex three dimensional object. Each of the carry-save adders (CSA blocks) is at least 8

Figure 5.7: Wallace Tree Multiplier (8×8 bits)

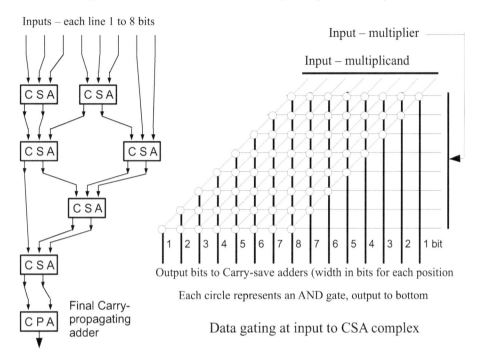

bits deep. The final carry propagating adder (CPA) is probably twice that.

- Various parts of the structure are skewed with respect to each other and are therefore at different depths from the viewer because of the shifting of the multiplicand according to the precision of the multiplier bits.

- The right-hand part of Figure **5.7** shows the input gating (multiple selection) here done by a simple ANDing of the shifted multiplicand by the multiplier bits.

- The displacement of the operands means that some have no low order inputs while others have no high significance bits. Many of the carry-save adders may be shorter, but the length generally increases towards the carry propagate adder.

- It is often possible to bring multiples into lower positions of the adder tree. Here it is done for two multiples, but Wallace shows multiples coming in much closer to the final adder.

- Wallace suggests recoding the multiplier using a form of Booth recoding so each pair of multiplier bits requests one of the multiplier multiples

{+2, +1, 0, -1, -2}. This halves the number of inputs to the adder tree, for a moderate complication to the input selection.

The Wallace tree multiplier is presented as an example of a family of parallel multipliers. Several variations and improvements exist, but without greatly modifying the basic idea. For example, some designs use, not a full adder, but a *counter*; a (7,3) counter takes 7 inputs and delivers a 3-bit value which counts the number of them which are 1. (An adder is a (3,2) counter). The regular structure of parallel multipliers makes then very suitable for VLSI implementation and most modern high performance processors use them. The fully-parallel multiplier (sometimes multipliers) may take a significant part of the chip "real estate" in most modern computers.

5.4   Division

Division, the inverse of multiplication, is the most difficult of the basic arithmetic operations. It is usually much slower than multiplication and some high performance computers even omitted it completely, preferring to program one of the "multiplicative" methods given later whenever division is needed.

In general, division takes two input operands, the *dividend* and the *divisor* and produces two results, the *quotient* and the *remainder*, such that

$$dividend = divisor \times quotient + remainder$$

with

$$| \, remainder \, | < | \, divisor \, |$$

Division is always performed by some repeated or iterated operation which constructs successively better approximations to the quotient. The traditional algorithms are based on additions and subtractions and are sometimes collected under the general term of "subtractive division". Most other algorithms assume the availability of a fast multiplier and use a sequence of multiplications to obtain the quotient; these may be described as "multiplicative division" methods.

5.4.1   Restoring and non-Restoring Division

Subtractive division algorithms have a working value, which is initially obtained from the dividend and from which successive divisor multiples are subtracted as the division proceeds. This "working value" has no single preferred name and is often known as the "partial remainder" or "partial dividend". Here and following Atkins [6], the shorter term "residue" will be employed.

All of the "subtractive" division methods assume an initial double-length dividend (corresponding to the double-length product in multiplication); a single-precision divisor is extended to double precision in the normal way, by sign-extending integers to the left, or zero filling fractions on the right. The division operates only on the more-significant part, which is shifted left as the division proceeds. This leaves vacated digits at the extreme right hand (least significant) end. By convention these places are filled with the quotient bits which conveniently fill the otherwise unused spaces; the whole dividend/quotient must be shifted left as a single entity. Thus the quotient is generated in the *extension* while the remainder is the final residue.

The simplest division methods, and the basis of all of the subtractive methods, are the restoring and non-restoring algorithms shown in Figure **5.8**. Both examples show $67 \div 7 \rightarrow 9$ (4 remainder). Restoring division is an exact parallel to standard pencil-and-paper long division, adapted to binary arithmetic.

Figure **5.8** is laid out in a conventional manner for division, with the added convention that down-arrows ($\downarrow$) show how successive dividend digits are introduced to the calculation. The basic division cycle for restoring division with positive operands is –

- Subtract the divisor from the residue

- If the result is negative, generate a quotient bit of 0 and restore the residue (either by adding back the divisor or not accumulating the difference).

- If the residue is positive, leave it unchanged and develop a quotient bit of 1

- In both cases, shift the residue left with respect to the divisor by one digit (or shift the divisor right with respect to the residue) discarding the most-significant bit of the residue and introducing a new least-significant residue bit from the dividend.

At the very end, when the last dividend digit has been processed, the residue becomes the remainder.

Each zero quotient bit corresponds to an "overdraw" in restoring division. If the residue has been already updated an extra step is needed to add back

Figure 5.8: Binary Restoring and non-Restoring Division

```
                      0   1   0   0   1              the quotient
0   0   1   1   1  )  0   0   1   0   0   0   0   1   1   the dividend
                 -    0   0   1   1   1   ↓   ↓   ↓   ↓   subtract
                      1   1   1   0   1              overdraw; digit = 0
                      0   0   1   0   0   ↓          restore
                      0   1   0   0   0              shift; new digit
                 -    0   0   1   1   1              subtract
                      0   0   0   0   1   ↓          success; digit = 1
                      0   0   0   1   0              shift; new digit
                 -    0   0   1   1   1              subtract
                      1   1   0   1   1              overdraw; digit = 0
                      0   0   0   1   0   ↓          restore
                      0   0   1   0   1              shift; new digit
                 -    0   0   1   1   1              subtract
                      1   1   1   1   0              overdraw; digit = 0
                      0   0   1   0   1   ↓          restore
                      0   1   0   1   1              shift; new digit
                 -    0   0   1   1   1              subtract
                      0   0   1   0   0              remainder = 00100
```

(a) Restoring Division

```
                      0   1   0   0   1              the quotient
0   0   1   1   1  )  0   0   1   0   0   0   0   1   1   the dividend
                 -    0   0   1   1   1   ↓   ↓   ↓   ↓   subtract
                      1   1   1   0   1   ↓          negative; digit = 0
                      1   1   0   1   0              shift; new digit
                 +    0   0   1   1   1              add
                      0   0   0   0   1   ↓          positive; digit = 1
                      0   0   0   1   0              shift; new digit
                 -    0   0   1   1   1              subtract
                      1   1   0   1   1   ↓          negative; digit = 0
                      1   0   1   1   1              shift; new digit
                 +    0   0   1   1   1              add
                      1   1   1   1   0   ↓          negative; digit = 0
                      1   1   1   0   1              shift; new digit
                 +    0   0   1   1   1              subtract
                      0   0   1   0   0              positive; digit = 1
                                                     remainder = 00100
```

(b) non-Restoring Division

the divisor and correct for the erroneous subtraction. One variation which eliminates the correction is *non performing* division. Here the result of each subtraction (divisor from residue) is monitored and the residue updated only if no overdraw occurs. The speed is increased by eliminating the correction step on perhaps 50% of the digits, but at the expense of more difficult control logic; the load/not-load condition depends on the current result whereas it is often more efficient to set it from *previous* data.

A more usual improvement is *non-restoring* division, in which an overdraw is allowed to stand but is corrected on the next step by an addition. The above rules are now modified.

- If the residue is negative add the divisor to the residue, otherwise subtract the divisor from the residue; the residue is always updated.

- If the result is negative, generate a quotient bit of 0; if the result is positive, develop a quotient bit of 1.

- Shift the residue left with respect to the divisor by one digit (or shift the divisor right with respect to the residue) discarding the most-significant bit of the residue and introducing a new least-significant residue bit from the dividend.

The result is that we always try to drive the residue towards or past 0, using divisor multiples of $+1$ or -1 as appropriate. The quotient bit is always set to the complement of the residue sign. With a positive result from a subtraction (residue $+ \rightarrow +$), the operation is just as with restoring division; we have a "successful" subtraction and develop a corresponding 1. A negative result from a subtraction (residue $+ \rightarrow -$) is similarly an overdraw and gives a 0 quotient bit. The initial subtraction which caused the overdraw and the following additions which try to correct it are equivalent to an initial multiple of 2^i and following multiples of $-2^{i-}, -2^{i-2}, \ldots$. The result is that for example, we write $1 = 8 - 7$.

5.4.2   Fast Subtractive Division

The fast subtractive division algorithms are extensions of non-restoring division and the inverse of standard digit-sequential multiplication. While restoring and non-restoring division were described as early as the Burks *et al* report [17], their extension to higher radix algorithms capable of developing several bits per step was performed in the late 1950s by Sweeney and Robertson [85] and Tocher [101] giving methods which are now referred to as "SRT algorithms".

All fast division algorithms expect a "normalised" divisor, usually of the form $0.1xx\ldots$ (if positive, and assuming fractions). At each stage we subtract from the residue the largest possible multiple of the divisor; that multiple becomes the next digit of the quotient. Just as with multiplication, we can use variants of shifting over 1s or 0s, or process a fixed number of bits per step (which is the usual case). A divider which generates n bits per step is a radix-2^n divider. The problem is in estimating the correct multiple (and quotient digit) and handling errors if the estimate is wrong.

All of the fast subtractive methods depend on the relation

$$p_{j+1} \;=\; r \times p_j - q_{j+1} \times d$$

where

$$
\begin{aligned}
p_j &= \text{the residue used in the } j\text{-th cycle,} \\
p_0 &= \text{the initial dividend,} \\
p_m &= \text{the remainder, and} \\
q_j &= \text{the } j\text{-th quotient digit}
\end{aligned}
$$

We also have that

$$
\begin{aligned}
r &= \text{the radix, eg 2, 4, 8, 16, } \ldots \\
d &= \text{the divisor, and} \\
m &= \text{the radix-}r \text{ digits in the quotient}
\end{aligned}
$$

Verbally, we can note that we subtract a multiple (q_j) of the divisor from the residue and enter the same q_j as the corresponding quotient digit. Note that *any* value of q_j will then satisfy the relation. By convention $0 \leq |q_j| < r$, this ensuring that a properly chosen value q_j will eliminate a digit of p_j and ensure that $|p_{j+1}| < |d|$ and p_{j+1} is in the range to allow the iteration to proceed.

The general idea is to use the high-order bits of the divisor and residue to estimate the divisor multiple which, subtracted from (or added to) the residue, forces the residue as close as possible to zero. The biggest problem for most division methods is in generating the correct value of q_j so that the residue is properly reduced and the generated digit is accurate. Most division algorithms require an accurate quotient digit to be forced into the quotient step. While it may be modified as it is entered, it cannot afterwards be changed. For high radices the digit estimation may require considerable logic.

The difficulty of estimating quotient digits has been discussed by Knuth [66] and also Atkins [6], both analysing high radix SRT division. Atkins discusses redundancy of the quotient representation (for example, 3 may be represented as either $2 + 1$ or $4 - 1$) and states that "With redundancy, the quotient digit ...need not be precise." Then from a detailed analysis of digit-estimation logic, he shows that the number of bits to be examined is at least that shown in Table **5.2**.

Table 5.2: Atkins' Estimates of Bits to be Examined

Residue bits	N_p	$=$	$2k + 3$ or $2k + 4$, and
Divisor bits	N_d	$=$	$2k + 5$
where the radix r is	r	$=$	2^{2k}

	Radix	Residue bits	Divisor bits
	4	5	7
[ht]	8	6	8
	16	7	9
	64	9	11
	256	11	13

A full discussion of SRT division is very complex; interested readers should consult Omondi [78] or some similar book. In any case, few authors recommend operation beyond radices of 4 or 8 (2 or 3 bits per step) because of the difficulties of estimating the quotient digits and preparing an appropriate tableau of divisor multiples.

5.4.3   Approximate Quotient Estimation

Traditional SRT division is complicated by the need to generate *precise* digit estimates at each cycle, leading to extensive estimation logic as discussed by Atkins. Two modifications have appeared in recent literature, both eliminating the need for precise estimation. Both rely on the property that, while it is easy to generate most of the quotient bits most of the time, it can be much more difficult to generate all of the bits all of the time. Perhaps 99%, or even 99.9%, of cases are relatively easy to handle; it is only the remaining 1% or 0.1% which are difficult and expensive.

Montuschi and Ciminiera [76] generate the best-estimate digit but reduce its precision if necessary. For example, they may estimate a 5-bit quotient digit but find on doing the arithmetic that only 3 bits are satisfactory and that using any more would give an unrecoverable overdraw. They then accept only those three bits. Their divider runs most of the time at near to its designed quotient bits per cycle, but every so often drops back to fewer quotient bits.

Fenwick [31] first of all places a small adder at the low-order end of the quotient so that the new quotient is *added* into the existing quotient. This allows previous estimates to be corrected if necessary. (Normal SRT methods just "jam" the quotient digit and *must* have it correct.) In case of extreme overdraw he allows the division to pause so that a correction step can be applied (this is just a normal add/subtract with no accompanying shift).

As a measure of the improvement, Atkins estimates that a radix-16 divider requires a 7×9 table (2^{16} entries)[6]. With a (6×6) table Fenwick gets a speed within 0.1% of 4 bits per cycle; even with a (4×4) table the speed is still with 10% of the limit, generating 3.7 bits per cycle. Fenwick also considers the effect of not having a tableau of divisor multiples (replacing multiples by appropriate combinations of shifted adds and subtracts) and shows that with his methods a radix-16 divider with a 5×5 bit estimation table can still deliver 3.78 bits per cycle, or 95% of the maximum.

5.4.4   Multiplicative Division

Multiplicative division uses iterative algorithms based on multiplications to get an approximation to the reciprocal of the divisor. Multiplying this reciprocal and the dividend yields the quotient (but not a remainder). This method has a long history, dating back to some of the early computers where even bit-wise restoring division was considered too complex for hardware. When division became reasonably understood and as long as it was not *too* much slower than multiplication, there seemed little need to deviate from the obvious subtractive algorithms. The ability of multipliers and dividers to share most of their logic was also an incentive to retain subtractive methods.

That situation changed when Wallace developed his fast multiplier [109], Section **5.3.5**, which was quite unsuited to division. This led to a resurgence in multiplicative division. Assume that the divisor d is a normalised fraction, an assumption which is usually true for floating-point arithmetic. The algorithms calculate the divisor reciprocal $a = 1/d$ and then get the quotient by multiplying the dividend and the reciprocal.

---

[6]A "7×9" table takes 7 bits and 9 bits as address bits for a conceptual 2^7 rows and 2^9 columns, or a total of 65 536 entries. A "4×4" table has only 256 entries.

Wallace proposes the following iteration, first setting $p \approx 1/x$ as an initial estimate

set	a_1	$=$	px	get $a_1 \approx 1$
and	b_1	$=$	p	the estimate
iterate	a_{n+1}	$=$	$a_n(2 - a_n)$	$(2 - a_n)$ is error in estimate –
				– adjust a towards 1
and	b_{n+1}	$=$	$b_{n+1}(2 - a_n)$	same adjustment for b and a

The process converges quadratically, doubling the significant digits at each step, with $a_n \to 1$ and $b_n \to 1/x$.

Knuth gives two other formulæ, both of which iterate to find the reciprocal [66][p 244]. Given a positive normalised fraction d, set $a_0 = 1$ and iterate.

$$
\begin{aligned}
a_{i+1} &= a_i(2 - da_i) \\
&= 2a_i - dx_i \\
a_{i+1} &= a_i + a_n(1 - da_i) + a_i(1 - d(a_i))) \\
&= a_i(1 + (1 - da_i)(1 + (1 - da_i)))
\end{aligned}
$$

The first formula is derived from the Newton-Raphson method for finding the root of a function and requires two multiplications per step. It is again quadratically convergent and has been used in many computers. The third is cubically convergent, each step tripling the number of significant digits. But it demands more arithmetic at each step and is no faster overall.

Wallace also gives a quadratically convergent iterative square root. Given $0 < x < 1$, set $a_1 = p^2 x$, $b_1 = p$. then iterate as below; b_n converges to $\sqrt{(1/x)}$

$$
a_{n+1} = a_n(3/2 - a_n)^2; \quad b_{n+1} = b_n(3/2 - a_n)
$$

5.4.5   Additive Refinement

The final example is a division method which depends only on cunning data-dependent subtractions and is unrelated to any of the standard methods. The original description by Svoboda [94] is for decimal arithmetic and its rationale is not easy to grasp. Its binary form is much easier to follow; again it assumes a normalised divisor $D = 1.0 \ldots 01x \ldots$. It has the unusual property that the divisor is constantly changing. It forms the basis of a method of calculating binary logarithms, given in Section **7.4**.

The basic principle is that we transform the divisor, so that it converges to 1.00...00, applying identical transformations to the dividend, which converges to the quotient. (It does not develop the remainder.) We illustrate it by calculating $N \div D$, where N is initially the dividend but is transformed into a sort of "residue" and eventually becomes the quotient.

At any stage, the divisor $D = 1 + 2^{-j} + \varepsilon$, where $\varepsilon < 2^{-j}$. In other words, the first fractional 1 is that for 2^{-j}. The basic step is the subtraction $D = D - D \times 2^{-j}$ or $D = D(1 - 2^{-j})$, using the most significant bit of D (which is known to be a 1) to eliminate the *second* significant 1 of the divisor. At the same time we calculate $N = N(1 - 2^{-j})$, multiplying the dividend/residue by the same amount (subtracting a similarly shifted copy); the ratio N/D remains the same. The operation is repeated until all of the internal 1s of the divisor are annihilated, leaving $\dot{D} = 1$ and the dividend N transformed into the quotient.

In words, shift the divisor right so that its most-significant 1 coincides with *second* 1 and subtract the shifted divisor; this corresponds to a multiplication of the divisor, driving it closer to 1.000.... Shift the dividend right by the same amount and subtract its shifted value from the dividend. Because the divisor and dividend are both modified by equivalent shifts of themselves, both are multiplied by the same factor and their ratio is unchanged.

This form differs from the original, decimal, method. There digits were eliminated until the left-half of the divisor was all-zero (apart from the leading 1), allowing the approximation $1/(1+x) = 1 - x$ to give the divisor reciprocal, which was then multiplied by the dividend to give the quotient. Also, the decimal elimination step used rather mysterious, and unexplained, factors which rather concealed the underlying rationale. (They are related to the reciprocals of the divisor digit.)

We illustrate the division with the example $3/5 = 0.6$

$$3/5 = .75/1.25 \quad = \quad \frac{0.110000}{1.010000}$$

$$= \quad \frac{0.110000 - 0.001100}{1.010000 - 0.010100} = \frac{0.100100}{0.111100} \quad \text{overdraw}$$

$$= \quad \frac{0.110000 - 0.000110}{1.010000 - 0.001010} = \frac{0.101010}{1.000110}$$

$$= \quad \frac{0.101010 - 0.000010}{1.000110 - 0.000100} = \frac{0.101000}{1.000010}$$

$$= \quad \frac{0.101000 - 0.000001}{1.000010 - 0.000010} = \frac{0.100111}{1.000000} = 0.609375$$

The second step suffers an overdraw with the significant bit of the divisor (the bit used to eliminate the other bits!) becoming zero. It is necessary to correct the overdraw and to repeat the operation with the operands shifted one place further to the right. The situation is analogous to that in restoring division, but *not identical* because the divisor here is constantly changing. However we can certainly make the correction by adding an appropriately shifted value to both numerator and denominator; as before doing the same operation to both leaves the ratio unchanged. The correct position aligns the most-significant 1 of the shifted denominator with the least significant 1 of its leading block of 1s. If the denominator is $0.1111100\ldots$, the subtraction is $0.1111100 - 0.0000111\ldots$. With non-restoring corrections, the example becomes

$$3/5 = .75/1.25 \quad = \quad \frac{0.110000}{1.010000}$$

$$= \quad \frac{0.110000 - 0.001100}{1.010000 - 0.010100} = \frac{0.100100}{0.111100}$$

$$= \quad \frac{0.100100 + 0.000100}{0.111100 + 0.000111} = \frac{0.101000}{1.000011}$$

$$= \quad \frac{0.101000 - 0.000001}{1.000011 - 0.000010} = \frac{0.100111}{1.000001}$$

$$= \quad \frac{0.100111 - 0.000000}{1.000001 - 0.000001} = \frac{0.100111}{1.000000} = 0.609375$$

As before, rounding has introduced an error into the last bit. The correct binary answer is 0.100110011001...

5.5 Division with Signed Numbers

Repeating the basic rules from Section **5.4**, the fundamental relations in division are –

$$\text{dividend} = \text{divisor} \times \text{quotient} + \text{remainder}$$

with

$$|\text{ remainder }| < |\text{ divisor }|$$

There is little problem with positive operands, but the fish-hooks arise with signed operands and the second relation which deals only with *magnitudes*. Does $-7 \div 2$ give a quotient:remainder pair of $\{-4\!:\!1\}$, or is the result $\{-3\!:\!-1\}$? Similar problems arise in each of the three cases where at least one operand is negative. The dividend may of course change by 1 depending on the sign of any non-zero remainder. These problems are essentially those of Floating-point rounding, discussed in Section **6.6**.

A conventional solution is that the remainder has the sign of the dividend. But the author has seen problems with Algol 60 where the real $\rightarrow$ integer function `int = entier(real)` is defined as yielding "the largest integer not greater than". For a positive result it truncates toward zero, as we might expect, but for negative it rounds *away* from zero. (Remember that an integer division in effect yields a non-integer result, equivalent to a real, which must be converted back to integer using the `entier` operation, even if no non-integer quantities are visible.) This alternate definition of the remainder sign means that algorithms such as Binary Search may need careful examination[7].

So the lesson is simple; be very careful of the result signs when dividing signed operands.

---

[7] A literature survey, done about 1990, yielded over 20 published variants of the "simple, fundamental" Binary Search algorithm, only *one* of which was actually correct in C. An Algol 60 version, while correct in Algol, did not transliterate easily into C, just because of this problem.

Send Orders for Reprints to reprints@benthamscience.net

Introduction to Computer Data Representation, 2014, 103-126

Chapter 6

Floating-Point Representations

Abstract: This chapter extends the earlier representations of integers to the equivalent of the real numbers of scientific calculation. It discusses the basic ideas, especially with reference to the IEEE 754 standard, and contrasting with descriptions of the IBM S/360 and Burroughs B6700 representations. There is extensive discussion of the requirements of ideal floating-point representations and the failings of practical implementations. Special mention is made of the requirements of range, precision and rounding. It concludes with examples of straight-forward calculations which can easily overwhelm many floating-point systems.

Keywords: Floating-point basics, IEEE 754 standard, Floating-point precision, Floating-point range, Floating-point rounding, Not a Number (NaNs), examples of range problems.

6.1 Introduction

Floating-point numbers extend the number system of a computer to include the very wide range of values needed by scientific or engineering computation. To some extent, the number system parallels the real numbers of mathematics (hence their frequent description as *real numbers*), but there are major differences from mathematical reals, some of which will be discussed later in greater depth.

The design (and use) of floating-point numbers is a very difficult and tricky area. Historically, most computers had their floating-point representations designed in a fairly ad hoc manner, with little attention to many of the finer points that will be raised later in this chapter. As a result, the floating-point arithmetic on many computers was often suspect, with differing accuracies or even results on different computers. (Sometimes a later computer even had to perpetuate the idiosyncrasies of a predecessor!)

Following an extensive analysis of the problems of floating-point number systems and computation, in 1985 the IEEE announced the IEEE 754 standard for floating-point numbers [58], a standard that addresses most of the previous problems with floating-point numbers. An initial broad outline will be followed later in the chapter with discussion of its more subtle aspects. Excellent discussions of floating-point numbers are found in the article by Goldberg [44] and the book "Computer Architecture", by Hennesey and Patterson [54]. Sterbenz [91] gives an earlier view of floating-point.

Floating-point numbers are at best an approximation to mathematical reals. Their ranges are limited, both towards the indefinitely large and towards the infinitesimally small and their precisions are also limited. Whereas there is always an infinity of reals between any two mathematical real values (no matter how close), this is far from true with floating-point numbers. With a standard 32-bit floating-point representation there are "only" about 16 million possible values between 1.0 and 2.0. Or there are only 16 values between 1.000 001 and 1.000 002, while 1.000 000 01 $\equiv$ 1.000 000 02 $\equiv$ 1.00. Confusion with true mathematical real numbers can cause major problems in programs that perform significant computation with low-precision numbers[1].

6.2 Basic Floating-Point Representation

It is appropriate to first review the conventional scientific representation, as it is a close analogue of many aspects of computing floating-point numbers. The representation, devised by Gauss about 1800, represents a value as two components, the numerically significant digits and an exponent giving the magnitude of the value.

The velocity of light, 299 792 458 ms^{-1}, is 2.997 924 58 $\times$ 10^8 ms^{-1} in more conventional (scientific) terms. (For many practical purposes we can use the

---

[1]The proper understanding of infinities and infinitesimals was a major achievement of 19th century mathematics. But there are now suggestions that these very concepts may be at the heart of some current problems in Physics (*New Scientist*, 17 Aug 2013, No 2930 "The End of Infinity", pp 32–35. (Perhaps true infinities and infinitesimals just do not exist in nature and the purity of mathematics is inappropriate to reality in these extremes.)

approximate value $300\,000\,000$ ms^{-1}, or 3×10^8 ms^{-1}.) The decimal point is naturally to the right of the last digit (the 8). To convert to scientific form, the point is first shifted so that it follows the first digit, a leftward shift of 8 places. A multiplier of 10^8 is included to correct for this shift.

For very large and very small numbers the scientific notation is very efficient. The charge on the electron is $0.00000000000000000160217653$ Coulomb or, even better, $1.602\,176\,53 \times 10^{-19}$ C. With the first form there is easily trouble counting zeros. Similarly, the number of atoms in one mole of gas is about 602214150000000000000000 or $6.022\,141\,5 \times 10^{23}$. The scientific form makes things easier in several ways –

1. The exponent indicates generally how large the number is (positive exponent) or how small (negative exponent). It also reduces the problems in counting many following or preceding zeros (I hope the counting was correct in the two examples!).

2. The number of digits tells how accurately the value is known. Thus a value of $98\,270$ known to an accuracy of ± 10 should be written 9.827×10^4 (the units digit is not certain), whereas if the last digit is certain, it should be written as 9.8270×10^4. Writing the speed of light as 3×10^8ms^{-1} means that we worry about only that first digit, whereas writing it as 3.00×10^8ms^{-1} means that the first 3 digits are correct. (Writing to another digit must be 2.998×10^8ms^{-1} when the last digit is rounded.)[2].

Computer real numbers are held in a similar way, except that values are usually binary[3]. A real value is held as two parts –

1. The *significand, fraction* or *mantissa* is often about 24 or 50 bits and usually gives a value $0.5 \leq V < 1.0$, with the binary point at or near the left-most bit.

---

[2]The converse seems to apply in the press and other popular writings. For example the statement that an aircraft was flying at an altitude of $30\,000$ feet may be translated into an altitude of 9144 metres, whereas 9000m might be more appropriate given the probable accuracy.

A more subtle example occurs with small probabilities; a failure probability of 6 parts per million (meaning somewhere between 5 and 7) becomes converted to 1 part in $166\,667$ (note that this is neither $166\,666$ nor $16\,668$), implying accuracy to the 6th digit. This leads to the comment that the more digits quoted, the less the accuracy! A similar effect is often seen in budgets and financial estimates. Something *estimated* to cost $\$1\,000\,000$ per week, with a *probable* daily overhead of $\$500$, gives the wondrously precise daily cost as $\$143\,357$.

[3]Many old purely decimal computers such as the IBM 1620 with only decimal arithmetic did naturally use decimal floating-point.

2. The *exponent* or *characteristic* is a smaller 7 to 12 bit value giving a multiplier for the significand. For most numbers the value for a significand S and an exponent E is $S \times 2^E$. The value could be written as a binary value with integral and fractional parts; the exponent tells by how many bits the binary point must be shifted to get the true external value from the internal representation.

6.2.1 Some Important Concepts

Several important concepts arise in dealing with computer floating-point numbers. They will be dealt with in some detail later on, but for now it is important to introduce them in general terms –

normalisation Equivalent forms for the velocity of light are –

$$2.997\,924\,58 \times 10^8$$
$$0.299\,792\,458 \times 10^9$$
$$0.002\,997\,92458 \times 10^{11}$$
$$29.979\,245\,8 \times 10^7$$

By convention, scientific numbers are always written with one decimal digit before the point, giving a *normalised* representation. The "engineering" representation on many calculators forces the decimal exponent to be a multiple of 3 to fit with the standard scale factors of most physical units (kilo, Mega, milli *etc*); the value before the point is then in the range $1\ldots999$.

Binary floating-point numbers are similarly normalised to the binary value $0.1xx\ldots$, or $1.xx\ldots$ by balancing a left shift of the digits with a decrease in the exponent (or a right shift of the digits with an increase in the exponent).

Some computers use a base of 8 or 16 for the floating-point representation. In these computers the binary values are shifted by 3 or 4 places (corresponding to the base of 2^3 or 2^4) until the left-most octal or hexadecimal digit is non zero, in the range 1–7 or 1–15 respectively.

range The range is determined by the exponent and determines how close to zero or far from zero a number may be. It is closely connected to the exponent form of scientific notation. An 8-bit signed exponent can have values from -128 to $+127$. The smallest representable number will be about 2^{-128} and the largest 2^{+127}. Remembering that $\log_2 10 \approx 1/0.3$, the smallest number is about 10^{-38} and the largest 10^{+38}. It is shown later that this range is quite inadequate for some calculations.

precision The precision is controlled by the significand (or fraction or mantissa) and gives the *accuracy* with which a number may be represented. Remember, again, that N bits equals about $0.3 \times N$ decimal digits. A standard 32-bit *real* has 23-bit precision, or not quite 7 decimal digits. A 64-bit *double* has 52-bits or 15 decimal digits. Even a 32 bit real can handle the accuracy of most physical measurements, but much of the precision is lost in lengthy calculations; this is the real justification for using 64-bit or 128-bit floating-point numbers.

rounding Floating-point arithmetic is subject to rounding and truncation errors. The significand can represent only so many bits; any less-significant bits must be discarded. Often, if the first discarded bit is a 1, we add 1 onto the significand to *round* the result. Thus 1.7 would round to 2, which is probably a better result than 1 (from just forgetting the bits).

But there are other options, such as truncating the number by just discarding the lost fractional digits[4]. But if +1.5 is rounded-up to 2, how should −1.5 be treated? Rounded up by adding 0.5 gives a result of 1; is it better to say that the positive *round-up* is matched by a negative *round-down*, both being examples of *round away from zero*? It is matters such as these that bedevilled earlier computer floating-point arithmetic and that are addressed in the IEEE 754 standard.

Truncation and rounding always cause some loss of precision. This loss is seldom important within even a few calculations, but is effectively a noise or unreliability imposed on the calculation result and once there it cannot be removed. In long sequences of calculations it leads to a progressive erosion or loss of less-significant digits, to the extent that calculations can all too easily lose *all* significance or meaning.

Care is needed when using real-number arithmetic. Some of the problems seem to disappear with "long" numbers, but really stay there and are never more than reduced.

6.2.2   Some Cautions

To conclude the general introduction to floating-point numbers it is important to give some cautions on their use.

---

[4]This problem is closely related to the sign of the remainder discussed in Section **5.5**.

- The 32 bit floating-point *real* or *float* on many computers is quite limited in comparison with many scientific calculators. Its range is about $10^{\pm 38}$, and its precision is not quite 7 decimal digits. Even short calculation sequences can overwhelm it. (A quite ordinary calculator may have a range of $10^{\pm 99}$ and a precision of 10 decimal digits.)

- Arithmetic with floating-point numbers is seldom exact. Great care must be taken as round-off errors accumulate in long calculation sequences. For example, one of the author's early experiences involved the solution of a set of 39 simultaneous equations (as many as the computer could handle). The 3–4 least significant decimal digits were quite meaningless (although this may have due largely to the deficiencies in floating-point implementation).

  Indeed, it is important to remember that the fundamental laws of arithmetic

  $$(A + B) + C = A + (B + C)$$

  and

  $$(A + B) \times C = A \times C + B \times C$$

  may be only approximately true with floating-point numbers in computing.

- Beware of computational techniques that involve differences of large quantities. This is related to the previous point. Say we have two values close to 1000, both with the last decimal digit uncertain, such as $1002 + x$ and $999 + x$ (both known to about 10 parts in 1000, or 1%). Subtracting gives a value $3 + x$, where the last digit is still uncertain, but the error is now 10 parts in 30, or about 30%. Two moderately accurate values have combined to give a value that is nearly meaningless. Some types of statistical calculation are especially sensitive to this problem.

- Be very careful if using floating-point arithmetic for financial calculations. Rounding errors may make it almost impossible to achieve reliable balances, especially if the number precision is barely adequate to represent the whole amount.

  The author is particularly suspicious of spreadsheets in this regard, having heard from other programmers of their attempts to balance accounts with floating-point arithmetic. The saving feature is probably that modern floating-point systems have sufficient precision to provide plenty of guard digits and probably use better rounding anyway.

6.3   IEEE 754 Floating-Point Representation

Although there were some significant exceptions (two of which are mentioned later), most floating-point number design had, by the 1970s, settled into a few variations on the following basic theme.

- The total representation length was 32 bits, largely following from the 16-bit minicomputers and, later, the 8-bit microcomputers of the time. Some computers provided an extended or long format of 48 or even 64 bits but these numbers used more memory (always an expensive resource) and had much slower arithmetic, especially with programmed floating-point. (Remember that some of these computers did not even have a multiply or divide instruction.) But 32 bits seemed to be adequate for most small computations, so why change?

  The 32 bits were further divided into a *fraction* or *mantissa* (now called the *significand*) of 24 bits including sign, and an 8-bit signed exponent.

- The significand was held in a sign and magnitude representation. On the smaller machines this may have been habit, but was also probably connected with the difficulties of implementing high-precision signed arithmetic when only lower-precision operations were available. In any case, many of the largest computers of the time also used sign and magnitude to simplify their very fast arithmetic units.

- The exponent was held in an *excess* or biased form, often excess 128. While the true reasons for this choice are doubtful, it has the significant advantage that an unsigned comparison (as 32-bit integers) "compares true" with more-positive values always comparing greater than more-negative values. When the fields of the floating-point number have the conventional order of {sign, exponent, significand} normalised floating-point numbers can be compared with a simple and faster integer compare. It also means that the smallest value is represented by all-zeros, giving a "clean zero" representation for a floating-point zero.

- Some computers, especially the PDP-11 and then the VAX series by Digital Equipment Corporation, used a *hidden bit* representation to get a little more precision.

  In conventional and traditional representations the significand is always normalised to the form $0.1xxxx\ldots$. But this means that the most significand bit is *always* 1, and therefore redundant (except where the significand is zero). With a hidden bit the significand is normalised to

1.*xxxx*... and the 1 removed before converting to external form. The 1 is automatically restored when the number is read from memory and broken into its components to perform arithmetic.

A floating-point zero is represented by an all-zero word; both exponent and significand are zero. An exact power of two, with only a single 1 in its representation is also represented by an all-zero significand but with a non-zero exponent.

But there were still some differences and incompatibilities, so that programs all to often gave different results on different computers. Some of the problems were to do with rounding, but others were concerned with error handling. For example, it was not uncommon for a computer to evaluate $\sqrt{-4} = 2$ and to set an error flag, which the programmer could interrogate (or ignore). Overflows and underflows were similarly handled in various and inconsistent ways. It is against this background that the IEEE developed its standard for binary floating-point arithmetic [58].

The IEEE 754 standard defines several number formats and precisions. The 32 bit format has a 1-bit sign, an 8-bit exponent with a bias of 127, and a 23-bit significand. The significand is always stored in normalised form with its most significant bit 1, but treating this 1 as a hidden bit. The bits are used as `sxxx xxxx xfff ffff ffff ffff ffff ffff` where `s` is the sign bit, `xx` ...`xx` are the exponent bits and `ff`...`ff` the (fractional) significand bits. The value of a number is then

$$(-1)^{sign} \times (1.0 + significand) \times 2^{(exponent - 127)}$$

The IEEE 754 standard has quite complicated rules on the rounding of numbers. It also has ways of representing underflowed and overflowed numbers and special error values called *Not a Number* (NaN), from cases like 0/0 or $\sqrt{-3}$. All of these aspects will be discussed later.

6.3.1   Higher Precision Numbers

As described earlier, the 32-bit representation is barely adequate for serious computation; the precision is limited and rounding errors accumulate very quickly so that some relatively short computations can become quite meaningless. Also, the number range of $10^{\pm 38}$ is too small to handle some physical quantities, or formulæ involving them. The original standard had rather vague

Table 6.1: Summary of IEEE 754 Binary Representations

Parameter	Format			
	Half Precision	Single Precision	Double Precision	Quadruple Precision
p	$h + 10$	$h + 23$	$h + 52$	$h + 112$
E_{max}	$+15$	$+127$	$+1023$	$+16\,383$
E_{min}	-14	-126	-1022	$-16\,382$
Exponent width in bits	4	8	11	15
Format width in bits	16	32	64	128

extensions to the "single" and "double" formats but these have now been clarified and extended to include a 128-bit "quadruple precision". There is also a 16-bit "half" precision.

The full format specifications are shown in Table **6.1**. The "h" in this table denotes the "hidden bit", so that the Single Precision format has 23 visible bits, plus the hidden bit, to give a total fractional precision of 24 bits.

IEEE 754 double precision uses a 53-bit significand (giving about 16 decimal digits of precision) and an 11-bit exponent with a bias of 1023 (a range of about $10^{\pm 300}$). The underlying principles are as for the 32-bit representation. The new quadruple precision representation has a 112-bit significand (over 30 decimal digits) and a range nearly $10^{\pm 5000}$. The Standard also describes a family of decimal floating-point representations, which are not discussed here.

6.3.2   Rounding in IEEE 754

The precise specification of rounding modes and operations is a major feature of the IEEE 754 standard. The standard specifies that all results are first produced as though to infinite precision and then rounded according to one of the following modes. (Remember that rounding occurs only if non-zero bits are to be discarded. No rounding or adjustment occurs if all of the discarded bits are zero.) This section emphasises the IEEE 754 standard; a general overview of rounding is given later in Section **6.6**.

It is convenient in the descriptions to use *intermediate result* as meaning the infinitely precise initial result referred to above. The standard uses *representable value* as the maximum precision approximation to the intermediate result; the intermediate result may coincide with the representable value if the

Table 6.2: IEEE 754 Rounding Modes

Intermediate Value	to nearest	towards $+\infty$	towards 0	towards $-\infty$
+1.4	+1.0	+2.0	+1.0	+1.0
+1.5	+2.0	+2.0	+1.0	+1.0
+1.6	+2.0	+2.0	+1.0	+1.0
−1.4	−1.0	−1.0	−1.0	−2.0
−1.5	−2.0	−1.0	−1.0	−2.0
−1.6	−2.0	−1.0	−1.0	−2.0
+2.5	+2.0	+3.0	+2.0	+2.0
−2.5	+2.0	+2.0	−2.0	−3.0
+3.5	+4.0	+4.0	+3.0	+3.0
−3.5	−4.0	−3.0	−3.0	−4.0

discarded bits are all 0, or may lie between two representable values.

Round to Nearest This is the default mode. The intermediate result will usually lie between two representable values; the nearest of these two values is chosen as the result. If the two are equally near, the one with a zero least-significant bit is chosen.

Directed roundings There are three directed rounding modes –

- Round towards $+\infty$. The result is the representable value closest to and not less than the intermediate result.

- Round towards zero. The result is the representable value closest to and no greater in *magnitude* than the intermediate result.

- Round towards $-\infty$. The result is the representable value closest to and not greater than the intermediate result[5].

The rounding modes are illustrated in Table **6.2**, assuming a low-precision value in which the *representable value* is an integer. The standard also specifies an ability to round a double precision result to single precision, while retaining the double precision representation. This may be useful in a compiler, or to combine a lower precision value and a wider exponent range.

---

[5]This corresponds to to the Algol 60 **entier** function mentioned in Section **5.5**.

6.3.3   Semi-Numerical Codes

The IEEE 754 standard has explicit representations for –

1. "infinite" values, such as arise from arithmetic overflows,

2. somewhat numerical Not-a-Numbers (NaNs) that may arise from invalid arithmetic but then propagate as operands through arithmetic operations,

3. a special class of very small *denormalized numbers.*

Table **6.3** shows all of the codings for the 32-bit single-precision representation, including the numeric values. This table shows the exponent e (as held in the representation), sign s and fraction or significand f (again as represented).

The conventions are similar in double precision, except that the maximum exponent of 2047 replaces the 255 and the bias becomes 1023 rather than 127.

The various codings have the meanings –

Infinities   Infinities may be result from overflow or division by zero (and are signalled if the trap is enabled). Infinities behave much as normal signed values, but propagate to produce infinite results, except that a division of a number by infinity produces 0.0 as a result. (The division ∞/∞ is undefined and gives a NaN.)

NaNs   NaNs may be *signaling*, to detect uninitialised operands or to extend operand types, or may be *quiet* to indicate some previous error. Generally a NaN will propagate through an arithmetic sequence; any arithmetic operation with a NaN yields a NaN, and any comparison with a NaN yields FALSE (a NaN comparison is always *unordered*). (Languages may include explicit tests for NaNs, such as the Java method `Double.isNaN()`.

Denormalized numbers   These allow the representation of values closer to zero than the usual minimum (say 2^{-127}, albeit with reduced precision.

Table 6.3: IEEE 754 Single Precision Codings

e	f	Meaning	Comment
$e = 255$	$f \neq 0$	NaN	Not a Number (coded by f)
$e = 255$	$f = 0$	$v = (-1)^s \infty$	signed infinity
$0 < e < 255$		$v = (-1)^{e-127}(1.f)$	normal number
$e = 0$	$f \neq 0$	$v = (-1)^{e-126}(0.f)$	denormalized number
$e = 0$	$f = 0$	$v = (-1)^s 0$	zero (signed)

6.3.4 Floating-Point Number Examples

1.25
- Written as a binary value with one bit to the left of the binary point, 1.25 is 1.0100000000 .... Omitting the first bit gives .010 000 000 0 ... as the significand.

- Now 1.25 is already normalised, without any shifting or alignment necessary and the number has an exponent of zero. Adding the bias of 127 gives a field value of 127, or 01111111, in the representation of the number.

- With a positive sign of 0, the representation becomes
  0 01111111 01000000000000000000000.
  Converting to hexadecimal gives 3FA00000.

14.0
- Written as a binary value, 14.0 is 1110.0000000000 ....

- To normalise, the binary point must be shifted three places to the left, giving a true exponent of +3 and a fraction of 1.1100000000 ..., which with the leading bit omitted is represented as .1100000000 ....

- Adding the bias of 127 to the exponent (+3) gives a represented value of 130, or a bit pattern of 10000010.

- With a sign of 0, the whole bit pattern becomes
  0 10000010 11000000000000000000000.
  Converting to hexadecimal gives 41600000.

0.1
- In binary, 0.1 is 0.00011001100110011001100 ....

- To normalise, the binary point must be shifted four places to the right, for a true exponent of -4 and a fraction 1.100110011001100110011001100 ..., or 0.100110011001100110011001100 ... with the leading bit omitted.

- Adding the bias of 127 to the exponent (-4) gives a represented value of 123, or a bit pattern of 01111011.

- With a sign of 0, the whole bit pattern becomes
  0 01111011 10011001100110011001.

- Converting to hexadecimal gives 3DCCCCCC. As the bits immediately following this pattern are 1100 ..., the last digit is rounded up to the next digit, or D, giving a final representation 3DCCCCCD.

6.4   Other Representations

6.4.1   IBM S/360 Format

This is an example of a design that is widespread and therefore important, but has some unfortunate design errors. It was developed when most computers had at least a 36 bit word length, but that had to be trimmed back to 32 bits for the IBM System/360, released in 1964. Some of the underlying design rationale is given by Sweeney [97] and Amdahl *et al* [2].

IBM S/360 floating-point numbers have, in single precision, a 24-bit fraction plus sign (sign & magnitude form) and a 7-bit exponent in excess-64 format. The fraction base is 16, so that a normalised fraction can start with any of the bit patterns $1xxx\ldots$, $01xx\ldots$, $001x\ldots$ or $0001\ldots$. The maximum exponent is 63, but this is associated with a base of 16, giving a maximum represented value of 16^{63}, or 7.2×10^{75}, or twice the range of most 32-bit floating-point representations. The smallest represented value has a (binary) minimum fraction $0.0001\ldots \approx 1/16$ and an exponent of -64; its value is $1/16 \times 16^{-64} = 16^{-65} = 5.4 \times 10^{-79}$.

Thus the base 16 gives twice the exponent range of most 32-bit representations. Against the wider range is a reduction in precision, which varies between 21 and 24 bits, or 6.3 (decimal) digits and 7.2 digits. A standard example of the problem relates to the value of π and is discussed in Section **6.6** and shown in Table **6.6**. The accuracy of a general calculation may depend critically on the exact arrangement of values within the calculation (which a compiler may helpfully rearrange).

The choice of base-16 exponent was justified largely on the grounds of increased range compared with many other 32-bit representations and because it minimised the number of normalising shifts in addition.

The S/360 included a 64-bit floating-point, and later a 128-bit representation while retaining the same exponent and range.

6.4.2 Burroughs B6700 Format

The Burroughs B6700 and its successors the Burroughs/Unisys A-series, are computers with many interesting and novel features. For example, each 48-bit word has a tag of 3 bits (later 4 bits) that identifies the type of word. Many tags make their words unavailable to users, and accessible only under system conditions, but a tag=0 identifies its word as a numeric operand. Furthermore, a single format includes both integers and floating-point; the computer truly works with *numbers*.

Figure 6.1: Layout of B6700 Number

47	43	39	35	31	27	23	19	15	11	7	3
	—	EX	EX								
0	MS	EX									
0	ES	EX				Mantissa					
0	EX	EX									
44	40	36	32	28	24	20	16	12	8	4	0

left bit	right bit	field width	function
47	47	1	unused (historical reasons)
46	46	1	mantissa sign
45	45	1	exponent sign
44	39	6	exponent (sign & magnitude)
38	0	39	mantissa (sign & magnitude)

The layout is shown in Figure **6.1**, including the 3-bit tag, with bits in columns and showing the extreme bit numbers of each 4-bit column or hexadecimal digit. The presentation is as in the B6700 manuals. The bit fields are labelled MS=Mantissa sign, ES=Exponent sign, EX=Exponent.

Both exponent and mantissa are held in sign and magnitude, but the mantissa is held as an *integer*, rather than the more conventional fraction. Any number with a zero exponent is an integer; an *Integerize* instruction will attempt to force a number into this form. Thus there is only one form of numeric operand; the meaning of a tag-0 word is unequivocal, unless it is interpreted bit-fields or characters.

The exponent has a base of 8 with the mantissa alignment in steps of 3 bits. The mantissa is 39 bits, giving a maximum integer (either sign) of

549 755 813 887 and a working precision of about 11 decimal digits.

A double-precision value uses two words, both with tag=2. The exponent of the second word (extended to use all 9 bits not used by the mantissa extension) acts as a *high-order* extension of the base exponent, while the mantissa is a *fractional* extension of the base mantissa. Extending a single precision value just involves appending an all-zero word and adjusting the tags from 0 to 2. Converting a double precision to single requires just dropping the extension word *provided that the exponent is positive and the extension exponent bits are zero*. Conversion with a non-zero exponent extension gives either 0.0 (-ve exponent) or overflow (+ve exponent).

The limiting values for the B6700 number representation are –

Largest single-precision value	$8^{63} \times (2^{39} - 1) = 4.313\,591\,466\,7 \times 10^{68}$
Least SP value (full precision)	$8^{-63} \times 2^{37} = 1.751\,623\,080\,4 \times 10^{-46}$
Least SP value (unnormalized)	$8^{-63} = 1.274\,473\,528\,9 \times 10^{-57}$
Largest double-precision value	$1.948\,829\,382\,0502\,807\,912\,446\,9 \times 10^{29\,603}$
Smallest normalized DP value	$1.938\,545\,857\,137\,585\,833\,556\,4 \times 10^{-29\,581}$

In contrast with the S/360, the B6700 format is saved by its greater word length. The basic precision is sufficiently high that the loss and granularity from the octal exponent is mimimal. While the single precision range is less that of the S/360, the precision is such that it is seldom necessary to escape into double precision. (Double precision may be needed to handle some intermediate values as shown in Section **6.5.3**.) The double precision format gives about 22 decimal digits of precision and a range $\approx 10^{\pm 29\,600}$ that is surely adequate for any problem! Its unique feature though is its representation that combines integer and floating-point into the one format.

6.4.3   A Final Curiosity

As a closing example of a representation, we give a number system that represents decimal numbers in binary [28]. The problem is that it is often necessary to perform calculations that are decimally exact, especially in financial calculations. While floating-point can be used, it requires care and appropriate use of guard digits[6].

---

[6]The imprecision of floating-point was a major problem when this example was first published, but has since been largely resolved by the adoption of the IEEE 754 standard.

This representation holds a *decimal* value d as a *binary* integer i with a scaling factor s, such that $d = i \times 10^s$ with some typical values shown in Table **6.4**.

Table 6.4: Examples of Decimal Binary Representation

value (d)	mantissa (m)	exponent (s)
27	27	0
3.82	382	-2
0.382	382	-3
6	6	0
6.000	6000	-3
3.141 59	314 159	-5
0.001 28	128	-5

The representation has several distinctive features –

1. The mantissa (significand) is an integer rather than the more usual fraction.

2. The exponent, probably also held as a binary integer, has an associated base of 10.

3. The mantissa is not normalised; all of its digits are significant and must be preserved. Trailing zeros in its decimal value are significant digits.

4. The mantissa contains only as many digits as are significant. (See the cases for 6 and 6.000 in the table.) Properly managed, this can reduce problems of unwarranted precision. For example, should 1 000 000/6 be treated as 166 667 (6 digits precision) or 1.67 (2 digits).

Alignment or normalisation of the mantissa requires multiplication or division by appropriate powers of 10. Multiplication by 10 is straightforward, but division may require some efficient constant-divisor technique (discussed in the original paper). The arithmetic techniques are derived from those of floating-point arithmetic –

Addition and subtraction resemble normal floating-point; the value with the larger exponent is first scaled left to align digits of like precision. However an addition overflow may have to be treated as a genuine numeric overflow; renormalisation would entail loss of significant low-order digits that may not be permitted.

Multiplication involves the multiplication of the mantissæ and addition of the exponents, just as in normal floating-point. However the fractional digits accumulate and it may be necessary to scale the product back to an appropriate precision. It could be desirable to have an instruction or hardware system status that specifies the precision from a multiplication.

Division definitely requires specification of the result precision, because division itself is poorly defined and may be inexact. The quotient exponent may be required to be zero (integer), either of the operand exponents, or even some other value. All cases can be accommodated by appropriate scaling of the inputs, but the choice comes from the application rather than any general principle.

6.5 Requirements of Floating-Point Numbers

The requirements of floating-point numbers are usually discussed under the categories of *range* and *precision*; many aspects have been already mentioned in passing. A related topic of *scaling invariance* is discussed in Section **11.9**.

6.5.1 Range

Scientific measurement, especially in physical sciences, involves quantities covering an enormous range of values. Examples here are given in line with normal usage; much smaller quantities are found in particle physics and much larger ones in cosmology.

length Two extreme named values are the Ångström (10^{-10}m used for atomic distances) and the megaparsec ($3.085\,6 \times 10^{22}$m used in astronomy).

mass Extremes here are the electron mass (9.109×10^{-19}kg), the mass of the Earth (5.976×10^{24} kg) and the mass of the Sun (1.99×10^{30}kg).

time A reasonable lower bound to everyday times might be the period of visible light, about 10^{-15}s. A corresponding reasonable upper limit might be the period of the Earth in its orbit (1 year $= 3.153\,6 \times 10^7$s), or even the age of the Earth (about 1.4×10^{17}s).

Even these values are misleading, because far more extreme values can occur in the course of calculations. Some examples that illustrate some problems of floating-point number range are given in Section **6.5.3**.

6.5.2 Precision

Looking at the formula for gravitational attraction in Section **6.5.3** indicates that 4 digits of precision might be adequate (no value is stated more accurately than that), while the second example in that section indicates a necessary precision of about 6 digits. This argument is quite misleading because experience, and analysis of arithmetic techniques, show that floating-point calculations can suffer from serious *round-off* error or loss of precision. It is not at all difficult to lose 4 or 5 digits of precision, or to get results that mean absolutely nothing! Thus numbers should usually represent values to several decimal places more than might be indicated by simple inspection of the input values.

To illustrate the effects of limited precision, assume that we are calculating the third side of a right angle triangle whose hypotenuse has been measured as 33.7cm and another side as 33.0cm; we must calculate the third side, using arithmetic to 1 fractional digit and rounding any less-significant digits. (The two values are actually in the ratio 101:99, which are two members of the Pythagorean triple {20, 99, 101} giving a true result of 6.67cm.)

The third side is then

$$\sqrt{(33.7^2 - 33.0^2)} = \sqrt{(1135.7 - 1089)} = \sqrt{46.7} = 6.8$$

If the calculation is done with 4 digits precision in total

$$\sqrt{(33.7^2 - 33.0^2)} = \sqrt{(1136 - 1089)} = \sqrt{47} = 6.855$$

These examples show the effects of limited precision, especially when taking the difference of two large similar values, as here. Thus we must ensure that there is adequate precision for the problem, and for the method of calculation.

6.5.3 Examples of Floating-Point Range Problems

The examples of this section all come from physics, reflecting both the author's background and the fact that physics is a ready source of calculations to strain many floating-point systems. Table **6.5** shows the constants as used in the examples.

The physics here just supplies convenient formulæ and values; the main purpose of this section is to show that underflows and overflows easily arise in the course of quite reasonable calculations, even where all visible values are well within range.

Table 6.5: Some Physical Constants (numerical values, MKS units)

$$
\begin{aligned}
e &= 1.602\,189\,2 \times 10^{-19} && \text{charge of an electron} \\
G &= 6.670 \times 10^{-11} && \text{the gravitational constant} \\
h &= 6.626\,176 \times 10^{-34} && \text{Plank's constant} \\
m_e &= 9.109\,534 \times 10^{-31} && \text{mass of electron} \\
M_e &= 5.976 \times 10^{24} && \text{the mass of the Earth} \\
M_s &= 1.99 \times 10^{30} && \text{the mass of the Sun} \\
R &= 1.496 \times 10^{11} && \text{the radius of the Earth's orbit} \\
\epsilon_0 &= 8.854\,19 \times 10^{-12} && \text{permittivity of space}
\end{aligned}
$$

Gravitational attraction   The gravitational attraction between the Sun and the Earth is

$$ F = G\frac{M_e M_s}{R^2} $$

Although the final result is 3.54×10^{22}, a value of about 1.2×10^{55} probably occurs during evaluation, unless the order of calculation is deliberately altered by using strategically placed parentheses to force a specific order of evaluation. But even the best-laid plans can fail ...

Although most programming languages allow parentheses to override normal precedence rules so that the user can control the order of calculation, it is not unknown for "optimising" compilers to ignore parentheses in favour of "mathematically equivalent" results, completely defeating the programmer's deliberate intentions and knowledge. A "good" optimiser can even override explicit assignments to intermediate variables, completely deleting the variables!

Bohr model of hydrogen atom   In the Bohr model of the hydrogen atom, the energy E_n of the nth stationary state is given by

$$ E_n = \frac{m_e e^4}{8\epsilon_0^2 h^2} \cdot \frac{1}{n^2} $$

The numerator (top line) of the fraction is 6×10^{-106}, and the denominator (bottom line) is 2.75×10^{-88}; the final value is about 2.18×10^{-18}.

Both numerator and denominator are outside the range of many representations, even though the final value is representable.

Ratio of electrostatic and gravitational forces The electrical and gravitational forces between two electrons both follow a similar inverse square law, giving a constant ratio, independent of distance. A standard example in physics is to calculate their ratio to demonstrate the relative weakness of gravity. The two forces are –

$$F_e = \frac{1}{4\pi\epsilon_0} \frac{e^2}{r^2}$$

and

$$F_g = \frac{Gm_e^2}{r^2}$$

with the ratio

$$
\begin{aligned}
F_e/F_g &= e^2/m_e^2 \times 1/(4\pi\epsilon_0 G) \\
&= 3.10 \times 10^{22}/7.423 \times 10^{-21} \\
&= 4.167 \times 10^{42}
\end{aligned}
$$

In this case a standard 32-bit IEEE 754 floating-point number cannot even represent the result.

6.6   Rounding

It frequently happens, perhaps even usually happens, that a value has more bits than are available in the chosen number representation. The represented value is then an approximation to the correct value because some of the less-significant bits must be discarded. The question then arises as to just how the retained bits should be adjusted to reflect the effect of those discarded. This is one of the most difficult aspects of floating-point design and is treated at length by Goldberg [44].

Before discussing rounding as such, it is necessary to introduce the concept of errors. In general an external value $\mathcal{V}$ is approximated by a representation $\mathcal{R}$; we hope that $\mathcal{V} \approx \mathcal{R}$. If the floating-point number $d.d\cdots d \times \beta^e$ is used to represent the value z to p digits with a floating-point base of β, the value is in error by $\mid d.d\cdots d - (z/\beta^e) \mid \beta^{(p-1)}$ units in the last place, or "*ulps*". While this error should never exceed $^1/_2$ ulp, the distribution of the error can be very important.

Another important measure is the *relative error*, defined as $(\mathcal{V} - \mathcal{R})/\mathcal{V}$; it should not exceed β^{p-1}. The relative error corresponding to $^1/_2$ ulp can vary by a factor of β between numbers with a small significand and ones with a large significand.

Table 6.6: IBM S/360 Representation of π (Single Precision)

	true value decimal	true value hexadecimal	truncated 6-digit hex.	decimal (from hex.)	rel.err. $\times 10^8$
π	$3.141592653\ldots$	$3.243F6A88\ldots$	$3.243F6$	3.141592026	20
$\pi/2$	$1.570796326\ldots$	$1.921FB544\ldots$	$1.921FB$	3.141592026	20
$\pi/4$	$0.785398163\ldots$	$0.C90FDAA2\ldots$	$0.C90FDA$	3.141592503	5
$\pi/8$	$0.392699081\ldots$	$0.6487ED51\ldots$	$0.6487ED$	3.141592502	5

This effect is shown in Table **6.6**, representing π in the IBM S/360 number format. With the fraction held as 6 hexadecimal digits, small values (such as 0001 1001 ... from $\pi/2$) have 3 leading and 21 significant bits, while other values (such as 1100 1001 ...) with $\pi/4$ have the full 24 bits of precision. The effect of the large base is to introduce a wobble in the precision of the representation; a hexadecimal base as in the S/360 can easily lead to the loss of a full decimal digit.

There are several versions of rounding, which will be illustrated by values such as 3.73 rounded to one fractional digit.

Truncation. In this form, which is strictly not rounding at all, the fractional digits are just forgotten, so that $+3.73$ and $+3.78$ both convert to $+3.7$. However the operation is not well defined with negative numbers. With sign-magnitude $-3.73 \to -3.7$, but with a complement representation $-3.73 \to -3.8$. (Remember that in 1s or 2s complement a low-order bit *adds on* to the value of the other bits.) It does not seem right that positive and negative numbers should behave differently. In particular $(-A) + (-B) \neq -(A + B)$ and commutativity fails.

Round to nearest. Here we examine the most significant of the discarded digits. In decimal arithmetic, if the discarded digit is $0 \ldots 4$, the retained digits are left unchanged. If the discarded digits are $5 \ldots 9$, then one is added to the retained digits, in the least-significant position. Equivalently, we add 0.5 to the result, allowing carry propagation as needed. In binary, one is added if the most significant discarded bit is a 1.

Round toward even. This resolves the problem of, for example, rounding 1.5 to an integer. It is identical to *round toward zero* except that if the discarded portion is precisely 0.5 of the least-significant digit, the least-significant digit is set to zero.

Round toward $+\infty$. In integer terms, if the value is an exact integer it is left unchanged. Non-integral values are rounded towards $+\infty$; $+1.3 \rightarrow +2$ and $-1.3 \rightarrow -1$.

Round toward $-\infty$. This version is similar to *round toward $+\infty$* but with rounding in the opposite direction; $+1.3 \rightarrow +1$ and $-1.3 \rightarrow -2$.

Round toward zero. This option is equivalent to truncation, *for sign-and-magnitude representations.* $+1.3 \rightarrow +1$ and $-1.3 \rightarrow -1$.

Books on statistics give two allegedly equivalent formulæ for calculating the sample variance s^2 of a population. (In all cases the sum is over the whole population.)

$$s^2 = \frac{\sum(x_i - \bar{x})^2}{n-1} = \frac{n\sum x_i{}^2 - (\sum x_i)^2}{n(n-1)}, \text{ where } \bar{x} = \frac{\sum x}{n} \text{ (the mean)}$$

Although these two forms are mathematically equivalent (indeed it is an elementary exercise to prove the equivalence), they are decidedly *not* equivalent in the approximate arithmetic of many floating-point systems. The right-hand form is superficially desirable because it involves only one pass through the data but it involves the difference of two large quantities and is therefore suspect. The left hand form is slightly more complex with two passes over the data, first to get the mean and then the variance, but avoids the difference of large quantities.

A test involved a sample of 1000 numbers, uniformly distributed in the range 999–1001 (1000 ± 1), evaluating the variance by both *square of differences* (the left-hand form) and by *difference of squares* (the right-hand form), with the results shown in Table **6.7**. The mean and range are chosen to be representative of reasonably accurate physical measurements, but with squared values barely representable with the 32-bit floating-point format (24 bits of significance).

The square of differences column shows a consistent value. Both formulæ in double precision agreed with this column in single precision, to 4 fractional digits. The right-hand column (difference of squares) is completely unreliable,

Table 6.7: Calculation of Variance of 1000 Values, with 32-bit Precision

mean	square of diffs	diff of squares
1000.02	0.33	0.20
999.98	0.33	-0.43
1000.00	0.34	-0.42
1000.01	0.32	0.54
1000.00	0.35	0.35
999.99	0.34	-0.33
999.99	0.33	1.53
999.99	0.33	-0.20
1000.03	0.33	1.47
1000.03	0.32	0.95

although its *average* of 0.37 is more or less consistent with the other values. Not only is this column unreliable from the spread of values, but some values are obviously wrong because the variance, being the square of a real value *must* be positive and some values are negative.

6.7   History of Floating-Point Computation

Although numerical values, both large and small, had of necessity been used in science for at least the previous 100 years, it was only in the early 19th century that the present systematic scientific number representation was introduced by Gauss (at a time when some die-hard mathematicians were still denying the existence, let alone the utility, of negative numbers!)[7]. The use of that representation in calculating devices was proposed by Torres y Quevedo in 1914 [102] and a computer using binary floating-point was built by Konrad Zuse (the Z-1 computer, 1936) [113]. Two relay calculators in 1944-45 also used floating-point arithmetic, the Bell Laboratories Mark V [63] and Howard Aiken's Mark II [1].

By the time of the Burks, Goldstine and Neumann report in 1946 [17] floating-point numbers were clearly accepted and were stated as being proposed for several computers. However they argued strongly against floating-

---

[7]A known large value at this time was the velocity of light (estimated by Rømer in 1675). From it came estimates of planetary distances, also large values. A small value came soon afterwards from the wavelength of light, determined by Young in 1817.

point, preferring the extra precision that resulted from integer representations. With the enormous amount of effort needed to prepare programs using neither assemblers nor compilers, the time spent analysing problems and arranging integer scaling was probably justified. (And memory was itself a rare and expensive resource; floating-point arithmetic usually needed software libraries using memory that might be better used on more data or a better algorithm.) With the introduction of high-level languages and compilers extensive pre-coding analysis of problems was no longer appropriate and floating-point arithmetic became accepted as a natural, and even essential, part of scientific computing.

Send Orders for Reprints to reprints@benthamscience.net

Introduction to Computer Data Representation, 2014, 127-132 **127**

Chapter 7

Logarithmic Representations

Abstract: Some types of calculation emphasise multiplication and division over addition and subtraction. Representing numbers as their *logarithms* accelerates multiplication and division, but slightly complicates addition and subtraction. This chapter gives a brief overview of logarithmic representations and their arithmetic.

Keywords: Logarithmic representations, logarithmic arithmetic, implementation of logarithmic arithmetic.

7.1 Introduction

Logarithmic numbers provide an interesting alternative number representation that is related to floating-point numbers and helps explain some aspects of floating-point representation. They were introduced to assist computation such as signal processing where only limited precision is needed and expensive operations such as multiplication often dominated the computation. With early processors using serial multiplication, or even programmed multiplication, the expense of multiplication was a very real problem. Although modern processors with fast combinational multipliers largely remove this need, logarithmic representations are still interesting.

An early paper by Mitchell [75] described multiplication and division with logarithms, and a logarithmic number system was described by Swartzlander and Alexopoulos [96]. Taylor [99] and then Yu and Lewis [111] describe actual hardware implementations. An overview of logarithmic number systems is included in a book by Koren [67].

The fast calculation of 2^x and $\log_2 x$, an essential adjunct to logarithmic representations, is described for example by Majithia and Levan [73] and Kingsbury and Rayner [65].

7.2   The Logarithmic Representation

Conventional scientific representation represents a real value R as a combination of fraction f and exponent x (both f and x may be signed), using a base b, usually 10, as

$$R = b^x f$$

Floating-point representations represent R by the number pair $\{x', f'\}$, where the exponent x' is the *integral* part of $\log_b R$ and the fraction or significand is $f' = \log_b f$, or $f' = R/b^x$. Floating-point is thus a mixed representation, with one part a logarithmic function of the original value and the other linearly related to the value.

A logarithmic representation simply takes the logarithm of R as fixed-point number, with a fixed division between integral and fractional parts. Working in decimal, with 3 integral places and 7 fractional places gives the following equivalences for some physical and other constants –

Value	representation
299 792 458	8.476 820 7
$6.626\,176 \times 10^{-34}$	$-33.178\,873\,7$
$6.022\,045 \times 10^{23}$	23.779 774 0
16 384	4.214 419 9
0.0025	$-2.602\,060\,0$

There are two signs on each number, just as with floating-point. That shown in the examples above corresponds to the exponent sign and is positive for large values ($|R| \geq 1$) and negative for small values ($0 < |R| < 1.0$). This sign is often handled as a biased or offset representation for the whole number, just as for the exponent of a floating-point number. Not shown in the examples here is the normal value sign, corresponding to the significand sign.

Binary logarithmic numbers usually assume a fraction (significand) of 1 so that it may be discarded (much like the "hidden 1" of DEC computers). The value is then represented solely by the exponent, which is now a true "fixed-point" number with defined integral and fractional parts.

7.3   Logarithmic Arithmetic

The usual rationale for using a logarithmic representation is to facilitate multiplication and division, which are done just by adding or subtracting the representations. The "value sign" is of course handled independently, according to the usual rules for operations on signed quantities. (If the logarithmic representations follow frequent practice for floating-point and use a biased representation, the bias must be subtracted after "multiplication" and added after "division", exactly as for exponent arithmetic in multiplication and division.)

Addition and subtraction are more difficult and are, in general, only approximate. The fundamental formulæ for the sum S and difference D are now

$$S = A + B = A\left(1 + \frac{B}{A}\right) \qquad \text{and} \qquad D = A - B = A\left(1 - \frac{B}{A}\right)$$

or, taking logarithms, using K_x to denote the finite-precision logarithm of x (or approximation to $\log_2 x$) and writing $X = B/A$,

$$K_S = K_A + \log(1 + X) \qquad \text{and} \qquad K_D = K_A + \log(1 - X)$$

Then, if $K_A \geq K_B$

$$\begin{aligned}
K_S &= K_A + \beta(K_B - K_A) \\
K_D &= K_A + \gamma(K_B - K_A)
\end{aligned}$$

where $\beta(x) = \log_2(1 + 2^x)$ and $\gamma(x) = \log_2(1 - 2^x)$.
If $K_A < K_B$

$$\begin{aligned}
K_S &= K_A + \beta(K_A - K_B) \\
K_D &= K_A + \gamma(K_A - K_B)
\end{aligned}$$

The evaluation of the awkward $\beta(x)$ and $\gamma(x)$ functions to adjust the larger operand is usually done with a Read Only Memory. Operands of n bit precision need 2^n words of ROM for each function, or $2n2^n$ bits of ROM.

Figure **7.1** shows the basic adder for logarithmic numbers. Little extra logic is needed to handle the (now simpler) operations of multiplication and division, as shown in Figure **7.2**. (The "bias" input in this last figure is used to compensate for the bias or offset when multiplying or dividing.)

The original paper quoted $n = 8$ for a precision of 8 bits; with modern technology a precision of 16–20 bits is quite feasible. But the size of the ROM

Figure 7.1: Logarithmic Arithmetic Adder/Subtractor

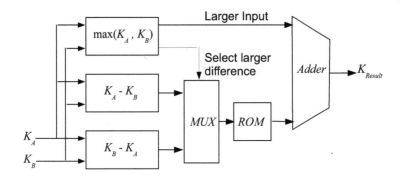

Figure 7.2: Complete Logarithmic ALU

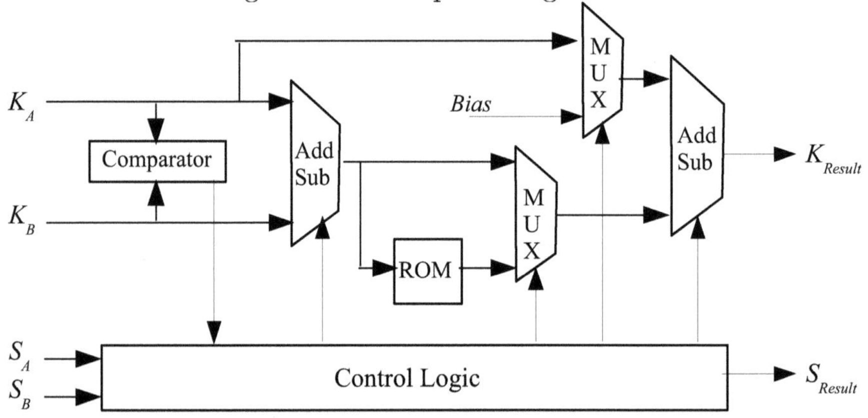

Add Sub = Adder/Subtracter; MUX = Multiplexer

can be reduced considerably at the expense of some extra complication, as described by Taylor *et al* [99]. They partition the main ROM into a cascade of a single initial ROM and several later ones in parallel, the whole providing a piece-wise approximation to the function. The later ROMs are designed to each cover a range of input values, such that some more-significant result bits are constant over the argument range covered by each later ROM. The initial ROM decodes the more-significant input bits to select the appropriate later ROM and provide the more-significant result bits in each case.

Yu and Lewis [111] go further in developing a 30-bit logarithmic arithmetic unit. The principles are similar to those of Taylor *et al*, but they use a much more complex ROM structure and value encoding, to achieve a speed comparable to that of conventional floating-point arithmetic units with similar technology.

7.4   Calculating Binary Logarithms

This section describes a simple method of calculating the binary logarithm of *normalised* binary numbers, based on the division method of Svoboda [94] described in section **5.4.5**[1].

Table 7.1: Table for Calculating Logarithms

	Decimal		Binary	
n	$z = 2^{-n}$	$\ln(1 + z)$	$1 + z$	$\ln(1 + z)$
1	0.5	0.584 963	100 000 000 000	100 101 011 100
2	0.25	0.321 928	010 000 000 000	010 100 100 110
3	0.125	0.169 925	001 000 000 000	001 010 111 000
4	0.0625	0.087 463	000 100 000 000	000 101 100 110
5	0.031 25	0.044 394	000 010 000 000	000 010 110 101
6	0.015 625	0.022 368	000 001 000 000	000 001 011 011
7	0.007 812 5	0.011 227	000 000 100 000	000 000 101 101
8	0.003 906 25	0.005 625	000 000 010 000	000 000 010 111
9	0.001 953 125	0.002 815	000 000 001 000	000 000 001 011
10	0.000 976 562 5	0.001 408	000 000 000 100	000 000 000 101
11	0.000 488 281 25	0.000 704	000 000 000 010	000 000 000 010
12	0.000 244 140 62	0.000 352	000 000 000 001	000 000 000 L001

The operation is based on values of 2^{-n} and $\log_2(1 + 2^{-n})$, as shown in Table **7.1**.

1. At each stage we have a number such as $x = 1001\ldots$, $x = 100001\ldots$, *etc*, with n 0s between the leading 1 and the next 1 bit.

2. Form a new $x = x - x \times 2^{-(n+1)}$, shifting x right n places so that its leading 1 coincides with the *second* 1 of the original x, and using this shifted value to eliminate that second 1.

---

[1]The origin of this algorithm is unknown, but a decimal version was used with the PDQ Fortran compiler for the IBM 1620 computer in the early 1960s—an early example of "shareware".

3. In parallel with the reduction of x, accumulate the stored values of $\log(1+2^{-(n+1)})$.

4. The above operations continue until all of the internal 1s have been eliminated.

The above algorithm generates binary (base 2) logarithms; for other bases it is necessary only to have the table of logarithms to the appropriate base. But a refinement is possible for natural logarithms, using the approximation

$$\ln(1+x) = x - x^2 + x^3 - x^5 + \ldots \text{ or } \ln(1+x) \to x \text{ for small } x$$

Eventually, for a number of N bits, $n > N/2$, and there are at least as many "leading" 0s as there are bits following the second 1. We can then use the identity and add the low-order half of x into the logarithm to complete the calculation, approximately halving the amount of computation.

Chapter 8

Characters and Text

Abstract: Characters are the most-visible aspect of computing. This chapter outlines the development of the EBCDIC codes (from card code), and ASCII (initially from paper tape), and the extension of these codes to include a full range of alphabets, to give UNICODE. Other topics include the collection of characters into text strings, and especially the problems of transmitting binary data over systems designed for handling text. Thus it describes UTF-8 and UTF-7 coding, as well as "punycode", for encoding Internet domain names with arbitrary alphabets.

Keywords: EBCDIC, ASCII, text strings, EBCDIC-ASCII incompatibilities, ASCII extension to UNICODE, UCS-2, UCS-4. MIME encoding, UTF-7. UTF-8, Punycode.

8.1   Historical Background

Computers must not only compute, they must also communicate those computations with people. They must accept information from people and deliver information to people. That requires some way of representing within computers the symbols of visual communication, or writing. As far as the human user is concerned, essential operations include –

- accepting numerical input and converting it to the internal form of the computer.

- accepting text as either information (names, addresses, *etc*) or as commands to control processing.

- manipulating text, including sorting collating and merging. This may include working with names for example as entities in their own right, or it may involve actually constructing sentences or other text.

- producing output in some appropriate form, hopefully in some aesthetically pleasing layout with supporting text and commentary to aid human understanding.

The English language requires a minimum of about 45 symbols—the digits 0 ... 9, the letters A ... Z (initially upper case only) and assorted punctuation such as ␣ . , ( ) / * + and -, where ␣ denotes the inter-word space. An alphabet of 45 symbols (the term "alphabet" is extended to include *all* displayed symbols) can be represented as 6 bits, which can in turn be regarded as small integers. That allows "characters" to be moved as integers within the computer, compared as integers, and even converted from one character to another using integer arithmetic. Later computers expanded the representation to 7 or 8 bit integers and then 16 bit integers as the alphabet grew to include an increasing number of symbols.

While there is no unique encoding for alphabetic (visible) symbols, they may be divided into three groups of desirable characteristics.

1. The digits 0 ... 9 have an inherent or natural order, following directly from their meaning. It is sensible to assign the digits 0 ... 9 to a set of 10 consecutive integers.

2. The letters (A, B, ... , Y, Z) (or α, β, ... , ψ, ω, *etc*) have a conventional (but still arbitrary) order. While successive letters should be assigned to increasing integers, these integers need not be consecutive or even form a dense block. The EBCDIC code (Section **11.6.1**) is a good example of a non-dense code.

3. The punctuation symbols have no inherent order and may be assigned in any suitable manner. It is usual to make the non-visible space code (a normal space) the numerically smallest of all character codes, letters, digits and punctuation.

The ordering of these classes is arbitrary—for example ASCII places digits lower than letters, while EBCDIC places them highest (and mingles some punctuation within letters).

In this chapter we make a strong distinction between the internal code of a character and its visible form, or "glyph". Thus the visible representation may be Roman, *emphasised* (or *italic*), **bold**, *slanted*, sans serif, CAPITALS, or `typewriter`. Even though the letters 'a', 'e' or 'i' appear with different shapes, the glyphs in the previous sentence are different visible representations of the same internal codes in each case. Thus, in ASCII, 'a' is always represented by 61_{16} and 'e' by 65_{16}; the desired font and style are part of the display mechanism rather than the internal encoding.

8.2   Development of Character Codes

Character encodings have come from two main sources, from punched cards and "unit record" equipment, and from paper-tape teleprinter and similar communication equipment. Only the paper-tape/teleprinter path is important for now (although this will surely surprise many people). As a detailed comparison of the two sources is largely irrelevant to the main discussion, this is deferred until Section **11.6**. An important aspect here, though, is codes for languages other than English; these are introduced as appropriate.

Table 8.1: Table of ASCII-67 Character Codes (• may be 0 or 1)

binary	hex	•000	•001	•010	•011	•100	•101	•110	•111
0000	0	NUL	DLE	SP	0	@	P	`	p
0001	1	SOH	DC1	!	1	A	Q	a	q
0010	2	STX	DC2	"	2	B	R	b	r
0011	3	ETX	DC3	#	3	C	S	c	s
0100	4	EOT	DC4	$	4	D	T	d	t
0101	5	ENQ	NAK	%	5	E	U	e	u
0110	6	ACK	SYN	&	6	F	V	f	v
0111	7	BEL	ETB	'	7	G	W	g	w
1000	8	BS	CAN	(	8	H	X	h	x
1001	9	HT	EM	)	9	I	Y	i	y
1010	A	LF	SUB	*	:	J	Z	j	z
1011	B	VT	ESC	+	;	K	[	k	{
1100	C	FF	FS	,	<	L	\	l	—
1101	D	CR	GS	-	=	M	]	m	}
1110	E	SO	RS	.	>	N	^	n	~
1111	F	SI	US	/	?	O	_	o	DEL

8.3   ASCII Character Encodings

Most computing now uses either the ASCII code shown in Figure **8.1** or various codes which are derived from ASCII (strictly ANSCII-67)[1]. The ASCII character encoding represents each character by a 7-bit value, giving a total of 128 possible characters, of which about 96 are used for written or visible symbols and 32 for transmission control and simple text layout. The characters are normally written in a table of 8 columns and 16 rows, so that the character encoding corresponds to the 3-bit column number followed by the 4-bit row number. Thus 'B' is represented by $x100\ 0010$, and 'k' $x110\ 1011$). The initial x is usually 0 but may be 1, even parity or odd parity.

The ASCII codes divide into four main groups, each 32 codes, taking 2 columns in Table **8.1**.

000x xxxx Transmission control codes.   The only ones of these which are important for now are

CR Carriage Return This code and the next are widely misunderstood and misused. The **CR** code is meant to return the print mechanism (or the display cursor) to the start of the current line, *without advancing a line.*

LF Line Feed The **LF** code is meant to advance one line, *without changing the horizontal position.* A "new line" is then properly coded as the pair "CR LF". Unfortunately some widely used systems have different conventions. Unix uses a single **LF** code as a "line separator", while the Macintosh uses a **CR** for the same function, and Windows retains the **CR-LF** pair. (So much for standards! In fact there is *another* control code, RS, intended as a record separator and, strictly, a line separator. **CR** and **LF** are really meant as printing control.)

HT Horizontal Tab This code signals a horizontal movement to the next "tabular stop", a term inherited from typewriters. Much computer software assumes preset "tab stops" at every 4 or 8 positions and uses some tabs as a form of "blank suppression".

There are some less-important formatting codes – **VT** (Vertical Tab) skips to a predefined vertical position (line) and **FF** (Form Feed) starts a new page. Other codes provide a hierarchy of *separators* –

---

[1]The earlier ASCII-63 had no lower case letters, had fewer punctuation symbols and different names for some control and transmission codes.

FS (Field Separator), GS (Group Separator), RS (Record Separator, equivalent to a new line) and US (Unit Separator).

ESC (Escape) introduces device-dependent control sequences.

The other codes are mostly used in data communications to control messages and to signal between stations.

On most computer keyboards these codes are generated by simultaneously pressing the CONTROL Key and some letter, changing the letter's 100 prefix to the 000 prefix for the control code. Thus "CTRL-C"→ ETX, "CTRL-J"→ LF, and "CTRL-M"→ CR.

001x xxxx Numeric and "specials" or punctuation.

010x xxxx Upper case letters (and some punctuation)

011x xxxx Lower case letters (and more punctuation)

Figure 8.1: Two "Extended ASCII-67" Character Codes

	A...	B...	C...	D...	E...	F...
...0	†	∞	¿	—	‡	
...1	°	±	¡	—	·	Ò
...2	¢	≤	¬	"	,	Ú
...3	£	≥	√	"	„	Û
...4	§	¥	*f*	'	‰	Ù
...5	•	µ	≈	'	Â	ı
...6	¶	∂	Δ	÷	Ê	^
...7	ß	Σ	«	◊	Á	~
...8	®	∏	»	ÿ	Ë	¯
...9	©	π	…	Ÿ	È	˘
...A	™	∫		/	Í	˙
...B	´	ª	À	€	Î	˚
...C	¨	º	Ã	‹	Ï	¸
...D	≠	Ω	Õ	›	Ì	"
...E	Æ	æ	Œ	fi	Ó	˛
...F	Ø	ø	œ	fl	Ô	ˇ

	8...	9...	A...	B...	C...	D...	E...	F...
...0	€			°	À	Ð	à	ð
...1		'	¡	±	Á	Ñ	á	ñ
...2	‚	'	¢	²	Â	Ò	â	ò
...3	*f*	"	£	³	Ã	Ó	ã	ó
...4	„	"	¤	´	Ä	Ô	ä	ô
...5	…	•	¥	µ	Å	Õ	å	õ
...6	†	–	¦	¶	Æ	Ö	æ	ö
...7	‡	—	§	·	Ç	×	ç	÷
...8	ˆ	˜	¨	¸	È	Ø	è	ø
...9	‰	™	©	¹	É	Ù	é	ù
...A	Š	š	ª	º	Ê	Ú	ê	ú
...B	‹	›	«	»	Ë	Û	ë	û
...C	Œ	œ	¬	¼	Ì	Ü	ì	ü
...D			-	½	Í	Ý	í	ý
...E	Ž	ž	®	¾	Î	Þ	î	þ
...F		Ÿ	¯	¿	Ï	ß	ï	ÿ

Old Macintosh (obsolete)   Windows 7 extensions

8.4   Extended ASCII Encodings

ASCII is itself limited to an essentially "English" character set, with none of the accents or other characters of other European languages and certainly no provision for Asian languages. As a first step towards satisfying this need, the "upper half" of the 8-bit code space can be used, extending ASCII to 224 printing characters (256 minus 32 communication control). Two such extensions, an older one as used on the original Macintosh computers, and the newer Windows 7 coding (essentially Unicode) are shown in Figure **8.1**.

ASCII in principle allows extension beyond this with its SO and SI codes (Shift-Out of standard set and Shift-In, back to standard set). A "non-ASCII" character will be preceded by the SO code to force a movement into the alternative alphabet; at the end of the special characters an SI code forces a move back to standard ASCII. (The action is very similar to what happens with the Baudot code, described in Section **11.6.2**.) A few simple alphabets can be accommodated in this way, but again standards proliferate. The problem will be addressed later in Section **8.7**, when Unicode is introduced.

8.5   Text Strings

We can usually assume that successive characters of text will be placed in adjacent bytes of memory and that later characters "extend" to higher memory addresses. At this level the text string itself is held in an array of 8-bit bytes or, for UCS-2, 16-bit byte-pairs.

Unfortunately this is where the confusion starts. Memory is addressed in bytes—agreed; bytes are collected into say 4-byte units called "words"— again agreed. But is a word addressed by its most significant byte (later bytes *less* significant), or least-significant byte (later bytes *more* significant)? Either is legitimate, provided that the interpretation is consistent within a computer, but there remains considerable scope for disagreement. Cohen [19] discusses these matters, illustrating many of the complexities that can arise and comparing them to the "big-endian"/"little-endian" wars in *Gulliver's Travels* [98]. His use of "big-endian" and "little-endian" for the two addressing types is now common currency. (A related topic is the direction of bit numbering discussed in Section **4.9.1**.)

In general there is little problem within a computer, but great confusion can arise when sending bytes as binary data *between* computers, as the bytes of, say a 4-byte word, must be marked as being sent in order of *increasing* or *decreasing* significance. One solution is found in the Unicode "Byte-order Mark", discussed in Section **8.7.1**.

With 32-bit words (4 characters to a word), the ASCII-coded string "A text sample." would be stored as

	characters	big-endian	little-endian
word 1	A te	41 20 74 65	65 74 20 41
word 2	xt s	78 74 20 73	73 20 74 78
word 3	ampl	61 6D 70 6C	6C 70 6D 61
word 4	e.	65 2E xx xx	xx xx 2E 65

If we assume that successive bytes (more generally, codes) of a character string (left to right) are placed in increasing memory addresses, there is still the problem of knowing how many codes belong to the current string. (Remember that bits are bits and bytes are bytes, with neither having any intrinsic meaning apart from that given by the programming context.) There are four approaches to defining the length of a string.

known length The length can be known to the program, either by being defined by the data type, or coded into the program. This is the least satisfactory solution, but is unavoidable in many languages without explicit string handling, and in standard Pascal.

delimiter code The string is terminated by a defined delimiter symbol. The C language uses the ASCII NUL code (0x00), but other codes such as ETX (0x03, End of Text) or RS (0x1E, Record Separator) are also reasonable. (It is also possible to use some combination of CR and LF, but the resulting confusion has been already mentioned.) A major problem is that the delimiter can *never* appear as a deliberate character in the text, which may be difficult to guarantee if the alleged "text" is received from somewhere else and may contain non-printing characters[2].

An older (and generally less-satisfactory) method was found in the old IBM 1620, where a string of characters (or digits) could be terminated at its high-address by a special "Record Mark" $0A_{16}$ (an invalid BCD code, card code 0-8-2, printing as ‡). A "Transmit Record" instruction copied the entire string, including the Record Mark, from its low-address.

---

[2]For this reason the Java language always encodes the UCS-2 symbol U+0000, corresponding to an ASCII NUL, as the 2-byte UTF-8 sequence 0xC0 0x80. If UTF-8 is ever processed as a C string, it cannot be terminated by an accidental embedded NUL.

Alternatively a "Transmit Field" instruction could copy a digit string (including Record Mark) from its high-address end back to its low address until terminated by a "flag bit".

count byte Many languages held strings in a byte array, with the first byte containing the length of the valid part of the string. With this system a string has a *defined maximum length*, corresponding to its allocated space, and a *current length* defined by its first byte, `byte[0]`. Two advantages are that *any* codes are legal within the string, and that if the string is accessible as a byte array the first character is at `byte[1]` and so on.

A disadvantage is that strings are limited to 255 characters, but this is seldom a problem unless an entire screen load or disk record is treated as a single string. Some systems, such IBM S/360 PL/I and Pascal, use a 16-bit length to avoid this problem and Delphi uses a 32-bit length.

associated variable This is really a version of the "count byte" method, but the length is much less tightly bound to the character storage. The storage area and length may be components of a data structure or record or may belong to the one object. In languages such as Java where the String object and its internal array which holds the string characters are separately allocated objects, the association in memory may be quite loose and the length and data may be far removed from each other. They are nevertheless connected by their membership of the same String object.

8.6 MIME Encodings

Electronic mail as first specified for the Internet in RFC 822 [21] assumes that all messages are "simple ASCII text", whatever that means[3]. There is no provision for transfer of data beyond 7 bits such as extended ASCII or binary; even 7-bit ASCII is not guaranteed for all characters. Various ad hoc solutions existed to allow such transfers, but they were not necessarily compatible with each other or suited to other applications.

The MIME standard (Multipurpose Internet Mail Extensions) as described in RFC 1521 [13] and RFC 1522 [77] extends the Internet electronic mail

---

[3] "RFCs" are the Internet standards. Originally just "**R**equests **F**or **C**omments" on proposals, they developed into a hierarchy ranging from preliminary proposals to established standards defining the operation of the Internet.

specification to allow the transfer of extended text, binary and other data. It is a large and comprehensive standard which specifies complete message formats and message headers. Here we describe only the character recodings, but readers must be aware that these are only a small part of the standard and should not be viewed in isolation. In particular, any attempt to generate these encodings should recognise the wider context and implications as stated in RFC 1521.

8.6.1   Problems Resolved by MIME

Some of these matters have been discussed earlier, but it is appropriate to collect them together here as matters specifically addressed in the MIME specification.

8-bit data RFC 822 electronic mail is limited to handling 7-bit characters. The "useful" set is even more restricted because many of the 128 possible codes have special functions such as formatting control and transmission control.

EBCDIC - ASCII incompatibility Although most email systems assume ASCII or similar encoding, this assumption is not always true. Some electronic mail systems used EBCDIC (section **11.6.1**), either within the computers or over the entire sub-network. Not all ASCII codes have EBCDIC equivalents, and *vice-versa*.

End of Line encoding Although RFC 822 specifies that lines shall be terminated by the pair CR LF (0x0D 0x0A) this requirement is not always respected. Some systems may convert to their own internal conventions and then back to the external standard form. This may raise problems if "almost-text" binary data contains isolated CR LF codes; they may be erroneously "converted"[4].

TAB (HT) codes may be changed to variable numbers of spaces by "helpful" software, or spaces may be converted to HTs. may be wrapped (converted to 2 lines) or truncated.

Trailing white space characters (SPACE, HT) may be discarded as invisible and therefore irrelevant, or lines may be helpfully padded to constant length (for example to simulate an 80-column punched card!).

---

[4]This was once a known problem when sending Postscript files by e-mail between some systems.

ASCII variants The ASCII standard is not necessarily respected by all mail implementations. The differences are small, but crucial if binary data transfer is to be guaranteed. RFC 1521 states that the only characters which are *known* to be preserved across all systems are –
- the letters A ... Z and a ... z
- the digits 0 ... 9
- the eleven special characters ' ( ) + , - . / : = and ?.

(Even a space is excluded because spaces may be stripped from the ends of lines, or replaced by tabs.)

Data modification Some systems modify data such as a line containing a single ".", or a line starting with "`From `". Neither treatment conforms to the standard, but it must be recognised that it occurs.

8.6.2 Quoted-Printable Content-Transfer-Encoding

This encoding is intended for data which is mostly printable ASCII characters, leaving the text mostly readable to humans.

1. **General 8-bit representation** Any octet[5] other than those signalling a line break may be encoded as "=XY", where XY is the hexadecimal representation of the octet's value. The hexadecimal digits for quoted-printable encoding are "0123456789ABCDEF" (upper case, never lower case). This is the required encoding, except where other rules permit. (The standard suggests the lower-case hexadecimal digits might be accepted on reception, but only as a courtesy rather than as a requirement.)

   When data is sent through EBCDIC gateways[6], RFC 1521 suggests "quoting" the characters ! " $ [\ ] ^ ` { | } and ~ .

2. **Literal Representation** Octets whose decimal values are in the range 33 ... 60 or 62 ... 126 *may* be represented as the corresponding ASCII characters ('!' ... '<', and '>' ... '~'). This allows most text to be represented in its natural form. (This set corresponds to the "visible" ASCII characters, excluding "=" (code 61) which is used as the escape into Quoted-Printable form.)

---

[5] The convention in communications is to use the formally-defined term "octet" rather than the informally-defined "byte", to emphasise that it is indeed an 8-bit data unit.

[6] Gateways convert between various transmission protocols. Early networking required the interconnection of DECNET, SNANet, CSnet and TCP/IP networks, *etc.* .... Gateways were then an essential, and fearsome, part of network communications, and often approached with some trepidation as email addresses had to include the gateways in order of traversal.

Table 8.2: The Base64 Coding Table

0	A	13	N	26	a	39	n	52	0
1	B	14	O	27	b	40	o	53	1
2	C	15	P	28	c	41	p	54	2
3	D	16	Q	29	d	42	q	55	3
4	E	17	R	30	e	43	r	56	4
5	F	18	S	31	f	44	s	57	5
6	G	19	T	32	g	45	t	58	6
7	H	20	U	33	h	46	u	59	7
8	I	21	V	34	i	47	v	60	8
9	J	22	W	35	j	48	w	61	9
10	K	23	X	36	k	49	x	62	+
11	L	24	Y	37	l	50	y	63	/
12	M	25	Z	38	m	51	z	(pad)	=

3. **White Space** Octets with decimal values 9 and 32 *may* be represented as ASCII TAB and SPACE, except at the end of a line. (Trailing white spaces *must* be encoded rather than left "in clear".) Rule 5 allows an "=" at the end of a line to signal a "soft" line break; this may follow directly coded white space characters. *When receiving a Quotable-Printed body, any trailing white space on a line should be deleted as it can be assumed to have been added in transit.*

4. **Line Breaks** A line break in the text body *must* be represented by a CR-LF in the Quoted-Printable encoding, irrespective of other internal conventions used within the message

5. **Soft Line Breaks** A Quoted-Printable line may not exceed 76 characters, not including the final CR-LF, but including all "=" codes. If longer lines occur (and Printed-Quotable encoding expands the text), the line must be broken with a "=" as the very last character on the broken line.

8.6.3   Base64 Content-Transfer-Encoding

The "Quoted-Printable" encoding is designed for documents with only a few unusual characters, but can expand documents to 3 times their original length. The Base64 encoding is designed for documents which are inherently binary with little visible meaning to a casual reader. At the cost of a 33% expansion it allows binary data to be transferred reliably over communication systems which are designed for purely textual transmission.

Encoding is performed by taking successive octet triples (24 bits) and then dividing each triple into 4 groups of 6 bits. Each 6-bit group is then used to fetch a character from the Base64 table, shown in Table **8.2**, so converting 3 octets into 4 characters. The input is extended if necessary by adding 0s on the right to complete an octet triple (8 or 16 bits added, 1 or 2 octets). The number of "padding" units added is signaled by following the encoded text by a like number of "=" characters.

These characters are chosen because they are *believed* to be preserved across *all* character recodings and translations. A version of Base64 encoding is used in the Unicode UTF-7 encoding as described in Section **8.7.4**, which should be consulted for encoding examples. The fundamental difference is that Base64 is meant for binary data of arbitrary length, whereas UTF-7 handles mixtures of text and binary.

8.7   Unicode—16-bit Encodings

8-bit codes such as ASCII and EBCDIC are really designed only for English text and hardly cater for even the simple accents of French and German. Extension to other alphabets such as Arabic, Cyrillic and Hebrew is difficult and expansion into the East Asian ideographics is even harder. Many extension systems have been proposed and used (ASCII and EBCDIC indeed provide SI and SO codes, Shift-In and Shift-Out just to handle alternative alphabets) but most are ad hoc solutions with little overall coherence.

Unicode provides a coherent extension of ASCII to allow the handling of many different alphabets, indeed most alphabets in current use. Instead of using a basic 8-bit code and escaping into versions for different alphabets, a single 16-bit unified code covers all written alphabets. ASCII codes, zero-extended to 16 bits, are the first few values. Other 8-bit prefixes identify Arabic, Hebrew, Thai, various Indian alphabets and the accented letters for some central European languages. About half the total space (30 000 symbols) is used is used for Chinese, Japanese and Korean ideographs, denoted as "CJK symbols" in the table of Unicode alphabets, Figure **8.4**.

The usual form of Unicode gives 16-bit codes, known as UCS-2. . Although this is believed to encompass all active languages, the standard also provides a 32-bit form, UCS-4. The higher "planes" of UCS-4 (UCS-2 is Plane 0) are generally allocated to less-usual symbols. For example, Plane 1 (from U+10000) is the "Supplementary Multilingual Plane" (SMP), with entries such as Cuneiform, hieroglyphs and archaic numbers. Full details are given in the Unicode 6.2 Standard [106].

Unicode symbols are normally represented by the prefix 'U+' followed by 4 hexadecimal digits. Thus the letter 'A' is represented as U+0041, and 'p' as U+0070. The first 256 codes (apart from transmission codes) are shown in Table **8.3**; they have the codes U+0020 – U+00FF. Here "sp" represents the normal space which may signal word breaks and line breaks; "nbsp" is the "non-breaking" space, essentially a normal character, but invisible and *not* allowing a new line.

Table 8.3: First Unicode Characters, with Latin-1 Supplement

	2...	3...	4...	5...	6...	7...	A...	B...	C...	D...	E...	F...
...0	sp	0	@	P	`	p	nbsp	°	À	Ð	à	ð
...1	!	1	A	Q	a	q	¡	±	Á	Ñ	á	ñ
...2	"	2	B	R	b	r	¢	²	Â	Ò	â	ò
...3	#	3	C	S	c	s	£	³	Ã	Ó	ã	ó
...4	$	4	D	T	d	t	¤	´	Ä	Ô	ä	ô
...5	%	5	E	U	e	u	¥	µ	Å	Õ	å	õ
...6	&	6	F	V	f	v	¦	¶	Æ	Ö	æ	ö
...7	'	7	G	W	g	w	§	·	Ç	×	ç	÷
...8	(	8	H	X	h	x	¨	¸	È	Ø	è	ø
...9	)	9	I	Y	i	y	©	¹	É	Ù	é	ù
...A	*	:	J	Z	j	z	ª	º	Ê	Ú	ê	ú
...B	+	;	K	[	k	{	«	»	Ë	Û	ë	û
...C	,	<	L	\	l	|	¬	¼	Ì	Ü	ì	ü
...D	-	=	M	]	m	}	-	½	Í	Ý	í	ý
...E	.	>	N	^	n	~	®	¾	Î	Þ	î	þ
...F	/	?	O	_	o	!	¯	¿	Ï	ß	ï	ÿ

The Unicode Standard [106] describes the full Unicode character set, together with extensive information on the treatment and behaviour of characters in different alphabets[7]. To people used only to the unaccented characters of English, with perhaps some awareness of Western European accents, the full requirements of other scripts are astounding. Even within English, the standard discusses the use of characters and their relation to "similar" char-

---

[7]Most of the description here is based on the earlier Standard V2.0 [105].

acters, revealing many subtleties of typography which users of most modern word processors blithely ignore.

The following description refers to character "glyphs", which are the *visible* representation of each character, as distinct from its *internal* representation. Thus we may have upper-case (A), italic (*A*), bold **A**, *etc.* together with lower-case equivalents, and all repeated for each font. Note too that a glyph in one size might not be a simple scaling of another size—some adjustment is often needed for consistent or pleasing appearance. The design of typefaces is a surprisingly complicated matter.

As an example we present the entries for the ASCII space, and the symbols ", ', and /. Each symbol is actually one of a set of symbols of similar appearance but quite different meaning and usage. The text lists each of these different symbols or usages, giving the 16-bit Unicode encoding where appropriate. Thus where we might in ignorance just use the "near enough" ASCII quotation mark ("), Unicode has specific encodings for opening and closing double quotes, double prime and double acute accent[8].

Spaces white-space
- space U+0020
- no-break space U+00A0
- figure space U+2007
- narrow no-break space U+202F
- word joiner U+2060
- zero width no-break space U+FEFF

Quotation Mark " = APL quote
- neutral (vertical), used as opening or closing quotation mark
- preferred paired quotation mark characters are 201C " and 201D "
- 02BA Modifier letter double prime
- 030B combining double acute accent
- 030E combining double vertical line above
- 201C left double quotation mark
- 201D right double quotation mark
- 2033 double prime

Apostrophe ' = Apostrophe Quote
- neutral (vertical) glyph having mixed usage

---

[8]The following list is taken directly from the Unicode Standard.
Some readers may prefer the less formal "single quote" and "double quote", or "opening and closing double quotes" over the more formal "paired quotation marks" or "left and right double quotation marks" of the Standard (codes 201C and 201D).

- preferred character for apostrophe is 02BC '
- preferred character for opening single quotation mark is 2018 '
- preferred character for closing single quotation mark is 2019 '
- 02B9 modifier letter prime
- 02BC modifier letter apostrophe
- 02C8 modifier letter vertical line
- 0301 combining acute accent
- 2018 left single quotation mark
- 2019 right single quotation mark
- 2032 prime

Solidus / = Slash, or virgule, or shilling (British)
- 01C0 latin letter dental click
- 2044 fraction slash
- 2215 division slash

Table **8.4** shows how the UCS-2 code space is allocated to the different alphabets, in the older Version 2.0 Standard.

8.7.1   UCS-2 Byte Ordering

While UCS-2 is defined as a 16-bit code, it will be often transmitted as a byte string, in order of increasing addresses. This immediately raises the question of big-endian *versus* little-endian addressing, as bytes transmitted from one machine may be interpreted as being in the opposite order on another, destroying the UCS-2 structure. For this reason UCS-2 strings may start with the code U+FEFF, a "byte order mark"; a computer receiving the sequence U+FFFE should recognise that all following byte pairs should be transposed to correct for the "endian" error.

The *byte order mark* has a rather curious position in the Unicode Standard, as reflected in the following comments from the Standard –

- "The *byte order mark* is not a control character that selects the byte order of the text; rather its function is to notify recipients which byte ordering is used in a file."

- "...employment as signature constitutes a particular use of a Unicode character and there is nothing in this standard itself that requires or endorses this usage."

Table 8.4: Some Unicode Layer-0 Page Allocations

Code Range	Name	Code Range	Name
U+0000 — 007F	C0 Ctrls & Basic Latin	U+2190 — 21FF	Arrows
U+0080 — 00FF	C1 Ctrls & Latin-1 Suppl	U+2200 — 22FF	Mathematical Operators
U+0100 — 017F	Latin Extended-A	U+2300 — 23FF	Miscellaneous Technical
U+0180 — 024F	Latin Extended-B	U+2400 — 243F	Control Pictures
U+0250 — 02AF	IPA Extensions	U+2440 — 245F	Optical Char. Recog.
U+02B0 — 02FF	Spacing Modifier Letters	U+2460 — 24FF	Enclosed Alphanumerics
U+0300 — 036F	Combining Diacritical	U+2500 — 257F	Box Drawing
U+0370 — 03FF	Greek	U+2580 — 259F	Block Elements
U+0400 — 04FF	Cyrillic	U+25A0 — 25FF	Geometric Shapes
U+0530 — 058F	Armenian	U+2600 — 26FF	Miscellaneous Symbols
U+0590 — 05FF	Hebrew	U+2700 — 27BF	Dingbats
U+0600 — 06FF	Arabic	U+3000 — 303F	CJK Symbols & Punct.
U+0900 — 097F	Devanagari	U+3040 — 309F	Hiragana
U+0980 — 09FF	Bengali	U+30A0 — 30FF	Katakana
U+0A00 — 0A7F	Gurmukhi	U+3100 — 312F	Bopomofo
U+0A80 — 0AFF	Gujarati	U+3130 — 318F	Hangul Compatibility Jamo
U+0B00 — 0B7F	Oriya	U+3190 — 319F	Kanbun
U+0B80 — 0BFF	Tamil	U+3200 — 32FF	CJK Letters & Months
U+0C00 — 0C7F	Telugu	U+3300 — 33FF	CJK Compatibility
U+0C80 — 0CFF	Kannada	U+4E00 — 9FA5	CJK Ideographs
U+0D00 — 0D7F	Malayalam	U+AC00 — D7A3	Hangul Syllables
U+0E00 — 0E7F	Thai	U+D800 — DB7F	High Surrogates
U+0E80 — 0EFF	Lao	U+DB80 — DBFF	High Private Surrogates
U+0F00 — 0FBF	Tibetan	U+DC00 — DFFF	Low Surrogates
U+10A0 — 10FF	Georgian	U+E000 — F8FF	Private Use Area
U+1100 — 11FF	Hangul Jamo	U+F900 — FAFF	CJK Compatibility 'graphs
U+1E00 — 1EFF	Latin Extended Additional	U+FB00 — FB4F	Alpha. Present-n Forms
U+1F00 — 1FFF	Greek Extended	U+FB50 — FDFF	Arabic Present-n Forms-A
U+2000 — 206F	General Punctuation	U+FE20 — FE2F	Combining Half Marks
U+2070 — 209F	Superscripts & Subscripts	U+FE30 — FE4F	CJK Compatibility Forms
U+20A0 — 20CF	Currency Symbols	U+FE50 — FE6F	Small Form Variants
U+20D0 — 20FF	Combining Diacriticals	U+FE70 — FEFF	Arabic Present-n Forms-B
U+2100 — 214F	Letterlike Symbols	U+FF00 — FFEF	Half- & Fullwidth Forms
U+2150 — 218F	Number Forms	U+FFF0 — FFFF	Specials

- Systems that employ the Unicode character encoding as their interchange code should consider prepending the U+FEFF *byte order mark* to each plain text file and removing initial *byte order marks* during processing. The *byte order mark* has a legitimate use as a zero-width no-break space in the middle of text streams; it should not be filtered there."

8.7.2   Special Unicode Characters

Many of the Unicode codes are non-standard in that they supplement existing characters, or have no defined character equivalences. Some are used to extend the existing characters, while others are reserved for private use.

Combining codes Many alphabets, indeed most alphabets, use a basic alphabet and supplement letters with "accent" or similar modifiers, to give modified letters such as Å, ø, è, é, ö, ñ and ç. Unicode provides many "combining" characters which modify or extend other "base" characters.

The simplest of these are the "diacritics" (diacritical marks in normal usage) which combine with *any* normal Unicode base character and include the European accents and some other "non-spacing" characters. While some of the modified characters are included in the basic Unicode pages, such as U+0080 ... 024F, the Unicode page U+0300 ... 037F contains a complete set of combining diacritics which may be applied to any base character (including non-Latin). In use, the base character comes first in the code stream and may be followed by one or more diacritics. If two diacritics both specify marks above the base character, the second is placed above the first; diacritics below the base similarly add downwards in order of presentation.

The situation is more complex in some other alphabets. For example some alphabets represent mostly consonants, with combining characters added to represent vowels. Sometimes, a combining mark which logically follows its base (and is so represented in Unicode) appears physically *before* the base. Again, in languages which are written from right to left, the Unicode sequence, including combining marks, is in the logical order of presentation. In all cases the base character is first in the Unicode stream, with combining marks following. Unicode specifies rules appropriate to each language and the Standard should be consulted for the handling of specific alphabets.

Surrogates Surrogate characters provide a way of extending Unicode to handle rare characters. Each character encoding has both a "high-surrogate" and a "low-surrogate", which must be adjacent codes and in that order. High surrogates extend from U+D800 ... U+DBFF and low surrogates from U+DC00 ... U+DFFF, each providing 1024 codes and over 1 million characters in combination. A portion of the high surrogate area (U+DB80 ... U+DBFF) is intended for private use, as described in the next item.

No public surrogates had been defined when the Unicode Standard 2.0 was published (July 1996).

Private Use Codes The standard reserves the codes U+E000 ... U+F8FF for privately defined codes. Use of these is by agreement between cooperating users, for vendor's logos and the like. By convention, an End User subarea extends up from U+E000 and a Corporate Use subarea extends down from U+F8FF. The standard allows the "promotion" of Private codes to Unicode standard codes.

The "private use surrogate" area is an extension of the Private Use area.

Compatibility Area and Specials The codes U+F900 ... U+FFFF provide miscellaneous glyphs and variants which can be mapped to other characters in the Unicode standard, but which need specific Unicode values for compatibility with pre-existing standards. It includes Latin ligatures, such as for 'ff' and 'fi', pointed Hebrew, Arabic and some special Chinese, Japanese and Korean characters.

This area includes U+FEFF (the byte order mark) and U+FFFE (the strong suggestion that byte-swapping is appropriate – see Section **8.7.1**).

8.7.3   UTF-8 Encoding

The standard or "canonical" 16-bit encoding is known as UCS-2. An alternative encoding, UTF-8, (UCS Transformation Format 8-bit) gives a way of representing UCS-2 characters (16-bit) within an 8-bit code stream. ASCII characters are unchanged, while others are packed into groups of bytes. A standard ASCII character is emitted "as is" in UTF-8 with a high-order 0 bit. Larger values are broken into 6-bit groups, from the least significant bit, as shown in Figure **8.2**. Each group except the most significant is prefixed by the bits "10" and emitted as a byte. The first byte starts with as many 1s as there are bytes in the code, followed by a 0 (a unary code). Only 2-byte and 3-byte codes are used for UCS-2 characters. (UTF-8 can also handle 32-bit UCS-4 codes and some extended alphabets.)

Figure 8.2: UCS-2 to UTF-8 Conversion Rules.

bits	Input bit pattern	encoding into successive bytes		
7	0 ... 0 GFED CBA	0GFE DCBA		
11	0 ... 0 KJI HGFE DCBA	110K JIHG	10FE DCBA	
16	0 ... 0 PONM LKJI HGFE DCBA	1110 PONM	10LK JIHG	10FE DCBA

Some examples of UCS-2 to UTF-8 encoding are shown in Figure **8.3**, encoding into 1, 2 and 3 bytes respectively.

Figure 8.3: Examples of UCS-2 to UTF-8 Encoding

UCS-2	UTF-8		
(16 bits)	byte 1	byte 2	byte 3
0000 0000 0010 1101	0010 1101		
0000 0011 0101 1110	1100 1101	1001 1110	
0010 1011 0111 1010	1110 0010	1010 1101	1011 1010

For the reverse direction, changing UCS-2 to UTF-8, the details depend on the number of leading 0s in the UCS-2 encoding.

- If there are 9 or more leading zeros (code $\leq$ 0x7F) the low-order 8 bits or right-hand byte are taken as the UTF-8 code. This case, and this case only, may be interpreted as an ASCII character.

- If there are 5 – 8 leading zeros, divide the 16 bits of the UCS-2 encoding as 0000 0xxx xxyy yyyy and form the two bytes
110x xxxx and 10yy yyyy.
These two bytes are the UTF-8 code. (Here, as before, the x field and y field may be any mixture of 0 and 1 bits.)

- If there are 4 or fewer leading zeros, divide the UCS-2 encoding as wwww xxxx xxyy yyyy, and then encode into 3 bytes as
1110 wwww 10xx xxxx 10yy yyyy.

The initial bits of the UTF-8 encoding determine the interpretation of that and following bytes –

0... The character is encoded in a single byte, equivalent to standard ASCII (or International Alphabet No. 5 - IA5).

10... The following 6 bits are used to continue whatever has been previously emitted for the partial UCS-2 encoding. (This byte must be the second or third byte of a 2 or 3 byte group.)

110... Emit 5 leading zeros and then the remaining 5 bits of this byte, as the first 10 bits of the UCS-2 code. One 10... byte must follow.

1110... Emit the remaining 4 bits of this byte and then, in order, 6 bits from each of the two following bytes, both of which must start with 10...

Example.

The UTF-8 bytes 20 E6 98 AF 20 43 61 6C 69 73 20 C7 9A 44 E5 BB B6 convert to UCS-2 according to Figure **8.4**.

Figure 8.4: Conversion of a UTF-8 String.

UTF-8 Bytes	UCS-2 codes	ASCII
20	0020	␣
E6 98 AF	662F	♣
20	0020	␣
43	0043	C
61	0061	a
6C	006C	l
69	0069	i
73	0073	s
20	0020	␣
C7 9A	01DA	♣
44	0044	D
E5 BB B6	5EF6	♣

The symbol ♣ denotes a non-ASCII character and ␣ a space. The final UCS2 encoded string is
0020 662F 0020 0043 0061 006C 0069 0073 0020 01DA 0044 5EF6.

8.7.4 UTF-7 Encoding

The Internet mail protocols [21] are based on 7-bit characters and do not easily handle the 16-bit UCS-2 or even the 8-bit UTF-8 codes. Although general encodings such as MIME (Section **8.6**, [13] and [77]) allow extension beyond 8-bit codes, they are not designed for Unicode; some Unicode characters may expand to as many as 9 octets in these representations[9]. Other problems arise if traffic must traverse systems using EBCDIC representations, because not all ASCII characters translate correctly to or from EBCDIC.

---

[9]A general UCS-2 character, encoded as U+PQRS and treated as individual bytes, may expand to the 6 characters =PQ=RS, where P, Q, R and S are hexadecimal digits. If the expansion makes the line exceed 76 characters an extra '=' must be included as a soft line break, giving an expansion to 7 characters. Finally, if the Unicode is encoded as 3 UTF-8 octets, and that UTF-8 is subject to MIME encoding, then each UTF-8 octet may expand to 3 octets. The result is a MIME code such as =UV=WX=YZ.

The UTF-7 standard [46] allows UCS-2 character codes to be transmitted with reasonable efficiency over 7-bit systems, allowing for EBCDIC/ASCII vagaries and even incompatible interpretations of the ASCII codes themselves. The standard specifies that UTF-8 encoding should be used wherever 8-bit transport is possible; UTF-7 is specifically for transmission over 7-bit "ASCII" systems.

UTF-7 takes the Base64 encoding from the MIME standard and adapts it to allow mixed or alternating sequences of ASCII and binary code. As far as possible, ASCII text is transmitted as plain characters. Other characters are translated according to the MIME Base64 conventions and the resultant codes placed in the output stream with a leading '+' as an introduction character and a trailing '–' Because not all ASCII codes are necessarily transmitted without corruption the direct encoding is limited to characters which are *believed to be* handled correctly by all systems and translations. Optionally, this set may be extended by other characters which are *probably* handled correctly, but some of which are illegal in RFC822 mail headers.

UTF-7 is based on several ASCII character subsets –

Set D The directly encoded characters include the upper case letters A ... Z, the lower case letters a ... z, the digits 0 ... 9 and the nine special characters ' ( ) , - . / : ? . (This set omits the characters "+" and "=", which have special meanings as UTF-8 and MIME escape codes.) These characters should be transmitted with no recoding other than stripping the high-order zeros.

Set O The Optional direct characters consist of the ASCII characters
! " # $ % * ; < = > @ [ ] ^ _ ` { — }
The characters " \ " and "~" are omitted from this group because they are sometimes redefined in ASCII variants. While these characters *may* be transmitted without recoding, many of them are illegal in mail headers and some might not pass correctly through translation. (This applies especially to the characters "[" ... "}" in the above list.)

Set B (Modified Base 64) The upper case letters A ... Z, the lower case letters a ... z, the digits 0 ... 9 and the special characters "+/". This group is much as defined for MIME Base64 in Table **8.2**, with the addition of a "/". These characters are used to encode 6-bit groups of binary digits, using the bits as 6-bit, 0-origin indices into the Set B characters. Thus the group 000000 will encode as A, and 001000 as H.

space characters the characters SP, TAB, CR and LF (in hexadecimal 20, 09, 0D and 0A)

The rules for representing 16-bit Unicode characters in UTF-7 are –

Rule 1 (direct encoding) Unicode characters in **set D** may be encoded directly as their 7-bit ASCII equivalents. Unicode characters in Set O may optionally be encoded directly.

Rule 2 (Unicode shifted encoding) The shift character "+" introduces any Unicode character sequence encoded as a sequence of characters in **Set B**. The bits from successive UCS-2 characters are regrouped into a sequence of 6-bit binary values which are used to fetch characters from the **Set B** array. Three UCS-2 characters translate into 8 bytes for transmission.

The sequence terminates on any character not in **Set B**, including the carriage return and line feed characters. The terminator "−" is absorbed; other terminators are processed normally. The special sequence "+ −" may be used to encode a single "+".

Rule 3 The characters space (32_{10}), tab (09_{10}), carriage return (13_{10}) and line feed (10_{10}) may be represented directly by ASCII, provided that there is no conflict with MIME encoding rules.

The following three UTF-7 examples are taken directly from RFC 1642. Note that they use descriptive terms for characters which are difficult to represent in ordinary text, such as <NOT IDENTICAL TO> and <WHITE SMILING FACE>.

- The sequence "A<NOT IDENTICAL TO><ALPHA>.", or "A $\not\equiv$ α" (hexadecimal 0041, 2262, 0391, 002E) encodes to A+ImIDkQ. .

  It is only the sequence ImIDkQ which needs to be examined; the initial "A" and the final "." translate directly to ASCII. The <NOT IDENTICAL TO><ALPHA> has the code 2262 0391 or 0010 0010 0110 0010 0000 0011 1001 0001 in binary. Grouping this into 6 bit units gives 001000 100110 001000 000011 100100 01$_{0000}$, with decimal values 8, 38, 8, 3, 36 and 16, building out the final group to 6 bits. Now select characters 8, 38, 8, 3, 36 and 16 from Set B above (the modified Base 64 set), giving I, m, I, D, k and Q respectively. Precede these by the "+" introduction code and note that the following "." is not part of the Base 64 and therefore terminates the encoded sequence. Adding the unconverted ASCII codes gives the final sequence `A+ImIDkQ`.

- The Unicode sequence "Hi Mom <WHITE SMILING FACE>!" (hexadecimal 0048, 0069, 0020, 004D, 006F, 004D, 0020, 263A, 0021) encodes to `Hi Mom +Jjo-!` .

  It is only the sequence `Jjo` which needs to be examined; the initial "Hi Mom " and the final "!" translate directly to ASCII. The <WHITE SMILING FACE> has the code 263A or 0010 0110 0011 1010 in binary. Grouping this into 6 bit units gives 001001 100011 1010$_{00}$, with decimal values 9, 35 and 40, building out the final group to 6 bits. Now select characters 9, 35 and 40 from Set B above (the modified Base 64 set), giving J, j and o respectively. Surrounding these by the "brackets" + and - and adding the unconverted ASCII codes gives the final sequence `Hi Mom +Jjo-!` .

- The Unicode for the characters for the Japanese word "nihongo" (hexadecimal 65E5, 672C, 8A9E) encodes to the UTF-7 `+ZeVnLIqe-`.

  Convert the hexadecimal to binary
  0110 0101 1110 0101 0110 0111 0010 1100 1000 1010 1001 1110 and group into 6 bits
  011001 011110 010101 100111 001011 001000 101010 011110.
  Select characters 25, 30, 21, 39, 11, 8, 42 and 30 from Set B, giving `ZeVnLIqe` and enclose in the brackets giving `+ZeVnLIqe-`.

- The Unicode is "Item 3 is <POUND SIGN>1.", or "Item 3 is £1." (hexadecimal 0049, 0074, 0065, 006D, 0020, 0033, 0020, 0069, 0073, 0020, 00A3, 0031, 002E).

  It is only the "£", with code 00A3 which needs to be converted. Its binary value is 0000 0000 1010 0011, converting to 000000 001010 001100, or 0, 10 and 12. The corresponding characters from Base 64 are `AKM`. Adding the introduction '+' and terminator '-' gives the final code "`Item 3 is +AKM-1.`"

8.8   The ISO/IEC 10646 Standard

At the same time as Unicode was under development, the International Standards Organisation (ISO) was developing its own universal alphabet, specified by ISO/IEC 10646. This standard defines two alternative forms of encoding –

- A four octet (31-bit) encoding with 2^{31} code values, conceptually divided into 128 *groups* of 256 *planes*, with each plane containing 256 *rows* of 256 *cells*. This encoding is known as UCS-4.

- The *Basic Multilingual Plane* or BMP which is just plane 0 of ISO/IEC 10646 and is encoded in 2 octets. This is the original UCS-2 encoding, but is now extended to include Plane 1 (the *Supplementary Multilingual Plane*) as described in Section **8.7**.

Unicode is identical in character definitions to the Basic Multilingual Plane of UCS-2; the two standards were deliberately aligned. In other ways though, Unicode is a subset of ISO 10646. Although Unicode implementations conform to ISO 10646, some additional constraints imposed by Unicode may allow implementations to conform to ISO 10646, but not to Unicode.

The UTF-8 encoding can extend to cover all UCS-4 characters, by allowing prefix bytes between 1110xxxx and 1111110x and up to 5 continuation bytes (10xxxxxx). The initial 1s of the first byte are a unary length for the whole code, just as for 16-bit UTF-8.

8.9   Internationalized Domain Names

This section summarises a particular Unicode recoding for Internet Domain Names. The coding is complex, and not really for use *within* computers, but rather *between* computers.

The Internet and its constituents were developed primarily in English-speaking countries, with the symbol alphabet limited "standard ASCII" with no accented letters. An important consequence was that many visible aspects of the Internet were restricted to "plain" text, such as domain names being restricted to { 'a' ... 'z', '-', and '_' }, with '.' being reserved as a separator. Domain names were furthermore case-insensitive with names being expected to be lower-case; as a special concession upper-case letters are acceptable, but equivalent to lower-case.

When the message content was expanded to Unicode, allowing symbols from all extant alphabets, it was only natural to allow domain names to similarly expand. Not only did this dignify national languages with extended or other alphabets, but it could also remove transliteration problems. For example, some Russian transliterations are "Tchaikovsky", "Chaikovsky", "Tchaikowsi", or

"Chebyshev", "Tchebyshev", "Tchebysheff". Allowing such words to be rendered in the native language allows unique representations.

At first sight UTF-7 might be regarded as suitable for multilingual names, but it encodes to both upper-case and lower-case letters, which can be legitimately forced to lower-case. The UTF-7 may also include '.' in the converted text. While this should be absorbed in machine conversion, it is nevertheless likely to impair human readability.

The Unicode names are instead converted to ... Punycode. For example, the German "Bücher" becomes "xn--bcher-kva", the 'xn--' prefix identifying this as a Punycode string. As of 2011 most browsers can correctly display Punycode domain names and some country or domain names have been approved[10].

A full discussion of Punycode is inappropriate here (it is complex and in any case used *between* computers rather than *within* computers!). Punycode is fully described in RFC 3490, including translation code.

8.9.1   Homographic Symbols

A possible problem in domain names arises from "homographic" symbols, where two or more symbols use the same glyphs, or very similar glyphs. Some examples were given in Section **8.7**, but none of these apply to valid domain names. Some possibilities, all legal in domain names, are

- Cyrillic small 'a' U+0430 and Latin small 'a' U+0061.

- Greek capital Alpha U+0391 and ASCII 'A' U+0041, and many other Greek and Cyrillic capitals.

- Greek small omicron 'o' U+03BF and Latin small 'o' U+006F. (In fact LaTeX provides only the Latin symbol.)

(The minus U+002D has variants, but these can be filtered from domain names as illegal symbols.) Look also at conflicts between Basic Latin and Cherokee (block U+13A0 to U+13FF) even though Cherokee is unlikely to be accepted into domain names.

---

[10]An Arabic-script International Domain Name was announced in early 2014.

Send Orders for Reprints to reprints@benthamscience.net

Introduction to Computer Data Representation, 2014, 159-190 **159**

Chapter 9

Universal (Variable Length) Codes

Abstract: Text compression requires numbers to represented as compactly as possible, especially the more-frequent values. This chapter describes various compact representations, and especially the "Universal Codes" to represent arbitrarily large values. Many of these codes are seldom mentioned in general literature.

Keywords: Shannon-Fano codes, Huffman codes, Elias' α, β, γ and ω codes, Rice codes, Golomb codes, start-step-stop codes, ternary comma codes, Fibonacci codes, Goldbach and Ibsen codes, Wheeler 1/2 code.

9.1 Compact Integer Representations

All of the number representations described earlier have used fixed or known lengths, making them simple for memory management and for arithmetic. But another class of number representations requires that an "average" number must be represented as compactly as possible. These representations typically arise in data compression and some examples later will be taken from this area[1]. There are two variants of the problem of "efficient" compact data representation.

---

[1]Reprinted with minor revisions from "Lossless Compression Handbook"©2003, K. Sayood (Ed), Chap 3, "Universal Codes" , Pages 55–78, with permission from Elsevier. The early sections are completely revised, and Section **9.13.2** on Ibsen codes is new.

A very important class of variable-length codes, and probably the best known, are the Shannon-Fano and, especially, the Huffman codes. These are associated with a finite alphabet of "source symbols", usually with known *a priori* probabilities. Each symbol is represented by a "codeword" that is dependent on the entire ensemble of symbol probabilities. Changing just one symbol probability may change several codewords. Although not important in the present context of unbounded source alphabets they are briefly described below in section **9.1.2**.

A different problem is addressed in this chapter. We wish to represent an arbitrary integer in as few bits as possible, preferably by an algorithm that recognises only the magnitude and bit pattern of the integer, with no table look-up or mapping. Equally, a simple algorithm should be able to recover an integer from an input bit stream, even if that particular integer has never been seen before, and generally irrespective of the surrounding bit patterns. The binary representation of the integer is often visible within the representation and other information is appended to indicate the length or precision. In contrast to the Shannon-Fano and Huffman codes, the population of source symbols is large and in principle unbounded.

These codes or representations are variously known as "universal codes" or as "variable-length codes". The two terms are generally interchangeable— "universal codes" can represent *any* integer, without word-length or similar restrictions, while "variable length" is simply descriptive.

9.1.1   Definitions

In all of this chapter we have a set of *symbols* that together constitute a *source alphabet* that is to be encoded into some more suitable form, such as a binary *coding alphabet*. A sequence of symbols constitutes a *message*; much of this discussion is really meaningful only when symbols are considered within the message of which they are a part. Although this restriction may be relaxed in other circumstances, we will for now assume that each *source symbol* is transformed into a single *codeword*; the coding is unique so that each symbol maps into one codeword and each codeword corresponds to a single source symbol. The symbol alphabet may be *finite*, such as the letters A ... Z, or may be *unbounded*, such as the integers 0, 1, 2, 3, ... This chapter will emphasise unbounded alphabets.

Each of the source symbols $\{ S_1, S_2, S_3, \dots \}$ has an associated probability $\{ P_1, P_2, P_3, \dots \}$. A fundamental result of Information Theory is that, to achieve the minimum average codeword length and overall shortest representation of the entire message, the length L_i of each codeword should be related to its symbol probability by

$$L_i = \log_2 \frac{1}{P_i} = -\log_2 P_i$$

Before proceeding, there several terms must be introduced –

equivalent code Two codes are equivalent if, for any source symbol, the codeword lengths for that symbol are the same, even though the bit patterns may be quite different. For example, the Elias γ and γ' codewords are permutations of each other, giving codes that are naturally equivalent.

instantaneous code If a succession of code words is examined as a serial bit stream, it is possible with an instantaneous code to recognise the boundaries between codewords from only the past history and without any look-ahead. Equivalently, no codeword is a prefix of another codeword. Except for some of the Fibonacci codes, most of the codes given here are instantaneous.

comma code A comma code uses a reserved bit pattern to terminate each codeword. The Ternary and Fibonacci codes use commas to terminate codewords.

9.1.2   Codes for Finite Alphabets

Both the Shannon-Fano and Huffman [56] algorithms exploit the known symbol probabilities to construct reasonably efficient codes. (The finite alphabet means that these are *not* "Universal" Codes.) Each source symbol (that may or may not be an integer) has a representation that is dependent on the probability of its own symbol and usually many other symbols and may have little relationship to the "natural" integer coding.

Shannon-Fano code The coding procedure starts with the source symbols ranked in decreasing probability. The coding itself proceeds as a repeated binary subdivision of a to-be-encoded portion of the source alphabet, allocating say a 0 to the "top" half and a 1 to the "bottom" half, ultimately forming a binary tree with the source symbols as its leaves. The codeword for each symbol is obtained by traversing the tree from root to leaf, collecting the 0s and 1s of the path.

Figure 9.1: Construction of Shannon-Fano and Huffman Codes.

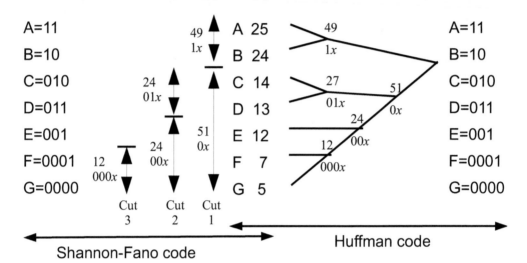

Huffman code The Huffman code similarly builds a tree with the source symbols as its leaves and obtains each codeword by traversing the tree from root to leaf. In contrast to the Shannon-Fano code, the Huffman code successively combines the two *least-probable* symbols into an intermediate symbol whose probability is the sum of its component probabilities. As with the Shannon-Fano code, each codeword is generated by traversing the tree from root to leaf, generating 0s and 1s according to the direction of branch.

Examples are shown in Figure **9.1** for the alphabet with symbol probabilities of {25%, 24%, 14%, 13%, 12%, 7% and 5%}. The average codeword length is 2.630 bits/symbol, compared with 3 bits for simple binary coding and the optimum 2.626. For this example the two codes are identical, but for larger alphabets the Huffman is usually slightly better.

The Huffman code as described assumes known static symbol probabilities, but realistic sources have differing probabilities, both overall and varying within each source. Solutions to cope with this "real world" situation include –

- The coder can perform a test run over part or all of the input and evaluate and transmit the Huffman tree (or the symbol probabilities).

- The coder can start with a known tree, possibly even equiprobable, and encode blocks of say 5 000 symbols. Within each block both coder and decoder accumulate symbol counts and, at the end of each block, both use those counts to recalculate the tree for the next block. No extra information needs to be transmitted, but the coding may be slightly less efficient than from the next method. It also has the cost of frequently recalculating the tree.

- Several authors have described methods for dynamically updating the Huffman tree, symbol by symbol. These are given in [87][p89ff], including commentary. Generally, if symbols do not occur many times within the source text it may be better to use a simple static Huffman code.

9.2   Polynomial Representations

Chapter **2** showed that integers can be represented as a polynomial in some implied base b, with the coefficients being the visible representation of the integer to base b. These representations for an integer N combine a visible *digit vector* **d** with an implicit *weight vector* **w**, such that $N = \mathbf{d} \cdot \mathbf{w}$, the scalar product of the two vectors. If successive terms of the weight vector are given by $w_{i+1} \approx bw_i$, we have a polynomial in some base b. Many, but not all, of the codes to be described are of this form.

Table **9.1** shows the first terms of the weight vectors for some of the codes to be described. The first line is the familiar binary representation, and the next two lines the Fibonacci numbers of order 2 and 3. (Section **9.12**.) The next line is the prime numbers, used for a representation based on the Goldbach conjecture. (Section **9.13**.) While all of the these codes use binary digits (0 and 1 in the visible representation), the last line is for a ternary code (base 3) with digits 0, 1 and 2. In this table, the binary and ternary examples are true polynomial representations, the two Fibonacci examples approximate polynomials, while the Goldbach or prime in no way resemble polynomials. All however provide valid weight vectors **w** for representations of the form $N = \mathbf{d} \cdot \mathbf{w}$.

In this table, as in much of the discussion of variable length codes, the weight vectors are shown with the least significant or smallest value to the left. This follows the practice in many codes of transmitting the bits in increasing numerical significance.

Usually each digit is bounded $0 \le d_i < b$ (but this restriction may be relaxed for redundant representations). Many variable length codes may be described

Table 9.1: Weight Vectors for some Variable Length Codes

Weights										Representation
1	2	4	8	16	32	64	128	256	...	Binary
1	2	4	7	13	24	44	81	149	...	Fibonacci, order 3
1	2	3	5	8	13	21	34	55	...	Fibonacci, order 2
1	3	5	7	11	13	17	23	29	...	Goldbach (primes)
1	3	9	27	81	243	729	2187	6561	...	Ternary

as polynomial representations with the base b non-integral and $1 \le b \le 2$. The digits d_i are always 0 or 1.

The base b representation of N has $\log_b N$ digits d_i. As the binary representation has $\log_2 N$ digits and $b < 2$, the base b representation expands relative to binary. The base b and expansion x are both descriptive of the representation and are related by

$$x = \log 2 / \log b, \text{ or } b = 2^{1/x}$$

To anticipate later developments, the bases and expansions of several codes are given in Table **9.2**. The simplest of these is the Elias γ code that, generating two bits[2] per binary digit, is equivalent to a number with a base of $\sqrt{2} = 1.414$. At the other extreme, the Fibonacci–3 (or "Tribonacci") numbers have a ratio between successive digit weights of

$$\frac{1 + \sqrt[3]{19 - 3\sqrt{33}} + \sqrt[3]{19 + 3\sqrt{33}}}{3} \approx 1.839$$

giving an effective number base of about 1.84 and an expansion, relative to binary, of $\log 2 / \log 1.839 = 1.137$.

Some of the codes add pairs of bits as the value grows; on average these have a small additive constant when calculating the length. Although their growth may be slower than codes that grow one bit at a time, this additive term may make them less attractive for small values. Similarly, the codes with smaller expansions often need a more complex length indication; the longer length indication may cancel any benefit from the smaller expansion.

---

[2]The term "bit" will always mean *binary digit* and is never used as an information measure. A codeword (the encoded collection of bits) is usually longer the binary representation of the value (also in bits).

Table 9.2: Effective Bases of Some Codes

Code	base (b)		expansion (x)
unary (α)	1	1	–
binary (β)	2	2	1
Elias γ	$\sqrt{2}$	1.414	2
Punctured γ	$2^{2/3}$	1.587	1.5
Fibonacci–2	$\frac{\sqrt{5}+1}{2}$	1.618	1.440
Ternary	$\sqrt{3}$	1.732	1.262
Fibonacci–3	see text	1.839	1.137

9.3   Length Indication

Every variable-length code must somehow specify the length of a codeword, normally using one of the two following methods (or a combination of the two).

- If the codeword prohibits certain combinations of bits, an illegal bit combination may act as a terminator or *comma*. For example an Elias α code is a sequence of N zeros followed by a terminating 1. Again, as the simple Fibonacci codewords can never contain two successive ones, the bit pattern 11 can act as a comma to terminate a codeword.

- The codeword may have two components, one giving the value and one the number of bits in the value. (And the length of the number of bits . . . , recursively.) The Elias γ code combines a binary value with an α code for its length. Ultimately of course every representation must somewhere contain a length of the first type to terminate a possibly recursive length definition.

9.4   Unary Codes

These are the simplest codes and are often at the foundation of more complex codes. They exist in two forms, each the bit-complement of the other, with rather different weight vectors and even interpretations according to the earlier description.

- The first form represents the integer n as $(n-1)$ zeros, followed by a terminating one. Here the weight vector is $\mathbf{w} = \{1, 2, 3, 4, \ldots\}$; most of the digits are 0 and the representation terminates on the first 1.

For example $6 \rightarrow 000001$ and $4 \rightarrow 0001$.

- The second form represents the integer n as $(n-1)$ ones, followed by a terminating zero. The weight vector is now $\mathbf{w} = \{1, 1, 1, 1, \ldots\}$.

  Now $6 \rightarrow 111110$ and $4 \rightarrow 1110$.

Both of these codes represent a minimum value of 1 and may be called "1–origin" representations. An alternate interpretation with n being the number of prefix digits ahead of the terminator allows 0 as a representable value (a "0–origin" representation). With this interpretation 3 would be represented as respectively 0001 and 1110. The two forms are equally valid, but sometimes the origin must be inferred from the context.

If we encode n as n ones rather than $(n-1)$ ones the weight vector can be interpreted as a polynomial with $b = 1$ ($b^i \equiv 1$ for all i). The unary code is therefore a polynomial code, with base $b = 1$ (which is good reason for its name)!

9.5   Elias and Levenstein Codes

These codes are the oldest of the variable length codes. The Elias gamma codes of this section are probably the most important variable length codes, combining simplicity with reasonable efficiency. They were first described by Levenstein [69], but the later description by Elias [25] is generally used in the English language literature.

Elias describes a whole series of codes –

alpha code The $\alpha(n)$ code is the unary representation, as described above.

beta code The $\beta(n)$ code is the natural binary representation of n, starting *after* the most significant 1. This is the most efficient representation of the value, but is usually combined with some other code or codes to indicate the length. $\beta(7)$ is 11, and $\beta(17)$ is 0001. The β code is of little use by itself because it has no length indication.

gamma code The γ code is an intermingling of the bits of the β code and an α code describing its length. Each numeric bit (from the β code) is preceded by a 0 *flag* bit (from the α code), with the whole terminating in the final 1 from the α code. (The beta component is encoded in reverse order, least-significant bit first.) This terminating 1 also supplies the most-significant 1 bit that was omitted from the β code. If the flag bits are marked by an overline, we have that

$$\gamma(1) = \overline{1} \qquad\qquad \gamma(2) = \overline{0}0\overline{1} \qquad\qquad \gamma(3) = \overline{0}1\overline{1}$$
$$\gamma(4) = \overline{0}00\overline{0}\overline{1} \qquad \gamma(5) = \overline{0}00\overline{1}\overline{1} \qquad \gamma(6) = \overline{0}100\overline{1}$$
$$\gamma(13) = \overline{0}10\overline{0}0\overline{1}\overline{1} \quad \gamma(23) = \overline{0}00\overline{1}01\overline{0}1\overline{1} \quad \gamma(44) = \overline{0}00\overline{1}0\overline{1}00\overline{0}0\overline{1}$$

gamma$'$ code The γ' code is a permutation of the γ code, with the flag bits (now an α code) preceding the data bits (a β code) and the terminating 1 of the α prefix doubling as the leading 1 of the β suffix. (The beta component is now most-significant bit first.)

$$\gamma'(1) = \overline{1} \qquad\qquad \gamma'(2) = \overline{0}10 \qquad\qquad \gamma'(3) = \overline{0}11$$
$$\gamma'(4) = \overline{0}\overline{0}100 \qquad\quad \gamma'(5) = \overline{0}\overline{0}101 \qquad\quad \gamma'(6) = \overline{0}\overline{0}110$$
$$\gamma'(13) = \overline{0}\overline{0}\overline{0}1101 \quad \gamma'(23) = \overline{0}\overline{0}\overline{0}010111 \quad \gamma'(44) = \overline{0}\overline{0}\overline{0}\overline{0}\overline{0}101100$$

For most of this document the term "Elias γ code" will be used interchangeably for the two variants; often it will actually mean the γ' code. Examples of the four codes are shown in Table **9.3**.

The Elias gamma code represents an integer of N significant bits with $2N-1$ bits, or equivalently an integer n is represented by $2\lceil \log_2 n \rceil - 1$ bits. (It is convenient to ignore the floor and ceiling operators in future discussions to simplify the mathematics. As most of the discussion involves only order of magnitude considerations or averages over many symbols, precise values are relatively unimportant. We therefore say that an Elias code represents an integer n in $2\log n - 1$ bits.)

The γ code can be extended to higher number bases where such granularity is appropriate. For example, numbers can be held in byte units, with each 8-bit byte containing one flag bit (last-byte/more-to-come) and 7 data bits, to give a base-128 code.

A polynomial code with base b multiplies the range of represented values by b for each added codeword digit. As doubling the range of a γ code requires *two* extra bits, we can regard the γ code as a polynomial code with base $b = \sqrt{2}$. The non-integral powers all have a coefficient or weight of 0, except for the last one that terminates the codeword and implies the most significant bit.

Some variants of the γ codes are much older than the systematic descriptions by Elias and Levenstein (1975 and 1968 respectively). For example, the IBM 1620 computer (c 1960) used BCD coding with a "flag" bit on each decimal digit (memory addressed by individual decimal digits). Numbers were

Table 9.3: Examples of Elias codes.

n	$\alpha(n)$	$\beta(n)$	$\gamma(n)$	$\gamma'(n)$
1	01	1	1	1
2	001	10	001	010
3	0001	11	011	011
4	00001	100	00001	00100
5	000001	101	01001	00101
6	0000001	110	00011	00110
7	00000001	111	01011	00111
8	000000001	1000	0000001	0001000
9	0000000001	1001	0100001	0001001
10	00000000001	1010	0001001	0001010
100	...	1100100	0000010000011	0000001100100

addressed at the least-significant digit and proceeded to lower addresses until terminated by a flagged digit—a precise implementation (or anticipation) of a BCD variant of the γ code. (A flag on the addressed digit denoted a negative number.)

9.6   The "Punctured Gamma" Code

> This section describes a variant of the Elias γ code. The text is largely copied verbatim from the author's original Technical Report [33]; an excellent commentary is given by Salomon *et al* [86, p112].

We start with the simplest of a family of new codes, called here $P1$. It is derived from the Elias γ codes, but with some major differences. Like those codes, it has two variants. In the γ code variant the data bits are written in reverse order with each 1 bit followed by a 0 for an "internal" 1 and a 1 for the most significant 1. Zeros are written "as is" with no following bit. The $\gamma\prime$ variant has the data part written in reverse order (most-significant bit last) preceded by an α code to indicate the number of 1 bits. It is not possible to merge the last bit of the prefix with the numeric bit as is possible with the $\gamma\prime$ code.

Thus in both variants the "count" part of the code counts the number of *ones* rather than the number of *bits* (as in the original γ codes).

The name "punctured code" is chosen by analogy with error correcting codes. A systematic ECC codeword resembles an Elias γ' code in having a clearly identifiable natural representation of its data, with added check bits to provide the error correction facility. A punctured ECC has some of the check bits deleted to provide a shorter codeword, much as some of the unary length bits of the Elias code are removed to provide the new, punctured, code.

Table 9.4: Comparison of Punctured and Elias Codes

Value	P1 Code	P2 Code	Elias	biased Elias	advantage (bits) P1	P2
0	**0**	**0**1	_	**1**	0	-1
1	1**0**1	**0**01	**1**	0**1**0	0	0
2	10**0**1	1**0**11	0**1**0	0**1**1	-1	-1
3	11**0**11	**0**001	0**1**1	00**1**00	0	1
4	1**0**001	10**1**01	00**1**00	00**1**01	0	0
5	110**1**01	100**1**1	00**1**01	00**1**10	-1	0
6	110**0**11	110**1**11	00**1**10	00**1**11	-1	-1
7	1110**1**11	**0**0001	00**1**11	000**1**000	0	2
8	1**0**0001	101**0**01	000**1**000	000**1**001	1	1
9	110**1**001	100**1**01	000**1**001	000**1**010	0	1
10	110**0**101	110**1**01	000**1**010	000**1**011	0	0
11	1110**1**101	100**0**11	000**1**011	000**1**100	-1	1
12	110**0**011	110**1**011	000**1**100	000**1**101	0	0
13	1110**1**011	110**0**111	000**1**101	000**1**110	-1	0
14	1110**0**111	111**0**1111	000**1**110	000**1**111	-1	-1
15	1111**0**1111	**0**0001	000**1**111	0000**1**0000	0	3
16	1**0**00001	101**0**001	0000**1**0000	0000**1**0001	2	2
...						
31	11111**0**11111	**0**000001	0000**1**1111	00000**1**00000	0	4
32	1**0**000001	101**0**0001	00000**1**00000	00000**1**00001	3	3
33	110**1**00001	100**1**0001	00000**1**00001	00000**1**00010	2	3

The code described (especially that corresponding to the $\gamma\prime$ code) will be described as the $P1$ code. For all cases except for a value of 0, the $P1$ codes start and stop with a 1 bit. If the represented value is biased by 1, encoding not n but $(n+1)$, and the doubled bit replaced by a single bit, we obtain a variant of the punctured code, the "$P2$ code". Table **9.6** shows the representations for the first few integers, together with the Elias code for the same value. The digit which marks the end of the prefix is shown in boldface; for the Elias code it is also the most significant 1. As the Elias code has no representation for 0, it must often use a "biased" version as shown in the table. Finally, the last column shows the advantage in bits in using the new $P2$ code as compared with the biased Elias code.

For small values the punctured codes are often 1 bit longer than the biased Elias, but for large integers they average about $1.5 \log N$ bits, in comparison with the $2 \log N$ bits of the Elias codes.

9.7   Elias ω and Even-Rodeh Codes

These codes have a length part and a value part. In the γ' code the length is given as an α or unary code; a natural progression is to specify the length itself in a form more compact than the α code. Elias does this with his δ code, using a γ code for the length, but quickly proceeds to his ω codes. Some very similar codes were described by Even and Rodeh [27] and it is convenient to treat the two together.

Both of the codes start with the value as a β code, preceded by its length. That length is then preceded by the *length of the length*, then the *length of the length of the length* and so on. The recursion stops when the length is sufficiently small, as shown in the examples below.

Table 9.5: Examples of Elias' ω and Even-Rodeh Codes.

Value	Elias ω code	Even-Rodeh code
0		000
1	0	001
2	10 0	010
3	11 0	011
4	10 100 0	100 0
7	10 111 0	111 0
8	11 1000 0	100 1000 0
15	11 1111 0	100 1111 0
16	10 100 10000 0	101 10000 0
32	10 101 100000 0	110 100000 0
100	10 110 1100100 0	111 1100100 0
1000	11 1000 1111101000 0	1010 1111101000 0

Some representative Elias ω codes are shown in Table **9.5**, with the groups of bits separated by blanks. Each length is followed by the most-significant 1 of the next length or value; the final value is followed by a 0. To encode the

Table 9.6: Lengths of Elias' ω and Even-Rodeh Codes.

Values	Elias	Even-Rodeh
1	**1**	3
2 – 3	**3**	3
4 – 7	6	**4**
8 – 15	**7**	8
16 – 31	11	**9**
32 – 63	12	**10**
64 – 127	13	**11**
128 – 255	**14**	17
256 – 512	21	**18**

value 69 as an Elias ω code –

1. Write the value (69) as a β code, with following 0   1000101 0

2. This value has six digits after the initial 1; write this bit count as a β code prefix   110 1000101 0

3. This length prefix has two following digits; write this count as another prefix   10 110 1000101 0

4. As this final length has only two bits, the code is complete.   10 110 1000101 0

The Elias ω code is decoded by reversing the encoding process. The initial group is either the single bit 0 (representing the value 1), or the bit pairs 10 or 11, with values 2 and 3 respectively. If a group is followed by a 0, its value is the value to be delivered. If a group is followed by a 1, its value is the β code for the length of the next group. Thus 15 is read as the sequence 3, 15 and 16 as 2, 4, 16.

The Even-Rodeh code is best described by its decoding algorithm. It is similar to the Elias ω code, but each group now gives the total number of bits in the following group, *including* the most significant 1. A different starting procedure is used, with values of 0–3 written as 3-bit integers. (Values of 4–7 are in "natural binary", with a following 0 as terminator.)

Both codes are especially efficient just before a new length element is phased in and inefficient just after it is introduced, as for 15 and 16 in the Elias ω code. The codes alternate in relative efficiency as their extra length components phase in at different values, as shown in Table **9.6**, with the shorter code in bold face.

Bentley and Yao [9] develop a very similar code while developing an optimal strategy for an unbounded search. They recognise a correspondence between the tests of the search and the coding of index of the search target, but do not develop the code to the detail of either Elias or Even and Rodeh.

Codes such as the Elias ω code are often described as *logarithmic ramp codes* because each coding group is approximately the logarithm of its successor.

9.8 Rice Codes

Rice codes [83] have a parameter k. To encode the value n, first form $m = 2^k$ and then calculate $n \div m$ and $n \bmod m$. The representation is the concatenation of $(1 + n \div m)$ as a unary code and $(n \bmod m)$ in binary. (Using $1 + n \div m$ allows for $n < m$.) An integer n is represented by $n/2^k + k + 1$ bits, (in line with the earlier approximations). Representative Rice codes are shown in Table **9.7**.

Rice codes differ from most other variable length codes in that they are very efficient over an intermediate range of values. But they are less efficient for small values (dominated by the remainder, $n \bmod m$) and for large values (dominated by the quotient, $n \div m$).

Table 9.7: Rice Codes for the First few Integers and Parameter k.

k	1	2	3	4	5	6
0	0	000	0000	00000	000000	0000000
1	10	001	0001	00001	000001	0000001
2	110	010	0010	00010	000010	0000010
3	1110	011	0011	00011	000011	0000011
4	11110	1000	0100	00100	000100	0000100
5	111110	1001	0101	00101	000101	0000101
6	1111110	1010	0110	00110	000110	0000110
7	11111110	1011	0111	00111	000111	0000111
8	111111110	11000	10000	01000	001000	0001000
9	1111111110	11001	10001	01001	001001	0001001
10	11111111110	11010	10010	01010	001010	0001010
11	111111111110	11011	10011	01011	001011	0001011

9.9   Golomb Codes

The Golomb codes [45] are designed to encode a sequence of asymmetric binary events, where a more-probable event with probability p is interspersed with less-probable events of probability q ($q = 1 - p$ and $p >> q$).

The sequence is represented by the lengths of successive runs of the probable event between occurrences of the improbable event. The Golomb codes have a parameter m, related to the probability p by $p^m = 0.5$, or $p = \sqrt[m]{0.5}$. A run of length $n + m$ is half as likely as a run of length n, indicating that the codeword for a run of length $n + m$ should be one bit longer than that for a run of length n. Golomb codes may be regarded as a generalisation of the Rice Codes, with a Rice(k) code identical to the Golomb(2^k) code.

Figure 9.2: Some Golomb Codes for the First few Integers and Parameter m.

$m \rightarrow$ $\downarrow n$	1	2	3	4	5
0	0	00	00	000	000
1	10	01	010	001	001
2	110	100	011	010	010
3	1110	101	100	011	0110
4	11110	1100	1010	1000	0111
5	111110	1101	1011	1001	1000
6	1111110	11100	1100	1010	1001
7	11111110	11101	11010	1011	1010
8	111111110	111100	11011	11000	10110
9	1111111110	111101	11100	11001	10111
10	11111111110	1111100	111010	11010	11000
11	111111111110	1111101	111011	11011	11001
12	1111111111110	11111100	111100	111000	11010
13	11111111111110	11111101	1111010	111001	110110
14	111111111111110	111111100	1111011	111010	110111
15	1111111111111110	111111101	1111100	111011	111000
16	11111111111111110	1111111100	11111010	1111000	111001

- If m is a power of 2 (corresponding to a Rice code), the codeword for n is a simple concatenation of $\alpha(1 + n/m)$ as a prefix, followed by the binary representation of $n \bmod m$ to $\log m$ bits (ie $\alpha(1 + n/m) : \beta(n \bmod m)$. The representations of a few values are shown below for different values of m. The α and β components are separated by a ':'.

$\downarrow n \quad m \rightarrow$	2	4	8
3	0:1	0:11	0:011
9	11110:1	110:01	10:001
14	1111110:0	110:10	10:110

This is a special case of that below, where $2^k = 2m$ and $j = 2^{k-1} - m = 0$.

- For other values of m, let k be the smallest positive integer such that $2^k \geq 2m$. The dictionary starts with $j = 2^{k-1} - m$ words of length $k - 1$, represented in binary to $k - 1$ bits. This initial group is followed by groups of m codewords for every word whose *length* $\geq k$. Each codeword is obtained by adding 1 to its predecessor, except that at the start of a group of m codewords the incremented value is then doubled to increase its length by appending a 0.

  For all but the first group, the values of n are *almost* represented by a prefix of $(n - j)/m$ 1s (an α code without the terminating 0), followed by $\beta((n - j) \bmod m + 2j)$ to k bits. The difference is that the second (β) component is allowed to overflow into the final 0 of the α prefix. Without the overflow, the initial 0 of the β code acts as the terminator of the initial α component. Thus for $m = 6, k = 4$ the code alphabet starts with $2^3 - 6 = 2$ words of length 3 (ie 000 and 001). To form the first group of 6 codewords, start with the word *following* the last member of the initial group and append a 0 ($001 + 1 \rightarrow 010 \rightarrow 0100$). The first group is then (0100, 0101, 0110, 0111, 1000, 1001). For successive groups of $m = 6$ codewords, add more leading 1s to the α code prefix. Construction of the $m = 6$ code is shown in Table **9.8**.

To decode the Golomb codes, it is clearly necessary to know the parameter m and thence the values of k, where $2^k \geq 2m$ and $j = 2^{k-1} - m$. We also need a, the number of leading 1s (that may be zero), and x the value of the next k bits starting with the first zero.

There are 3 cases –

$$n = \begin{cases} a2^k + x & \text{if } 2m = 2^k \\ am + y/2 & \text{if } x < j \text{ and } 2m \neq 2^k \\ am + x - j & \text{if } x \geq j \text{ and } 2m \neq 2^k \end{cases}$$

- In the simplest case, $2m = 2^k$, there are $a + k + 1$ bits in the codeword and each leading 1 contributes an extra 2^k to the value.

Table 9.8: Construction of Golomb Code for $m = 6$

n		n		n		n	
0	:000	8	10:100	16	110:110	24	1111:000
1	:001	9	10:101	17	110:111	25	1111:001
2	0:100	10	10:110	18	111:000	26	11110:100
3	0:101	11	10:111	19	111:001	27	11110:101
4	0:110	12	11:000	20	1110:100	28	11110:110
5	0:111	13	11:001	21	1110:101	29	11110:111
6	1:000	14	110:100	22	1110:110	30	11111:000
7	1:001	15	110:101	23	1110:111	31	11111:001

- In the next case, we are dealing with the "overflow" at the start of each group and $a + k - 1$ codeword bits. As the value part has one bit fewer than the prefix indicates, we need to halve the value of y. The bit pattern $y/2 = 0$ always corresponds to a multiple of m.

- For the final case, which is usually the most frequent, note the codeword groups start with a value of $2j$ at an offset of j from a multiple of m. Combining the two adjustments gives the represented value as $am+x-j$. There are $a + k$ bits to the codeword.

Examples of Golomb codes are shown in Figure **9.2**.

The Golomb and Rice codes tend to be very efficient for moderate values, but large values are dominated by the long α code prefix, while small values are represented less efficiently than in the Elias γ codes.

9.10   Start-Step-Stop Codes

These codes [37] are defined by three parameters i, j, k. The representation may be less clearly related to the value than for Elias γ and Rice codes. If the last parameter k is finite these codes handle only a finite alphabet; an infinite alphabet requires that $k = \infty$.

The codewords contain both a prefix and a suffix. The code defines a series of blocks of codewords (β code) of increasing length, the first block with a suffix of i bits, the second with $i + j$ bits, then $i + 2j$ bits and so on, up to a final suffix length of k bits. A unary prefix gives the number of the suffix group. Thus a 3, 2, 9 code has codewords with suffixes of 3, 5, 7 and 9 bits

Table 9.9: Code Values for a 3, 2, 9 Start-Step-Stop Code.

Codeword	Range
0xxx	0–7
10xxxxx	8–39
110xxxxxxx	40–167
111xxxxxxxxx	168–679

and prefixes of 0, 10, 110 and 111 (omitting the final 0 from the last prefix) as shown in Table **9.9**.

Table 9.10: Special Cases of Start-Step-Stop codes

Parameters			generated code
i	j	k	
n	1	n	a simple binary coding of the integers to $2^n - 1$
0	1	∞	the Elias γ' code.
n	n	∞	the base 2^n Elias γ' code
n	0	∞	a code equivalent to the Rice(n) code

The start-step-stop codes can generate many of the other codes, or codes equivalent to them, as shown in Table **9.10**.

9.11 Ternary Comma Codes

All codes so far have used binary coding. If we consider bit-pairs we can represent the values 0, 1, 2, comma [30]. Table **9.11** shows the ternary comma code representation for the first few integers and some larger ones, with "c" representing the comma (coded as 3).

It will be seen later that the ternary code is one of the better ones for large values. It is also quite simple to encode and decode. The comma principle can be extended to larger number bases, but becomes increasingly inefficient for small values because the comma consumes a large amount of code space but conveys little information. The higher radix Elias γ codes would seem preferable.

Table 9.11: Ternary Codes for Various Integers.

value	code	bits	value	code	bits
0	c	2	11	101c	8
1	0c	4	12	102c	8
2	1c	4	13	110c	8
3	2c	4	14	111c	8
4	10c	6	15	112c	8
5	11c	6	16	120c	8
6	12c	6	17	121c	8
7	20c	6	18	122c	8
8	21c	6	19	200c	8
9	22c	6	20	201c	8
64	2100c	10	1000	1101000c	16
128	11201c	12	3000	11010002c	18
256	100110c	14	10000	111201100c	20
512	200221c	14	65536	10022220020c	24

9.12 Fibonacci Codes

These are codes based on the Fibonacci or Zeckendorf number representations discussed in Chapter **2**. To recapitulate, a value N can be represented as the scalar product of two vectors, a visible *digit vector* **d** and an implicit *weight vector* **w**, such that $N = \mathbf{d}.\mathbf{w}$ (the scalar product of **d** and **w**). For a decimal representation $\mathbf{w} = \ldots, 1000, 100, 10, 1$ and for binary $\mathbf{w} = \ldots, 16, 8, 4, 2, 1$.

The Fibonacci codes use as a weight vector the Fibonacci numbers $\{1, 2, 3, 5, 8, 13, 21, 34, 55, 87 \ldots\}$, where each later number is the sum of its two predecessors. This gives the "Zeckendorf" integer representation $Z(N)$ [112], with some examples given in Table **9.12**. (All representations have the least-significant bit to the left.)

The crucial property of the Zeckendorf representation is that it never has two consecutive ones (by the definition of the Fibonacci numbers any two adjacent ones are equivalent to a single more-significant 1.) We can therefore produce a variable length code by just writing the Zeckendorf representation least-significant bit first and following its most significant 1 by another 1; the illegal combination of successive 1s acts as a terminator. These codes are also shown in Table **9.12**.

Codes based on the Fibonacci numbers were first described by Apostolico and Fraenkel [3], and later by Fraenkel and Klein [40]. We start with the simpler, but later, codes of Fraenkel and Klein.

Table 9.12: Zeckendorf Representations and Fibonacci Codes

N	$Z(N)$	code	N	$Z(N)$	code
1	1	11	10	01001	010011
2	01	011	20	010101	0101011
3	001	0011	30	1000101	10001011
4	101	1011	40	10010001	100100011
5	0001	00011	50	00100101	001001011
6	1001	10011	60	000100001	000100001
7	0101	01011	70	010001001	0100010011
8	00001	000011	80	101000101	1010001011
9	10001	100011	90	0010000001	00100000011

9.12.1   Fraenkel and Klein Codes

The Fraenkel and Klein C^1 code is just the "Fibonacci" code described in Table **3.5.3**.

Their C^2 code is obtained by omitting all of the $F(N)$ representations that start with a 0, so obtaining codewords of the form $1\ldots1$. An alternative approach is to take the representations $F(N-1)$ and add a prefix 10. As a special case, the value 1 is represented by a single 1 bit. In contrast to the C^1 codes, the C^2 codes do not use "self-contained" codewords as each codeword overlaps its neighbours. However the C^2 code does allow a more compact representation for the smallest value.

The C^3 code is obtained by taking all values of $F(N)$ of some length, say r bits, and writing down the block twice, first with a prefix of 10 and then with a prefix of 11. Every codeword of C^3 has an initial 1-bit, no codeword has more than 3 consecutive ones (and any consecutive ones appear only as a prefix), and every codeword except $C^3(2)$ terminates in 01.

Some examples of these codes are shown in Table **9.13**, together with the codeword lengths. There is relatively little difference between them; all are better for some values and worse for others. Measurements by Fraenkel and Klein on recoding simple English text show that C^1 and C^3 give very similar performance, and are definitely superior to C^2. But C^2 has a shorter representation for 1 and may be better for more highly skewed distributions. These

Table 9.13: Fraenkel and Klein's Codes

N	C^1	C^2	C^3	$L(C^1)$	$L(C^2)$	$L(C^3)$
1	11	1	101	2	1	3
2	011	101	111	3	3	3
3	0011	1001	1001	4	4	4
4	1011	10001	1101	4	5	4
5	00011	10101	10001	5	5	5
6	10011	100001	10101	5	6	5
7	01011	101001	11001	5	6	5
8	000011	100101	11101	6	6	5
9	100011	1000001	100001	6	7	6
10	010011	1010001	101001	6	7	6

codes illustrate the general principle that a code that is better for very small values is often poorer for large values and *vice versa*.

9.12.2   Higher-order Fibonacci Representations

Traditional Fibonacci numbers involve the sum of *two* predecessors. In an "order-m" Fibonacci sequence each number is the sum of its m predecessors. (The order-3 numbers are often known as the "Tribonacci numbers".) The first few Fibonacci numbers of orders 2 and 3 are shown in Table **9.14**.

Table 9.14: Fibonacci Numbers of Orders 2 and 3

$F_1^{(2)}$	$F_2^{(2)}$	$F_3^{(2)}$	$F_4^{(2)}$	$F_5^{(2)}$	$F_6^{(2)}$	$F_7^{(2)}$	$F_8^{(2)}$
1	1	2	3	5	8	13	21

$F_1^{(3)}$	$F_2^{(3)}$	$F_3^{(3)}$	$F_4^{(3)}$	$F_5^{(3)}$	$F_6^{(3)}$	$F_7^{(3)}$	$F_8^{(3)}$
1	1	2	4	7	13	24	44

These higher-order Fibonacci numbers can be used to generate higher-order analogues of the Zeckendorf representation, with the property that they have no runs of k consecutive 1s if $k \geq m$. Thus an order-3 representation has no runs of 3 or more 1s. We assume throughout this section that the Fibonacci numbers F_k are of order-3, unless otherwise stated.

A simple order m code for N is simply $Z(N)$ (bits in either order), followed by a 0 and then m 1s. This code is not that efficient, but is useful as an introduction to the better codes of the following sections.

9.12.3 Apostolico and Fraenkel Codes

Apostolico and Fraenkel [3] develop several codes using the higher-order Fibonacci numbers. Their emphasis is not so much on variable length codes *per se* but rather on codes that are robust under occasional data corruption [3]. We restrict our discussion to order-3 representations, whereas they consider the general case of order-m codes.

They describe two codes, a "C_1" code (our AF_1) and then a "C_2" code (our AF_2, which is simpler than the AF_1 code). The description here is different from theirs; the original paper should be referred to for much of the underlying theory and justification.

We number the Fibonacci numbers differently from Apostolico & Fraenkel. They assume that $F_1 = 2$ for all $m \geq 2$. As the *Fibonacci Association* has the convention[4] that $F_1 = F_2 = 1$ and $F_3 = 2$ for $m = 2$, we assume that all Fibonacci sequences start with $\{F_1 = 1, F_2 = 1, F_3 = 2, \ldots\}$, preceded by an appropriate number of 0s for $m > 2$.

Table **9.15** shows examples of the Apostolico & Fraenkel codes (their C_2 and C_1 codes, our AF_2 and AF_1 codes, for order 3) and some new Fibonacci codes of Section **9.12.4**.

The Apostolico-Fraenkel AF_2 Codes

These codes represent the value 1 with $m - 1$ consecutive 1s. Larger values are encoded as the Zeckendorf representation $Z(N - 1)$, most-significant bit leading, followed by a suffix of 0 and then $(m - 1)$ 1s. (The termination comes from these 1s and the first 1 of the next codeword; the code is not instantaneous.)

The Apostolico-Fraenkel AF_1 Codes

These codes involve a transformation or mapping to remove many "awkward" codewords. For the order–3 codes we start with the order-3 Fibonacci numbers F_k from Table **9.14** and calculate the cumulative sums $S = \sum F(k)$ of those numbers, as shown in Table **9.16**.

---

[3]Because these are "comma" codes, a one-bit error can at worst split one value into two, or merge two into one; the error does not propagate.

[4]See any recent issue of *Fibonacci Quarterly* for this and related conventions.

Table 9.15: Apostolico and Fraenkel's Codes, with New Fibonacci Codes

| | Apostolico & Fraenkel | | New Fibonacci Codes | |
| | AF_2 | AF_1 | | NF_3 |
N	order 3	order 3	order 2	order 3
1	11	111	11	111
2	1011	0111	011	01111
3	10011	00111	0011	11110
4	11011	10111	1011	001110
5	100011	000111	00011	101110
6	101011	010111	10011	01111
7	110011	100111	01011	0001110
8	1000011	110111	000011	1001110
9	1001011	0000111	100011	0101110
10	1010011	0010111	010011	1101110
11	1011011	0100111	001011	001111
12	1100011	0110111	101011	101111
13	1101011	1000111	0000011	00001110
14	10000011	1010111	1000011	10001110
15	10001011	1100111	0100011	01001110
16	10010011	00000111	0010011	11001110

To encode a value N –

1. Find k such that $S_{k-1} < N \leq S_k$.

2. Find $Q = N - S_{k-1} - 1$.

3. Encode $F_{k+1}+Q$ in an order-3 Zeckendorf representation, most significant bit first.

4. Delete the leading 10 from this codeword and attach the suffix 0111 as terminator. (The codeword *always* has a prefix of 10, by virtue of step 2.)

The values 1 and 2 have the special codewords $1 \rightarrow 111$ and $2 \rightarrow 0111$.

To encode the value 11 (their example) –

1. Find k such that $S_{k-1} < 11 \leq S_k$; $k = 5$, $S_{k-1} = 8$.

2. $Q = 11 - 8 - 1 = 2$.

3. Encode $F_{k+1} + Q = 13 + 2 = 15$ in an order-3 Zeckendorf representation, giving 10 010.

4. Delete the leading 10 and add the suffix 0111 to give 010 0111 as the final codeword.

Again, to encode 40, we find $N = 7$ and $Q = 11$; encode $44 + 11 = 55$ to give first 1001100 and thence 01100 0111 as the final codeword.

Table 9.16: Development of the Apostolico-Fraenkel AF_1 Codes

k	1	2	3	4	5	6	7	8
F_k	1	1	2	4	7	13	24	44
$S = \Sigma F_k$	1	2	4	8	15	28	52	96
Range	-	-	3–4	5–8	9–15	16–28	29–52	53–96

The second step ($Q = N - S_{k-1}$) needs explanation. Consider the order-3 representations of $F_k \leq N < F_{k+1}$ as shown in Table **9.17** for the range $13 \leq N < 24$, (ie $F_6 \leq N < F_7$), with the digit weights in the first row and greater weights to the right. By the Fibonacci definitions, there are ($F_{k-1} + F_{k-2}$) values in this range; the F_{k-1} smaller ones end with . . . 01 and the F_{k-2} larger with . . . 11. The adjustment $Q = N - S_{k-1}$ eliminates all representations with most-significant bits . . . 11. Thus a received bit sequence . . . 0111 *always* corresponds to the numeric bits . . . 01.

The AF_1 code is then just two bits longer than the Zeckendorf representation whereas the simpler AF_2 code is three bits longer than the Zeckendorf representation after absorbing the most-significant 1 bit into its terminator 1110. By discarding some of the possible codewords the AF_1 code is slightly longer for larger values. Against this it is inherently 1 bit shorter than the simpler code; the two effects largely cancel.

From Table **9.2**, the Fibonacci-3 (or "Tribonacci") codes have an effective base $b = 1.839$ and an expansion $x = 1.137$. But they follow the general trend that a more compact code (smaller x) tends to have a more complex length indication that may offset (or even overwhelm) the smaller expansion.

The first order-3 Zeckendorf code above presented the bits in increasing significance, followed by the suffix 0111. In the AF_1 code the bits are presented in *decreasing* significance, again with a suffix 0111. Now consider the AF_1 code with its bits in *increasing* significance, so that the code for 11 is 010 0111 and for 40 is 11010 0111. But these codes are respectively 01001 11 and 1101001 11, shifting the break to give a different emphasis to the two components. Both are the representations of $F_{k+1} + Q$ with a suffix of 11.

Table 9.17: A Range of Order-3 Zeckendorf Representations

N	digit weights					N	digit weights				
	1	2	4	7	13		1	2	4	7	13
13	0	0	0	0	1	19	0	1	1	0	1
14	1	0	0	0	1	20	0	0	0	1	1
15	0	1	0	0	1	21	1	0	0	1	1
16	1	1	0	0	1	22	0	1	0	1	1
17	0	0	1	0	1	23	1	1	0	1	1
18	1	0	1	0	1						

So an alternative way of generating a code equivalent to the AF_1 code is to generate $Z(F_{k+1} + Q)$, least-significant bit first, and append a suffix 11.

9.12.4   The "NF_3" Order-3 Fibonacci Code

As the order-3 Fibonacci codes may end with either one or two consecutive 1s, the terminator must allow the two cases to be distinguished. Apostolico and Fraenkel solve the problem by eliminating those codes whose Zeckendorf representations end in . . . 11.

The "NF_3 code" here was first described in Sayood [87]; its description is copied here. It transmits the order-3 Zeckendorf representation least-significant bit first (using $F(N)$) and follows its most significant 1-bit with a suitable comma or terminator as described later. With the order-2 code, the most-significant bit pattern (LSB first) is always . . . 01 and a single 1 bit acts as an unambiguous terminator. With the order-3 code the most significant bit pattern may be either . . . 011 or . . . 01. The terminator must be a run of 111 but it is also necessary to decide how many of those 1s have numeric significance.

The FN_3 code uses the following rules for the terminator.

- If $F(N)$ ends with . . . 01, add the terminator 110, so that the codeword ends with . . . 01 110.

- If $F(N)$ ends with . . . 011, add the terminator 11, so that the codeword ends with . . . 011 11.

The bit immediately after the terminating sequence 111 indicates how many numeric 1s to retain. But the isolated terminator 111 can be retained as a unique representation for the minimum value. It always follows on immediately from another terminator, occurs at the start of the codeword and can be decoded without ambiguity. While the codeword lengths are similar to those of the Apostolico & Fraenkel C2 code (a few are 1 bit shorter), the NF_3 code is much simpler to generate. Examples of the NF_3 code are shown earlier in Table **9.15**.

Table 9.18: Terminators for Order-5 Fibonacci Code

numerical bits	final code
...01	...01.1111.0
...011	...011.111.10
...0111	...0111.11.110
...01111	...01111.1.111

The principle can be extended to higher order Fibonacci codes, but with increasingly expensive terminators. An order-m code must be built out to have m terminating 1s, but then needs a code to say how many of those 1s are numerically significant. The result is that an order-5 code needs on average a 5 bit terminator, as shown in Table **9.18**, with dots inserted to separate the components of the terminator. The terminator lengths in this table are Huffman coded according to their probabilities. While the order-5 code is inherently quite efficient, its costly terminator means that it is shorter than the order-3 Fibonacci code only for values over about 1 million. Fibonacci codes of order greater than 3 are expected to be useful only in special circumstances.

9.13 Constant Hamming-Weight Codes

A very recently discovered family of variable length codes is self-delimiting by always stopping on the *second* '1' of the representation.

9.13.1 Goldbach Codes

A famous proposition in Number Theory is the "Goldbach Conjecture", that every even number is the sum of two primes[5]. Although not even yet proved in a mathematical sense, it is certainly believed to be true and has been ex-

---

[5]Letter by Christian Goldbach to Leonhard Euler 7 June 1742, restated by Euler

perimentally verified for values to at least 4×10^{17}. The Goldbach Conjecture leads to a curious variable-length integer representation.

Remember the earlier equation that an integer N can be represented as the scalar product $N = \mathbf{d} \cdot \mathbf{w}$, where $\mathbf{d}$ is the visible *digit vector* and $\mathbf{w}$ is an implicit *weight vector*. Now let $\mathbf{w} = \{1, 3, 5, 7, 11, 13, 17, 19, \ldots\}$, the sequence of primes. The first few even numbers can then be represented as in Table **9.19**. (The representations are not necessarily unique as shown by the two entries for 8; all except the smallest values have multiple representations.)

Table 9.19: Some "Goldbach" Even Integer Representations

N	Sum	representation
4	$1 + 3$	11
6	$1 + 5$	101
8	$3 + 5$	011
	$1 + 7$	1001
10	$3 + 7$	0101
12	$5 + 7$	0011
14	$3 + 11$	01001
16	$5 + 11$	00101
18	$7 + 11$	00011
20	$7 + 13$	000101

Table 9.20: Some "Goldbach" General Integer Representations

N	Sum	representation
3	none	
4	0+1+3	011
5	1+1+3	111
6	0+1+5	0101
9	1+3+5	1011
10	0+3+7	00101
13	1+5+7	10011
14	0+3+11	001001
15	1+3+11	101001

Codes based on this principle have been developed by Fenwick [34]. For example, the first bit is an even/odd switch with a weight of 1, with later bits having weights $\{1, 3, 5, 7, 11, 13, 17, 19, \ldots\}$. The representation is therefore terminated by the second 1-bit *after* the first place. It is usual to encode a biassed value, because the code as given does not handle values 0, 1, 2, or 3. Examples are given in Table **9.20**. Other versions of these codes use a gamma code to represent the lengths of runs of zeros.

9.13.2 Ibsen Code

Jørgen Ibsen [57] has developed an improved constant Hamming weight code by abandoning the assumption that each bit should have a specific weight. (This section has been added for this publication; it is, apparently, otherwise unpublished.) A version of his code is illustrated in Table **9.21**.

Table 9.21: Some "Ibsen" Integer Representations

N	Sum	representation
1	0+1	11
2	0+2	101
3	1+2	011
4	0+4	1001
5	1+4	0101
6	2+4	0011
7	0+7	10001
10	3+7	00011
11	0+11	100001
15	4+11	000011
16	0+16	1000001

The *first* 1 has a weight of $\{0, 1, 2, 3, 4, \ldots\}$ (the number of preceding 0s), while the final terminating 1 has a weight based on the total "area" of all preceding codewords. For a codeword of length ℓ, the final bit has weight $2 + \ell(\ell - 3)/2$ and the codeword represents values from $2 + \ell(\ell - 3)/2$ to $\ell(\ell - 3)/2 + \ell$.

9.14   Choice of Codes

Variable length codes are designed for the efficient coding of values with differing probabilities (unknown to the decoder). If, in a message, an integer n

occurs with a probability P_n, we know from Information Theory that the shortest overall message coding results if each code has $\log_2(1/P_n)$ bits, for all values of n. Thus a "good code" will have shorter representations for more-frequent values and longer representations for less-frequent values. The following points come from the author's experience.

- The Rice codes are a good choice for a peaked distribution, with few very large or very small values and a preponderance of middle values. The Rice parameter allows the coding to adjusted for the known distribution of encoded values.

- The author has used variable length codes mostly in lossless data compression where the message is dominated by small values [36]. The probability distribution tends to follow a $P_n \propto n^{-1}$ law, or even $P_n \propto n^{-2}$, with the smallest symbol having a probability of 0.5 or 0.6.

  Here the good codes tend to be those with the simplest structure, either the Elias β code or the Fraenkel-Klein C^1 codes. The main difference here is the β code represents the smallest value by one bit, whereas the C^1 uses 2 bits, but the C^1 code is more efficient for large values. Therefore, for very skew value distributions, with highly-probable small values, use the β code, and for less-skew distributions use the C^1 codes. The differences though, tend to be small,

Finally, note that all of these codes follow the "keep it simple" philosophy, Seemingly clever ideas are all too often counter-productive.

9.15   Wheeler Codes

We conclude with a rather different variable-length code. Instead of using binary (mostly) for the codeword, this uses symbols from the source alphabet and is used only for encoding symbol runs.

Symbol runs often occurred in formatted "unit record" equipment, which used blanks to give correct field alignment. As long strings of blanks were expensive to transmit or store, the data was often subjected to some form of run-length encoding, replacing consecutive identical symbols by a count of the replaced symbols. Often this was only for embedded blanks, because trailing blanks were easily replaced by End-of-Line symbols). For example a special introduction code (such as ASCII ESC) might be followed by two coded decimal digits, allowing runs of up to 99 blanks. Runs are important too in data compression, often as part of pre-processing, and this is where they will usually be encountered.

The method here, communicated by David Wheeler [110] [6] can encode runs of any symbol within a text string. Wheeler's original description is rather complex and difficult, but is given first; a simpler one will follow.

Wheeler's description Assume that the string "xx" is interpreted as the start of a following run of N xs. The run length N may be zero, and x is interpreted to mean the binary representation of the symbol x (which is usually a byte). Having determined the run length, we convert that length to a bit stream where the 0-bits, in increasing significance, have the values $1, 2, 4, 8, \ldots$ and the 1-bits $2, 4, 8, 16, \ldots$. This encoding is emitted from the least-significant bit, representing each 0 bit by x and each 1 bit by $x + 1$ (the symbol whose binary representation is 1 greater than that for x). If the string terminates in $x + 1$ or $x + 2$ stuff an extra $x + 2$ into the encoded symbol stream (It will be removed during decoding)[7].

In a standard binary code all 0s have a weight of 0, and 1s have weights $1, 2, 4, 8, \ldots$ respectively (the powers of 2). In the Wheeler code successive 0s have weights $1, 2, 4, 8, \ldots$ and successive 1s have weights $2, 4, 8, 16, \ldots$. The code is terminated by any character other than x or $x + 1$. The first few encodings are shown in Table **9.22**. The name "Wheeler 1/2" arises because the first bit has a weight of 1 or 2, which Wheeler writes as 1/2. Remember that if the run of xs is followed by $x + 1$ (or $x + 2$) the code $x + 2$ is always forced into the output stream; a terminating $x + 2$ is *always* removed on decoding.

An alternative explanation Still using "/" to mean "or", the digit weights can be written as $(0+1)/(1+1)$, $(0+2)/(2+2)$, $(0+4)/(4+4)$, *etc.* Thus each weight is a standard binary weight, *plus* a 2^k weight for digit k. In a representation of n bits these constant weights add to $2^n - 1$; adding a further constant 1 turns these into 2^n or a single more-significant 1. Thus the Wheeler code for N is the same as the binary code for $N + 1$ with the most-significant 1 deleted, as may be seen from the last column of Table **9.22**. The Wheeler 1/2 code is little more than a reinterpretation of a binary representation.

---

[6]Wheeler claimed to not know the origin of the code, but it is quite probably his own.

[7]If this sounds complex, do not worry—many other people also think so!

A much simpler way of generating the Wheeler code for N suppressed symbols then is to encode $N+1$ in binary and ignore the most-significant or final bit. The "length" is now rather more obvious because an empty run (no more symbols following the introduction string) must decode as a 1. When decoding, the number is handled as binary, with a 1 implied by whatever symbol terminates the sequence; the count is then decremented by 1.

Table 9.22: Bit Weights and Coding in Wheeler 1/2 Code

Bit weights			Sums	value N	reverse binary $N+1$
1/2	2/4	4/8			
0			1	1	01
1			2	2	11
0	0		1+2	3	001
1	0		2+2	4	101
0	1		1+4	5	011
1	1		2+4	6	111
0	0	0	1+2+4	7	0001
1	0	0	2+2+4	8	1001
0	1	0	1+4+4	9	0101
1	1	0	2+4+4	10	1101
0	0	1	1+2+8	11	0011
1	0	1	2+2+8	12	1011
0	1	1	1+4+8	13	0111
1	1	1	2+4+8	14	1111

We now present a more general version of the Wheeler code which can handle runs of any symbol. (This is also due to Wheeler.) Assume that some symbol X encodes (say in ASCII) to some binary integer x and assume that a run is signalled by the two symbols "XX" (two consecutive symbols signal a run – 'X' denotes any symbol). Then find the *run length* ℓ or number of following Xs.

Encode –

- Transmit the length $\ell + 1$ in binary, least-significant bit first, encoding each 0 bit as x and each 1 as $x \oplus 1$ (Exclusive Or).

- The most-significant 1-bit of the length is signalled by a symbol whose code is neither x nor $x \oplus 1$.

- If the symbol following the run encodes as either $x \oplus 1$ or $x \oplus 2$, stuff a symbol $x \oplus 2$.

Decode –

- Convert $x \to 0$ and $x \oplus 1 \to 1$, building a binary number from the least-significant bit.

- Terminate decoding on any symbol neither x nor $x \oplus 1$, interpreting it as the most-significant 1 (and preserving it as the next symbol for any further processing).

- Discard any symbol $x \oplus 2$ which terminates a run.

Table 9.23: Example of Wheeler's Run-length Code

String	lengths		coded string	comment
	run	coded		
12334	2	1	12334	code 1
1233334	4	3	123334	code 01
12333334	5	4	1233334	code 001
123333334	6	5	1233234	code 101
1299999998	7	6	1299889!	code 110 – (stuff ! $= 9 \oplus 2$)
125551	3	2	1255771	code 10, jam 7
12446	2	1	124466	code 1, jam 6

Note here that as ℓ must be at least 1, the encoded length is usually 1 more than the number of suppressed symbols. The method actually works if *each and every* symbol is assumed to start a run, but inefficiencies may follow from the stuffed $x \oplus 2$ symbols. It is more usual to signal a run by two or more consecutive identical symbols; the actual offset is decided by experiment.

For an example assume that we have a string of decimal digits, with two identical symbols signalling a run, as in Table **9.23**.

Chapter 10

Checksums and Error Control

Abstract: Much computer data is prone to errors, especially when transmitted in space (or in time, as in data storage). The corresponding need for error detection and correction has been recognised from the very beginning of electrical computation. *Error correction* is a large and complex subject which is just touched-on here, but *error detection* is a much simpler, but seldom discussed subject and is the main emphasis of this chapter. After a brief mention of parity checks in textual data transmission, the emphasis is on checksums for verifying strings of decimal digits. Check-digit algorithms include the Luhn, those used in ISBN codes, and the Verhoeff and Damm checks, both based on advanced number theory. The chapter concludes with discussion of the more-powerful message checksums, especially those of Fletcher and Adler, and the Cyclic Redundancy checks.

Keywords: Parity codes, Hamming codes, modular arithmetic, Luhn checksum, ISBN checksum, Verhoeff checksum, Damm checksum, Fletcher checksum, Adler checksum, CRC checksums.

10.1 Introduction

This chapter is perhaps somewhat out of place in this book as it does not really deal with *data representation*. But computer data is frequently exchanged with the outside world, usually by recording or transmission media[1]. As all of these

---

[1]Error detection is often necessary even when transferring data within a computer as a special case of transmission.

operations are potentially error-prone, it is sensible to include some mention of methods to ensure data integrity. Another justification is that there seemed to be few, if any, collected accounts of checksums and related error detection techniques.

But a preliminary comment is appropriate. This chapter presents several algorithms of varying complexity and varying error-handling ability. Unfortunately the better algorithms are often complex and subtle. While complexity is of little account when buried in immutable subroutines it can be positively dangerous if the code is accessible. It is then all too liable to be "improved" by programmers who *think* they know how it works. A good general rule is to remember "KISS" ("Keep It Simple Stupid"), especially if the code is at all accessible,

10.2   Error Control Codes

Computing has always had to live with errors, especially in data transmission and data recording. Sometimes these errors are only a nuisance and a simple retry can obtain satisfactory, accurate, data. But sometimes an error can be serious, and perhaps even disastrous if an accurate original copy is inaccessible.

Two related, but somewhat parallel disciplines, have developed to deal with the handling of erroneous data, both part of the general theme of "Coding Theory" and collected under the generic title of "Error Control".

Error Detection extends the ideas of parity to provide powerful and reliable detection of errors, usually by appending a "checksum" of 8, 16 or 32 bits to the data. The checksum is carefully designed to be sensitive to the probable errors: a checksum for manual data entry must be sensitive to digit transposition and repetition, while one for data transmission must detect long bursts of errors. A detected error invariably leads to an alarm of some sort and request for data re-entry or retransmission.

Error correction is required if the original data is remote either in space (such as telemetry) or in time (such as data recording), with the original somehow inaccessible. In both cases the transmitted data must carry sufficient redundant information to allow the original to be reconstructed in the presence of an error. While methods for handling single-bit errors have been known for many years and errors of just a few bits for nearly as long, few data errors are that simple. The methods for coding on physical transmission or recording media mean that many single errors at the *physical* level become bursts of errors at the *data* level. Burst error correction is then important, but is unfortunately a very difficult topic.

Despite the division of error control into two fields, many of the techniques in one can be applied to the other. In particular, the better error detection codes are based on polynomial generators and Galois field arithmetic. Exactly the same techniques can be applied to some of the simpler error correcting codes, perhaps just by choosing a different generator polynomial. A consequence of this convergence is that a suitable long checksum can often provide some degree of error correction over a short message. An example is found in the ATM cell header which is protected by an 8 bit checksum (or "Header Error Control" field—HEC), far longer than is usually needed for the 32 bits of the header. Although it is designed for *error detection*, the HEC can provide some *error correction* as well.

This chapter emphasises codes for error detection where it is possible to repeat the entry or transmission. Codes for error correction are touched on only briefly, describing Hamming codes one of the older and simpler error correcting codes. A full discussion of error correction codes is far beyond the intended scope of this book.

10.3   More on Parity

The basics of parity were introduced in Section **4.9.10** where a single parity bit is added to a byte, word, or other simple data unit. Simple parity is fine for detecting very occasional errors, but becomes less satisfactory for higher error probabilities and for longer data.

With a bit error probability of p and assuming independent errors, the probability P_k of an n-bit message having k errors is

$$
\begin{aligned}
P_0 &= (1-p)^n \\
P_1 &= n(1-p)^{n-1}p \\
P_k &= \frac{n(n-1)\ldots(n-k+1)}{k!}(1-p)^{n-k}p^k
\end{aligned}
$$

for small p, then $P_2 \approx \dfrac{(np)^2}{2}$ (the probability of an undetected error)

Unfortunately a single parity bit detects only *odd* numbers of errors and does not detect even numbers of errors. For a message of 12 500 octets ($n = 100\,000$) and a bit error probability $p = 10^{-6}$, the probabilities are

P_0 90.5%   probability of no errors

P_1 9.05%   probability of one error

P_2 0.45%   probability of two errors (undetected)

$P_{k>0}$ 10.5%   probability of at least one error

P_{odd} 10.0%   probability of any odd errors (detected)

P_{even} 0.50%   probability of any even errors (undetected)

Thus even though 10.5% of messages have detected errors and should be retransmitted, 0.5% of the messages contain undetected errors and are falsely reported as "correct".

Except where errors are *very* infrequent, practical error control uses much more powerful and complex checking functions, with the checking spread over several inter-related checking bits, so that even a single error affects several parity bits and multiple errors are unlikely to cancel out and give a "false positive". Many of the checks described here are for strings of decimal digits, while others apply to sequences of bytes or octets.

Figure 10.1: Horizontal and Vertical Parity on a Message

char	P	a	r	i	t	y		c	h	e	c	k	s	
hex	50	61	72	69	74	79	20	63	68	65	63	6B	73	HP
VP	0	1	0	0	0	1	1	0	1	0	0	1	1	0
MSB	1	1	1	1	1	1	0	1	1	1	1	1	1	0
	0	1	1	1	1	1	1	1	1	1	1	1	1	0
	1	0	1	0	1	1	0	0	0	0	0	0	1	1
	0	0	0	1	0	1	0	0	1	0	0	1	0	0
	0	0	0	0	1	0	0	0	0	1	0	0	0	0
	0	0	1	0	0	0	0	1	0	0	1	1	1	1
LSB	0	1	0	1	0	1	0	1	0	1	1	1	1	0

As a simple extension of parity, Figure **10.1** shows an ASCII message with both character (vertical) parity and message (horizontal) parity as was used on some early ASCII terminals with block-mode transmission. The top row shows the characters of the message and the line below that their encoding in (7-bit) ASCII. Below that row VP shows the even *vertical parity* of each character based on the bits as shown in the remaining rows. At the extreme right, the column headed HP shows the *horizontal parity* for the entire message, where each bit is the Exclusive-OR of all preceding bits in that row (or bit-position within the characters). It is again even parity, though odd parity can be used if desired in either case. An error is usually signalled if the vertical parity fails for *any* character or if the overall horizontal parity fails.

The 2-dimensional parity is much better than the simple 1-dimensional parity in detecting errors; errors will escape detection only if they occur in fours, in positions on the corner of a rectangle. (If it is known that only one error has occurred, then that error can be corrected at the intersection of the failing row and column parities.) It was soon superseded by the much more powerful CRC-16 checks, described in Section **10.7.10**.

10.4   Hamming Codes

The Hamming Code [50] is one of the oldest and simplest of the error-correcting codes and is a good example of a Single Error Correcting (SEC) code. For the simplest non-trivial case (and the one which is the usual example) take 4 data bits and 3 parity bits and arrange them in a 7-bit word as $d_7d_6d_5p_4d_3p_2p_1$, with the bits numbered from 7 on the left to 1 on the right. The bits whose numbers are of the form 2^k are used as parity bits, with the other bits used as data, as in Figure **10.2**.

Figure 10.2: Example of Hamming Correction

The raw data	1	1	0	1					
Bit numbers	7	6	5	4	3	2	1		
position data for Hamming	1	1	0	.	1	.	.		
generate even parities	.	.	.	0	.	1	0		
combine for codeword	1	1	0	0	1	1	0		
bit#6) corrupted	1	0	0	0	1	1	0	syndrome	
generate syndrome	1	0	0	0	1	1	0	1	1	0
syndrome = 6, bit error at		↑							

On transmission set the parity bits as below, transmitting the entire 7-bit word as the codeword.

$$p_1 = d_3 \oplus d_5 \oplus d_7 \quad \text{(the bits with a "1" in the bit number)}$$
$$p_2 = d_3 \oplus d_6 \oplus d_7 \quad \text{(the bits with a "2" in the bit number)}$$
$$p_4 = d_5 \oplus d_6 \oplus d_7 \quad \text{(the bits with a "4" in the bit number)}$$

On reception, calculate the "syndrome" $S = \{s_4 s_2 s_1\}$ from the equations

$$s_1 = p_1 \oplus d_3 \oplus d_5 \oplus d_7$$
$$s_2 = p_2 \oplus d_3 \oplus d_6 \oplus d_7$$
$$s_4 = p_4 \oplus d_5 \oplus d_6 \oplus d_7$$

If $S = 0$, then the bits are all correct. If $S \neq 0$, then it gives the number of the bit in error (assuming just one error).

The Hamming code is easily extended to longer words, by using each bit number 2^k as a parity bit, but does not extend to correcting more than one error. The example used here is often written as a (7,4) code; each codeword has 7 bits, with 4 of those for user data. A general SEC Hamming Code is described as a $(2^k - 1, 2^k - 1 - k)$ code. Examples are the (15,11) and (31,26) codes.

Adding a single parity bit gives a code which is able to detect two errors if an internal parity fails, but the overall parity still succeeds, giving a Single Error Correcting, Double Error Detecting (SEC-DEC) code.

The simpler Cyclic Redundancy codes of Section **10.7.10** give similar performance to Hamming codes, but are more easily extended to correct multiple errors.

10.5   Modular Checkdigits and Checksums

Most of the checks described here use some form of modular arithmetic, deriving some relatively large value from the data and reducing that value to a smaller one by taking its remainder on division by some modulus. In very simple cases we may just use a modulus of 10 (which delivers the units decimal digit), or 256 (to give the least significant 8 bits). Generally the modulus is chosen using some less obvious criterion which maximises the ability to detect errors. The simpler techniques use ordinary numerical division and are more suitable for software calculation, while others use polynomial division and are better for hardware implementation. For example, many checking algorithms work best if the modulus is a prime number. Ordinary parity is the simplest example of modular arithmetic, taking the sum of the bits modulo 2.

10.5.1   Modular Arithmetic

When adding or subtracting mod p, it is necessary only to divide every value by p and take the positive remainder. Multiplication and division require more care.

We say that a "number a is congruent to a' modulo m" if both a and a' give the same remainder on division by m. This relation is written

$$a \equiv a' \bmod m$$
$$b \equiv b' \bmod m$$

Consider the particular case $m = 12$, $a = 21$ and $b = 20$. Then

$$a' = 9 \text{ and } b' = 8$$

and

$$ab \equiv a'b' \equiv 0 \bmod 12$$

despite neither a nor b being congruent to zero modulo 12. Only for a prime modulus do we have that if a product is zero, then at least one factor is zero. Given that many checksums work by forcing an overall value to be congruent to zero, this is a very important requirement.

10.6   Parity and Arithmetic Checksums

In the following descriptions we will use the generic term "digit" for the basic data. Depending on the context it may be a decimal digit (range $0 \ldots 9$), a byte (range $0 \ldots 255$), a 32-bit word (range $0 \ldots 2^{31} - 1$), *etc.* In many respects the algorithms are similar for all cases.

For simplicity the term "checksum" will include terms such as "parity" and "check-digit". "Digit" will include "byte", "character" and "word" as whatever is the major data unit entering into the calculation. More usually though, the term "check digit" is used where the entities being checked are decimal digits (human readable) and the check is itself a decimal digit (or is usually decimal).

logical sum A checksum is formed by bit-wise Exclusive-ORing together all the bytes or words of the message.

$$\{0010, 1010, 1001, 0001, 0110\} \rightarrow 0110$$

Each bit of the checksum is the Exclusive-OR of the corresponding bits of each data word, as shown in the horizontal parity of Figure **10.1**. Problems with this approach are that errors have limited effect on the checksum, and that it does not detect transpositions (unimportant for data transmission, but crucial for data entry).

arithmetic sum This resembles the logical sum, except that the Exclusive-OR is changed to a conventional arithmetic addition. With this change, the carries give some inter-dependence between bits of the checksum, but it is still insensitive to data transpositions.

With most computers the obvious addition uses 2s complement, reducing the sum modulo 2^N for an N bit word. However, with the carries propagating from least- to most-significant bits, the more-significant bits are much more sensitive to errors than are the less-significant bits. Changing to 1s-complement addition (adding modulo $2^N - 1$ rather than modulo 2^N), allows the "end-around" carry to give an overall symmetry to the operation with low-order checksum bits affected by changes in high-order data bits.

This is the checksum used in TCP/IP (section **3.4**). While it is computationally simple and better than a simple Exclusive-OR, it is not as good as the Fletcher or Adler checksums described later.

Tests on real data by Stone *et al* [93] show that the TCP/IP checksum is not good for many types of real-world data, such as character strings and even real numbers where there may be high correlations between adjacent words. They show that checksum values are far from uniformly distributed, and that the 16-bit TCP/IP arithmetic checksum may be no better than a 10-bit CRC.

10.7 Digit Checksums

The checksums of this section are all designed to check decimal numbers, and especially ones which are manually entered. Frequent errors during manual data entry are duplication or deletion of digits, transposition of adjacent digits and substitutions such as "667" for "677". Simple parity and arithmetic sums have the disadvantage that all digits are treated identically; to handle transposition errors the digits must be treated differently so that the checksum is also dependent in some way on the position of each digit. Most of the examples for digit checksums use systematically varying weights for successive digits. Wagner and Putter discuss using decimal check digits for a particular application [108].

In general a "good" checksum includes some aspect of each character's position as well as its value. Thus the simple 1s complement sum or Exclusive OR checks are "poor" because they take no account of position. The Luhn and ISBN-13 checks are better because of their alternating weights, but are still inferior to most of the others discussed here, all of which include the position in some way or another.

The examples will assume a string of decimal digits

$$\dots d_6 \; d_5 \; d_4 \; d_3 \; d_2 \; d_1 \; d_0$$

where the subscript corresponds to the power of 10. The digits $d_6 \dots d_1$ will be the supplied data and d_0 the checksum digit.

10.7.1   Luhn Algorithm

This algorithm was described in 1954 by H.P. Luhn of IBM [70]; it is now in the public domain and widely used. This check, discussed briefly in [14][p 49], is given as an example of a very simple checksum which involves minimal computation and is appropriate to electromechanical equipment, such as the IBM 026 Card Punch. It will detect adjacent transpositions (but not $09 \leftrightarrow 90$) but because of the simple repeating pattern of weights is insensitive to many other errors.

Form the sum of the *even* digits plus twice the *odd* digits.

$$s = \sum d_{2i} + 2 \times \sum d_{2i+1}$$

and the check digit is the 10s complement of the last digit of s. Thus the check digit c is

$$c = 10 - \left(\sum d_{2i} + 2 \times \sum d_{2i+1} \right) \bmod 10$$

Wagner and Putter [108] describe a similar algorithm (possibly the same one given that they provide more details) which is used for some account numbers and is known as the "IBM check". The possible difference is that when a digit is doubled and exceeds 10, the two digits of the sum are added. Thus $2*3 \to 6$, while $2*7 \to 14 \to 5$.

10.7.2 Modular Check

This method is described by Hamming [52][p 28 ff] but is widely used in many other contexts as well. All digits are weighted by their position in the input number. While it might seem natural to have the weights increasing from left to right, the usual "sum of sums" algorithm assigns weights increasing from right to left.

The value (including checkdigit), must have $\sum (i+1)d_i \bmod m \equiv 0$.

To generate the sum without multiplication (or even prior knowledge of the number of digits), progressively form the sum of the digits, in order left to right, and at each stage add the sum into a running "sum of the sums." To illustrate with the successive digits $p\ q\ r\ s\ t$.

Message	Sum	Sum of Sums
p	p	p
q	$p+q$	$2p+q$
r	$p+q+r$	$3p+2q+r$
s	$p+q+r+s$	$4p+3q+2r+s$
t	$p+q+r+s+t$	$5p+4q+3r+2s+t$

Hamming [52] gives an example of checksumming a combination of the letters "A"... "Z", digits "0"... "9" and space "␣". This gives an alphabet of 37 symbols, conveniently a prime number.

10.7.3 ISBN Checks

Two examples of widespread checksums are the ISBN (International Standard Book Number).[2] The ISBN numbers give a unique identifier for books, with separate codes for each different version of a book (paperback, hard cover, different publishers, *etc.*) There are two formats, the earlier ISBN-10 with 10 digits, and the later 13-digit ISBN-13. Their internal structures are different (and irrelevant here) but the two have quite different validity checking.

---

[2]For this section I depart from normal practice and explicitly refer you to the Wikipedia entries such as "ISBN" and "EAN", which are not easy to summarise.

ISBN-10 checksum The ISBN was first defined in 1970 as a sequence of 10 decimal digits indicating the country, the publisher, a sequence number for the book and a final check digit. The digits are combined with a "sum of sums" as above and reduced modulo 11 to give a check digit, written as the final, 10th, digit of the ISBN. With a modulus of 11, the check digits can range from 0 to 10. While we could just ignore values with a check digit of 10, that wastes $^1/_{11}$ of the available numbers. Instead, a check digit of 10 is represented by "X", giving an ISBN such as 0 7112 0232 X.

To compute the checksum, calculate $\ldots 8d_7 + 7d_6 + 6d_5 + 5d_4 + 4d_3 + 3d_2 + 2d_1$, reduce the sum modulo 11 and take the 11s complement of the result as the check digit. Including the check digit within the sum should give a "check" of 0.

$$c = 11 - \left(\sum (i+1)d_i\right) \bmod 11$$

To illustrate the verification of an ISBN, consider the example above –

digit	sum			sum of sums		
0	$0 + 0$	$= 0$		$0 + 0$	$= 0$
7	$0 + 7$	$= 7$		$0 + 0$	$= 7$
1	$7 + 1$	$= 8$		$7 + 8$	$= 15$
1	$8 + 1$	$= 9$		$15 + 9$	$= 24$
2	$9 + 2$	$= 11$		$24 + 11$	$= 35$
0	$11 + 0$	$= 11$		$35 + 11$	$= 46$
2	$11 + 2$	$= 13$		$46 + 13$	$= 59$
3	$13 + 2$	$= 16$		$59 + 16$	$= 75$
2	$16 + 2$	$= 18$		$75 + 18$	$= 93$
X	$18 + 10$	$= 28$		$93 + 28$	$= 121 \equiv 0 \bmod 11$

The final sum of sums is a multiple of 11, showing that this is a valid ISBN.

ISBN-13 As is all too often the case with fixed-length identification numbers, the ISBN-10 format eventually became too small for the number of books. Also, because the ISBN was often printed as a bar code (which codes were little used when the ISBN-10 was defined in 1970) it became desirable to include book numbers within the overall "EAN" international bar-code product numbering scheme. The ISBN-13 standards were published in 2005 and became mandatory in 2007.

The ISBN-13 numbers start with prefix of 978, followed by 9 data digits, which include publisher and title, and a final check digit. The number may be written using spaces or hyphens as field separators. (The 978 prefix is effectively a "Bookland" country code; the 979 prefix is also available for books.)

The ISBN-13 check digit calculation is quite different from that of ISBN-10, but follows that of the EAN standard. It is similar to the Luhn algorithm, Section **10.7.1**, but with different alternating weights. The digits, from left to right, are alternately multiplied by 1 or 3, and the products summed modulo 10 to give a value ranging from 0 to 9. The 10s complement of that modulo-10 sum is the check digit. Using subscripts to denote the multipliers, the ISBN number 978-0-12-62086-0 may be written (first 12 digits only)

$$9_1\, 7_3\, 8_1\, 0_3\, 1_1\, 2_3\, 6_1\, 2_3\, 0_1\, 8_3\, 6_1\, 0_3$$
$$= \quad 9 + 21 + 8 + 0 + 1 + 6 + 6 + 6 + 0 + 24 + 6 + 0$$
$$= \quad 90$$

The sum modulo 10 is 0, and its 10s complement, also 0, becomes the check digit (confirming the given value).

The checking is not as powerful as that of ISBN-10; for example if two adjacent digits differ by 5, their transposition will not be detected. But transpositions are likely only with human input and should not occur with machine reading, as is now usual with these numbers. However the check digit is always decimal, avoiding the 'X' of ISBN-10. But see later, Section **10.7.7**, for more details.

10.7.4 ID Checksum

This is a variation of the modular checksum which is often used for personal ID number checksums and the like. In this case the digit weights are successive powers of 2 and a check digit again makes the result 0 modulo 11. More formally, the checkdigit is calculated as

$$d_0 = c = 11 - \left(\sum 2^{i+1} d_i\right) \bmod 11$$

and then, for a 6-digit number with checkdigit,

$$2(d_0 + 2(d_1 + 2(d_2 + 2(d_3 + 2(d_4 + 2(d_5 + 2d_6)))))) \bmod 11 \equiv 0$$

(Taking digits from the left, double the *sum-so-far* and add in the next digit.) The polynomial may be written in a more familiar form as

$$\left(\sum_{i=0}^{n} 2^i d_i\right) \bmod 11 \equiv 0$$

To confirm that 6051001 is indeed a valid checked number in this system

$$6 \times 64 + 0 \times 32 + 5 \times 16 + 1 \times 8 + 0 \times 4 + 0 \times 2 + 1 \times 1 = 473$$

As $473 = 43 \times 11$ the result is $(0 \bmod 11)$ and is correct.

In contrast to the ISBN13, values with a checkdigit of "10" are rejected.

A possible variation using a modulus of 7 allows all numbers to be handled (no rejects) but at the cost of decreased error detection. This possibility has not been investigated. However Wagner and Putter [108] describe a similar modulo 97 code which appends *two* check digits.

10.7.5   Verhoeff Checksum (Dihedral Group)

This method is discussed in detail by Wagner and Putter [108], who cite both Verhoeff's original paper [107] and its rediscovery by Gumm [49]. The algorithm uses operations in the dihedral group D_5, which is related to symmetries of a pentagon. In particular, multiplication in D_5 is not commutative, so that $a * b \neq b * a$, where $*$ denotes multiplication in D_5. Instead of addition using a simple pattern of weights to differentiate the incoming digits, the digits are first subjected to a "Permutation", (perhaps more correctly a "substitution") where each is replaced by another, the permutation function depending on the digit position. The permuted digits are then multiplied in D_5 to give the checksum.

The algorithm is most easily implemented with supporting tables which, together with the algorithms, are shown in Figure **10.3**

Multiplication table (M) This is a 10 by 10 matrix where each element corresponds to the product of its indices (0-origin) in D_5.

Inverse (I) This gives the multiplicative inverse of i, so that $i * \text{Inv}[i] \equiv 0$ in D_5.

Permutation Function (F) The successive digits are combined by an equation $f_1 a_1 * f_2 a_2 * \ldots * f_n a_n$, where the successive f_i are permutation functions, defined by successive applications of an initial function. Note that $F[i, j] \equiv F[i \bmod 8, j]$.

The two functions assume that the digits to be checked are in positions $1 \ldots n$ of the array `dig` with `dig[0]` the check digit.

Figure 10.3: Tables and Code for Verhoeff (Dihedral) Check

$$M = \begin{pmatrix} 0 & 1 & 2 & 3 & 4 & 5 & 6 & 7 & 8 & 9 \\ 1 & 2 & 3 & 4 & 0 & 6 & 7 & 8 & 9 & 5 \\ 2 & 3 & 4 & 0 & 1 & 7 & 8 & 9 & 5 & 6 \\ 3 & 4 & 0 & 1 & 2 & 8 & 9 & 5 & 6 & 7 \\ 4 & 0 & 1 & 2 & 3 & 9 & 5 & 6 & 7 & 8 \\ 5 & 9 & 8 & 7 & 6 & 0 & 4 & 3 & 2 & 1 \\ 6 & 5 & 9 & 8 & 7 & 1 & 0 & 4 & 3 & 2 \\ 7 & 6 & 5 & 9 & 8 & 2 & 1 & 0 & 4 & 3 \\ 8 & 7 & 6 & 5 & 9 & 3 & 2 & 1 & 0 & 4 \\ 9 & 8 & 7 & 6 & 5 & 4 & 3 & 2 & 1 & 0 \end{pmatrix}$$

$$I = \begin{pmatrix} 0 & 4 & 3 & 2 & 1 & 5 & 6 & 7 & 8 & 9 \end{pmatrix}$$

$$F = \begin{pmatrix} 0 & 1 & 2 & 3 & 4 & 5 & 6 & 7 & 8 & 9 \\ 1 & 5 & 7 & 6 & 2 & 8 & 3 & 0 & 9 & 4 \\ 5 & 8 & 0 & 3 & 7 & 9 & 6 & 1 & 4 & 2 \\ 8 & 9 & 1 & 6 & 0 & 4 & 3 & 5 & 2 & 7 \\ 9 & 4 & 5 & 3 & 1 & 2 & 6 & 8 & 7 & 0 \\ 4 & 2 & 8 & 6 & 5 & 7 & 3 & 9 & 0 & 1 \\ 2 & 7 & 9 & 3 & 8 & 0 & 6 & 4 & 1 & 5 \\ 7 & 0 & 4 & 6 & 9 & 1 & 3 & 2 & 5 & 8 \\ 0 & 1 & 2 & 3 & 4 & 5 & 6 & 7 & 8 & 9 \\ 1 & 5 & 7 & 6 & 2 & 8 & 3 & 0 & 9 & 4 \end{pmatrix}$$

```
// Assume n digits, in dig[1]..dig[n], with d[0] the check

int checkDihedral(int n, int dig[])
  {
  int i, check = 0;
  for (i = 0; i <= n; i++)
    check = M[check] [F[i \% 8] [dig[i]]];
  return check == 0;       // OK if check == 0
} // end checkDihedral

void computeDihedral(int n, int dig[])
  {
  int i, check = 0;
  for (i = 1; i <= n; i++)
    check = M[check] [F[i \% 8] [dig[i]]];
  dig[0] = I[check];
  } // end computeDihedral
```

In contrast to the simpler mod-11 algorithms, the dihedral check has the advantage that *any* combination of data digits can be checksummed. There is no need to reject those with an unrepresentable check digit. This advantage comes at the cost of a much less comprehensible algorithm, which depends on rather inaccessible mathematics.

Despite the undoubted quality of the dihedral algorithm, Wagner and Putter caution against its use, especially in commercial applications which may be maintained by less-skilled programmers who do not understand the mathematics[3]. (This aspect may be less important now that programmers are used to invoking mysterious and often complex algorithms through Application Interfaces such as Java packages.) In their paper, they describe a system where the customer wanted 4 check digits for 8 data digits; their solution involves three nested checks. First is a mod-11 check on the 8 data digits, expanding to 9 digits. Next is a mod-97 check on those 9 digits, to a total of 11 digits. Finally, the 11 digits are subjected to a mod-10 "IBM check". The resulting code may be inferior to one using 4 check digits and based on advanced mathematics, but its three stages are comprehensible to users with modest mathematical ability. Comprehensibility is often preferred to intellectual excellence.

10.7.6   The Damm Checksum

A similar and newer algorithm, also based on advanced mathematics (but now using a quasigroup of order 10 rather than the dihedral group) was described by Damm in 2004[4]. It is remarkably simple and uses the single array of Figure **10.4**. Assuming a number with digits numbered left to right $d_1 d_2 d_3 d_4 \ldots$ and a "working digit" w we then –

1. Set $w = 0$

2. Successively set $w = M[w, d_i]$, working from the left (row w, column d_i of the matrix).

3. Append the final w as the check digit.

---

[3]Similar comments were made by Knuth when describing what is now called the "Knuth-Morris-Pratt" pattern matching algorithm. An earlier version of the algorithm, carefully designed according to finite-state machine theory was, within a few months, "hacked" beyond recognition by well meaning but ignorant programmers.

[4]The Wikipedia entry "Damm Algorithm" is apparently one of the few readily accessible sources, as the formal descriptions are minor parts of Damm's German PhD thesis.

Figure 10.4: Table for Damm Checksum

	0	1	2	3	4	5	6	7	8	9
0	0	3	1	7	5	9	8	6	4	2
1	7	0	9	2	1	5	4	8	6	3
2	4	2	0	6	8	7	1	3	5	9
3	1	7	5	0	9	8	3	4	2	6
4	6	1	2	3	0	4	5	9	7	8
5	3	6	7	4	2	0	9	5	8	1
6	5	8	6	9	7	2	0	1	3	4
7	8	9	4	5	3	6	2	0	1	7
8	9	4	3	8	6	1	7	2	0	5
9	2	5	8	1	4	3	6	7	9	0

Generating the check digit for the string 2314 gives the following successive values for w. $w = 0$; $w = M[0, 2] = 1$; $w = M[1, 3] = 2$; $w = M[2, 1] = 2$; $w = M[2, 4] = 8$, giving the check digit as 8. Leading zeros do not affect the check digit.

Validating the check digit is exactly the same, except that we now include the final, check, digit in the calculation; the digit from this stage is always zero for a valid check. (Note that the matrix M has all zeros on the diagonal; if say the preceding digits give a check of x, the check digit itself should be x, so yielding a zero from the matrix diagonal.)

10.7.7   Comparison of Digit Checksums

It is useful now to compare the more complex Verhoeff and Damm checksums against the earlier ISBN13 checksum of section **10.7.3**; these three are designed to check numbers or strings of decimal digits, whereas many of the other checks really apply to characters or more complex entities. (We neglect the Luhn algorithm as being a simpler version of the ISBN13.) The results from testing about 2 million values are given in Table **10.1**.

All checks reliably detect single errors, as do the Verhoeff and Damm for adjacent transpositions. The ISBN13 check will not detect adjacent transpositions of two digits whose difference is 5, as $1 \leftrightarrow 6$ or $8 \leftrightarrow 3$.

For more-complex errors, note that *any* burst can do no more than leave its intermediate check value as a wrong decimal value, just as would be produced

Table 10.1: Undetected Error Probabilities

	Single errors	Adjacent transposition	non-Adjacent Transposition
ISBN13	0.0%	6.25%	58.41%
Damm	0.0%	0.0%	11.06%
Verhoeff	0.0%	0.0%	11.76%

by a single digit error at the end of the burst. Thus any burst error is equivalent to a single-digit error, (unless it yields the correct intermediate check digit, with a probability of 10%). Full tests of digit-pair errors have not been done, but it is reasonable to expect a failure rate of around 10%, in line with the results for transpositions of separated digits. This test is therefore for only transpositions of non-adjacent digits.

The ISBN13 check suffers badly because all even digit positions have the same weight, as do all odd positions. The result is that about half of all transpositions (even $\leftrightarrow$ even positions, odd $\leftrightarrow$ odd) cannot be detected. The two more complex checks give very similar results, both failing about 11% of the time. There is little to choose between them, but the Damm check is certainly simpler.

10.7.8   Fletcher Checksum

The Fletcher checksum [38] [59] was developed for the Transport Layer (Level 4) of the OSI communication model. It is fundamentally a sum of sums method, with all additions done modulo 255. (But note that 255 is *not* prime!) Thus to add in the digit d_i we calculate

$$
\begin{aligned}
s1 &= s1 + d_i \bmod 255 \\
s2 &= s2 + s1 \bmod 255
\end{aligned}
$$

with initial values $s1 = 1; s2 = 0$. If the checksum is at the end of the message (the usual case) the two check-bytes are set to $B_1 = s1 - s2$ and $B_2 = -2s1 + s2$ to make the checksum including the two check bytes sum to zero. Testing for correct transmission is a little different from many checksums, because the result is correct if *either* $s1 = 0$ or $s2 = 0$. An error is signalled only if *both* sums are non-zero.

If the checksum bytes are at position n and $n + 1$ of an L-octet message (numbering $0 \ldots L - 1$), then

$$
\begin{aligned}
b_n &= (L - n) \times s1 - s2 \text{ and} \\
b_{n+1} &= s2 - (L - n + 1) \times s1
\end{aligned}
$$

The Fletcher checksum is stated to give checking nearly as powerful as the CRC-16 checksum described below, detecting –
- all single-bit errors,
- all double-bit errors,
- all but $0.000\,019\%$ of burst errors up to length 16, and
- all but 0.0015% of longer burst errors.

10.7.9   Adler Checksum

The Adler checksum [22] is a development of the Fletcher checksum and generates 16-bit sums and a 32-bit checksum. It was devised particularly for the GZIP text compressor. For each digit (or byte)

$$
\begin{aligned}
s1 &= s1 + d_i \bmod 65\,521 \\
s2 &= s2 + s1 \bmod 65\,521
\end{aligned}
$$

The checksum is the 32-bit value $65\,536 * s1 + s2$, transmitted most- significant byte first. The values are initialised with $s1 = 1$, $s2 = 0$ to give a length-dependent checksum for all-zero data.

Note that the modulus 65 521 *is* prime, removing one doubtful feature about the design of the Fletcher checksum[5].

10.7.10   Cyclic Redundancy Checks

These are the most important and widespread of the error-detecting codes for text or other data of arbitrary length. They are especially suitable for hardware implementation at very high operating speeds and are used in most data communications systems. They are still based on modular arithmetic, but with some major changes from the earlier examples –

---

[5]A similar algorithm with modulus 9973 gives a checksum of 8 decimal digits $(10\,000 * s1 + s2)$.

1. The "number system" is changed from the conventional and familiar integers to one of *finite fields*, specifically the Galois Field $GF(2)$. All of the arithmetic is performed modulo 2, as in point 3 below.

2. The bits are regarded as coefficients in polynomials. This allows the very highly developed and powerful mathematics of finite fields and polynomial fields to be applied to the theory of error control coding, both error detection and error correction.

   The expression as polynomials also allows a convenient representation for bit vectors which often have many zero elements. Only the terms corresponding to 1s appear in the polynomial and they very conveniently have the bit position shown explicitly as the exponent. Thus these two representations are equivalent

   $$1\ 0\ 0\ 1\ 0\ 1 \Longleftrightarrow x^5 + x^2 + 1$$

   as are also
   $$1\ 0\ 0\ 0\ 0\ 0\ 1\ 1\ 1 \Longleftrightarrow x^8 + x^2 + x + 1$$

   The polynomial variable is truly a dummy variable with little significance to most of the coding process. It could be regarded as a "carrier" for the exponents.

3. Numerical arithmetic in integers is replaced by logical operations on the bits in the $GF(2)$ finite field. Addition and subtraction are now *both* equivalent to an Exclusive-OR ($\oplus$) and multiplication is equivalent to a logical AND ($\wedge$). (In both cases, regard the bits as numerical values, do the numerical operations and take the result modulo 2.) There is no carry propagation between bits, which immediately removes one of the main impediments to fast addition.

   Practically, this change means that the arithmetic can be done very easily and quickly by simple logic. While not developed to any great extent here, this is a great incentive for using these methods in fast hardware.

The most visible operation for cyclic redundancy checks is polynomial division, as shown in Figure **10.5**. Except for the slightly changed subtraction rules the overall method is precisely that of traditional long division (decimal). The divisor, which is always a constant, is normalised with its most-significant bit a 1. (In practice its least significant term is also a 1, giving a polynomial of the form $x^N \ldots 1$. Technically, $g(x)$ is *monic*.) Because there is no carry propagation in subtraction, the divisor can be subtracted from the partial remainder whenever the most significant bit of the remainder is a 1; there is no

Figure 10.5: Polynomial Division — $x^3(x^6 + x^3 + 1) \div x^3 + x + 1$

```
                    1 0 1 0 1 1 0
      1 0 1 1  )  1 0 0 1 0 0 1 0 0 0
              -  1 0 1 1
                 0 1 0 0
                   1 0 0 0
                -  1 0 1 1
                   0 1 1 1 0
                  -  1 0 1 1
                     1 0 1 0
                  -  1 0 1 1
                     0 1 0
```

concept of a "trial subtraction" or compensation for overdraws as needed in integer division. The form of the dividend and the way it is written in this example are deliberately chosen to fit with the use of polynomial division in forming CRCs ($i(x) = x^6 + x^3 + 1$ and $g(x) = x^3 + x + 1$).

When we apply polynomials to checksum generation, the transmitted data forms a 1-dimensional bit stream, with earlier bits corresponding to higher-powers within the polynomial. There are several polynomials involved in transmitting data and checking for correct transmission –

information polynomial $i(x)$ The information polynomial is the transmitted data as provided by the user (usually including headers, addresses and other transmission control information). The information polynomial is usually transmitted without modification.

generator polynomial $g(x)$ The information polynomial is divided by the generator polynomial and the remainder from that division is appended as the checksum. Usually zeros corresponding to the degree of $g(x)$ are appended to $i(x)$ before the division.

codeword polynomial $c(x)$ Appending the checksum from the division to the information polynomial forms the codeword polynomial, which is what is actually transmitted.

error polynomial $e(x)$ During transmission one or more bits of $c(x)$ may be corrupted. The corrupted positions may be regarded as a polynomial, the *error polynomial* $e(x)$.

received codeword $v(x)$ This is what is received after corruption in transit. As $e(x)$ marks the corrupted bits in the transmitted data, then clearly $v = c \oplus e$, assuming a term-by-term exclusive-OR, or $v(x) = c(x) + e(x)$.

In more detail, if r is the degree of $g(x)$,

1. append r low-order zeros to $i(x)$, to form $x^r i(x)$.

2. calculate $(x^r i(x) \bmod g(x))$, the remainder on division by $g(x)$

3. append that remainder to $i(x)$ to form $c(x)$, the transmitted codeword. Thus the transmitted codeword

$$c(x) = x^r i(x) - (x^r i(x) \bmod g(x))$$

is always a multiple of $g(x)$. (Step 1 ensures that the whole of $i(x)$ is processed by $g(x)$ and also creates a space into which the remainder may be written.

4. On reception compute

$$
\begin{aligned}
r(x) &= v(x) \bmod g(x) \\
&= e(x) \bmod g(x) + c(x) \bmod g(x) \\
&= e(x) \bmod g(x) \text{ , as } c(x) \bmod g(x) \equiv 0 \text{ by construction}
\end{aligned}
$$

An error will be undetected if and only if $e(x)$ is a multiple of $g(x)$. The design of the generator polynomial $g(x)$ therefore determines the ability to detect errors and is in turn determined by its relationship to $e(x)$.

- If there is single-bit error, then the error polynomial is $e(x) = x^i$, where i determines the bit in error. If $g(x)$ contains two or more terms it will never divide $e(x)$ and all single-bit errors will be detected.

- If there are two single-bit isolated errors, then $e(x) = x^i + x^j$, or $e(x) = x^j(x^{i-j}+1)$ if $i > j$. If $g(x)$ is not divisible by x, then all double errors will be detected if $g(x)$ does not divide $x^k + 1$ for all k up to the maximum message length. Suitable $g(x)$ may be found by computer search; for example $x^{15} + x^{14} + 1$ does not divide $x^k + 1$ for any $k < 32\,768$.

- If there is an odd number of bits in error, then $e(x)$ has an odd number of bits. As no polynomial with an odd number of terms has $(x + 1)$ as factor, [6] we make $g(x)$ have $(x+1)$ as a factor to detect all odd numbers of errors.

- A polynomial code with r check bits will detect all burst errors of length $\leq r$. A burst error of length k can be represented as $x^i(x^{k-1} + \ldots + 1)$. If $g(x)$ has a constant term it will not have x^i as a term, so if the degree of $(x^{k-1} + \ldots + 1)$ is less than that of $g(x)$, the remainder cannot be zero.

- If the burst is of length $r+1$, the remainder $r(x)$ will be zero if and only if the burst is identical to $g(x)$. If all bit combinations are equally likely, the probability of the intervening $r - 1$ bits all matching is $1/2^{r-1}$.

- For a longer error burst, the probability of an undetected error is $1/2^r$.

Many of the terms in this description of CRC codes actually arise from the use of polynomial techniques in *error correction* developing and improving on what Hamming Codes showed possible. The key difference in block error-correcting codes is the remainder from dividing $v(x)$ by $g(x)$ is known as the *syndrome* $s(x)$ and can be used to determine the error vector $e(x)$ and thereby correct any errors. Although the mechanics are similar, the design of $g(x)$ is quite different from what was described for *error detection*.

10.7.11   Examples of CRC Polynomials

As a preliminary observation, the polynomial x^8+1 generates a simple longitudinal parity over a message of 8-bit characters, and similarly for other character lengths. [There are two bits in $g(x)$, which in the data stream correspond to similar bits of two adjacent data characters. The effect of this "window" is to Exclusive-OR bits of each data character into the corresponding bit of an overall parity character.]

Some standard error-checking polynomials are –

---

[6] Assume that $e(x) = (x + 1)q(x)$. Then, because $e(x)$ has an odd number of terms, $e(1)$ must be equal to 1. But $e(x) = (x + 1)q(x) = (1 + 1)q(x) = 0.q(x)$ which is always 0. Therefore the assumption must be false.

CRC-12 $x^{12} + x^{11} + x^3 + x + 1$
CRC-16 $x^{16} + x^{15} + x^2 + 1$
CRC-CCITT $x^{16} + x^{12} + x^5 + 1$
IEEE 802 $x^{32} + x^{26} + x^{23} + x^{22} + x^{16} + x^{12} + x^{11} + x^{10} + x^8 +$
                       $x^7 + x^5 + x^4 + x^2 + x + 1$
ATM HEC $x^8 + x^2 + x + 1$
ATM AAL3/4 $x^{10} + x^9 + x^5 + x^4 + x + 1$

CRC-12 is used for 6-bit character codes in some older banking and flight-reservation systems.

The 16-bit codes (CRC-16 used largely in North America, and CRC-CCITT in Europe) can detect all error bursts of 16 or fewer bits, all errors with an odd number of bits, and 99.998% of bursts of 18 or more bits.

The "ATM HEC" is the Header Error Control code used in ATM cells (Asynchronous Transfer Mode). It covers the 4 preceding octets and can correct all single errors and detect many multiple errors.

The "ATM AAL3/4" is used to verify the user data of each ATM cell in the ATM Adaptation Layers 3 and 4.

The "IEEE 802" checksum has been adopted in many communications systems apart from the IEEE802.x standards, including Fibre Channel and ATM AAL-5.

In some cases the details of the checking are changed. For example, with X.25 frames, using the CRC-CCITT polynomial.

- The shift register is initially preset to all 1s,

- the check digits are inverted as they are shifted out after the information bits,

- the receiver includes the check field in its calculation, and

- the result must be 1111 0000 1011 1000.

Although the "IEEE 802" generator polynomial is very widely used in many communications systems it is used with several variations.

In 802.3 Contention Bus (Ethernet) –

- the first 32 bits of the data are complemented,

- the entire frame including header and user data is divided by the generator polynomial,

- the FCS bits are inverted as they are shifted out after the information bits,

- the receiver checks that the FCS generated from the preceding received data matches the received FCS

and in 802.5 Token Bus –

- the 32-bit register for the checksum is initialised to all 1s,

- the entire frame including header and user data is divided by the generator polynomial,

- the check bits are inverted as they are shifted out after the information bits,

- the receiver includes the check field in its calculation, and Calculation

- the result, including the received checksum, must be
  $x^{31} + x^{30} + x^{26} + x^{25} + x^{24} + x^{18} + x^{15} + x^{14} + x^{12} + x^{11} + x^{10} + x^8 + x^6 + x^5 + x^4 + x^3 + x + 1$
  or, in binary, 1100 0111 0000 0100 1101 1101 0111 1011

10.8   Further Developments

This chapter has just touched on some very large and important areas, which go far beyond what is appropriate in this book, in particular –

Error Correcting Codes   These have been developed far beyond the simple Hamming Codes described in Section **10.4**. As with the Cyclic Redundancy Checks, most codes are described by polynomial methods using the mathematics of finite fields. A good description of error correcting codes is given by Blahut [10], with a simpler introduction by Arazi [4], but these pre-date some very important recent developments such as

"Turbo Codes". Hamming [52] gives an excellent introduction to coding in conjunction with Information Theory, but without going far into error correcting codes.

The power of modern error correcting codes is demonstrated in a Compact Disk player [55]. Even minor surface scratches and dirt can cause some data loss and a 1mm disk blemish can cause a data loss of 1500 bits. Compact Disc players therefore need excellent error correction and use some of the most powerful error correcting codes. These codes (technically a cross-interleaved Reid-Solomon code) can completely correct an error burst (data drop-out *etc*) of 4000 data bits. At a Bit Error Rate (BER) of 10^{-3} the uncorrected error rate is less than one in 750 hours and is undetectable at a BER of 10^{-4}. (To further conceal any audible error, any uncorrectable data is surrounded by a "fade-out" and a "fade-in" to give a brief silence rather than a noise.)

Message Authentication More-complex checksums include the "Message Digests" (also known as "Message Signatures" or "Cryptographic Hash Functions") which are now used to authenticate messages whose integrity must be guaranteed. They must detect interference which is malevolent rather than accidental, requiring a quite different design process and performance analysis. They are also used for software distribution, checking files of hundreds of megabytes for which simpler checks are inadequate. They are really a development of cryptography and their whole discussion and theory comes from that area. In passing it should be mentioned that Cyclic Redundancy Codes are very weak cryptographically and should not be used for authentication or message security.

Table 10.2: MD5 and SHA1 Digests for Three 1-byte ASCII Files

1	SHA1	356a192b7913b04c54574d18c28d46e6395428ab
1	MD5	c4ca4238a0b923820dcc509a6f75849b
2	SHA1	da4b9237bacccdf19c0760cab7aec4a8359010b0
2	MD5	c81e728d9d4c2f636f067f89cc14862c
3	SHA1	77de68daecd823babbb58edb1c8e14d7106e83bb
3	MD5	eccbc87e4b5ce2fe28308fd9f2a7baf3

Two earlier message digest routines are MD5 and SHA1 (there are newer functions, such as SHA-3, but these two give the spirit of the functions).

Both have source code freely available on the Internet. MD5 calculates a 128 bit digest (16 hexadecimal digits and SHA1 a 160-bit digest (20 digits); there seems to be no good reason for prefering either one[7]. Table **10.2** shows the digests for three trivial 1-byte files, containing the single ASCII digits '1', '2' and '3' (no end-of-line). Note the significant change from one file to the next; each file differs from its predecessor in only a single bit, but the digests are completely different.

Data Scrambling At the physical level, where data bits are encoded on the physical medium, few data transmission techniques tolerate long sequences of 0s or 1s, or sometimes other regular repeated patterns. Information is "scrambled" or randomised to minimise regularities and ensure regular data transitions.

This is often done by *dividing* the data stream by a suitable *scrambling* polynomial and transmitting the *quotient* as the data. The receiver *multiplies* the data by the same polynomial to recover the original data. (The order of division and multiplication could be reversed, but division is much more prone to *catastrophic error propagation* in response to transmission errors and should be avoided in the receiver.) Some typical scrambler polynomials are –

$$x^7 + x + 1 \quad \text{V.27 4800 bps,}$$
$$x^{23} + x^5 + 1 \quad \text{V.29 9600 bps,}$$
$$x^{20} + x^3 + 1 \quad \text{V.35 48 000 bps,}$$
$$x^{16} + x^{13} + 1 \quad \text{Bell System 44Mb/s T3}$$

The scrambler polynomials do not of themselves assure satisfactory operation; a long string of 1s or 0s may cause the shift register to freeze in an all-1 or all-0 or other repetitive state. In the V.35 standard for example, an "Adverse State" is recognised if, for 31 bits, each transmitted bit is identical to the bit 8 before it. An Adverse State causes line data to be complemented.

10.9 Historical Comments

The use of error-detecting and even error-correcting codes predates computers. As a very simple example, with telegrams minor errors in letters could be corrected from the context, but not digit errors. The digits were often all repeated, in order, at the end of the message as a form of redundancy check.

---

[7]But check the current literature because the security of all functions is under continual examination; new weaknesses are frequently discovered and improved functions announced.

An even better example comes from commercial code books. In the days of manual transmission (Morse code, or teleprinters for very advanced work), transmissions were expensive, relatively open to public scrutiny, often commercially sensitive and certainly liable to transmission errors. Many organisations used commercial codebooks with 5-letter groups for frequent words or phrases. Using code groups shortened the data (reducing the cost) and also provided a measure of security by concealing the information. Transmissions were however prone to errors and the codes often included error-control mechanisms. Apart from the expected errors of transpositions and character reversals, other errors peculiar to Morse code included splitting and joining characters. Figure **10.6** indicates some possible errors from splitting the code for one letter into two letters.

Figure 10.6: Examples of Morse Code Corruption

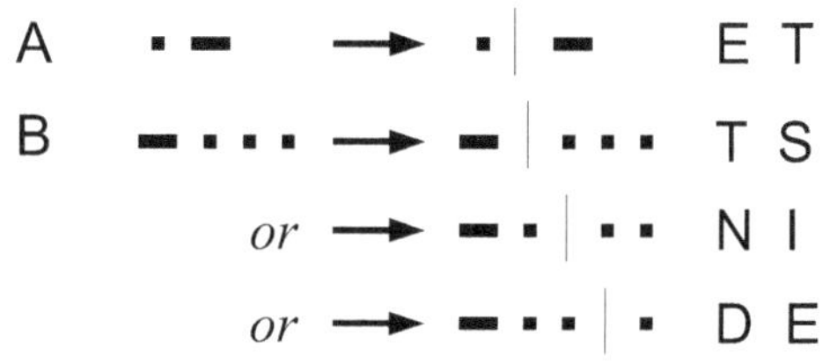

For example, in 1930 "Bentley's Second Phrase Code" [8] claimed the following properties for its codes[8].

1. There was a difference of two letters between any two codewords, including the spare codewords.

2. The reversal of any pair of consecutive letters in any codeword will not form a valid codeword.

3. The reversal of any three consecutive letters in any codeword will not form a valid codeword.

4. The mutilation of any pair of consecutive letters in any codeword by a pause-error in transmitting by Morse will not give another valid codeword.

---

[8]It is salutary to note that the book defines over 100 000 codes, all prepared without a computer.

Some codes replaced single words or currency amounts, but many 5-letter codes corresponded to quite long, but frequent, messages. There were many unused codes which customers could use for private messages.

Many of the early computers such as the Bell System relay machines used constant-parity codes (such as the 2-out-of-5 codes described in Section **11.7**) and included extensive checking facilities. Apparently Richard Hamming was using one of these computers in the late 1940s on problems which could run over the weekend, but was continually frustrated by errors which froze the machine part way through the calculation. It was from considering that problem and trying to rectify that situation that he developed the "Hamming codes" which could not only detect errors (which the machine designers already knew about and handled) but could correct them. These were described in Section **10.4**.

From that time designers of major computers have been well aware of the need to handle errors. Many errors arise from transmission or similar noise and are known as "soft" errors; they may be overcome just by retrying the operation. While other, "hard", errors may need an actual physical repair computers can be designed to recover from hard errors and reconstitute the correct results "on the fly". Apparently on at least one occasion a major computer suffered a logic failure during an acceptance test, but the error correction allowed the test to continue satisfactorily.

Chapter 11

Miscellaneous Topics

Abstract: This chapter contains a variety of topics, especially a history of numbers, justification for binary bits, good number representations, the history of 'word', 'bit' and 'byte', a history of character codes, a variety of decimal codes and Roman numbers.

Keywords: History of number representations, why use 0s and 1s, good and bad representations, history of byte, kilobytes and Megabytes, character codes, decimal codes, Roman Numbers, scaling invariance.

This chapter is a miscellany of material more or less related to previous topics. Some of it is historical background, some expands on less-important technical details, and some is, well, just interesting.

11.1   A Brief History of Number Representation

As discussed in Chapter **1**, there is a clear distinction between several types of numbering systems. An accessible introduction to these concepts and the history of numbers is found in Guedj [48], from which much of this section is taken. An (exceedingly!) comprehensive discussion of the history of numbers is given by Ifrah [61] who describes number representations in an enormous number of civilisations and societies. A later and smaller volume discusses numbers in relationship to computing (Ifrah [60]).

Minimal The very simplest level has no true number system at all and is found in simple societies of ("primitive"?) peoples who live in small groups and have little need of counting. Ifrah [61] shows that people can immediately recognise random collections of up to four objects, but no further unless some regularity allows fast mental arithmetic or some other technique. This limit is reflected in these very simplest numbering systems, with words for *one, two, three, four, many* or perhaps even *one, two, many*. In some languages there are different grammatical inflexions and constructs for the *one, two, three, four, many* cases, in contrast to the *singular, plural* of English.

Descriptive number systems are typically oral such as "two thousand, six hundred and seventy three", but often expressed in quite different terms. They let us talk about quantities, but not much more. In general, each society seems to have developed its own descriptive number system.

Representational systems such as "MMDCLXXIII" allow us to write values in a more or less convenient manner; the important word here is *write*. These systems are largely an adjunct to written alphabets and some languages just used abbreviations for say the "hundreds" word. Some authors claim that the earliest of these number systems actually predate written text—written symbols were first used for accounting and written words arose from the need to describe or annotate the values.

Many of these systems are described by Ifrah as *additive representations*. The Greeks for example used their 24 letters (plus three older symbols) for the 27 values $1 \ldots 9$, $10 \ldots 90$ and $100 \ldots 900$, covering an adequate range of values for most people. Table **11.1** shows lower-case letters; earlier representations used the upper-case equivalents. Using the codes shown in Table **11.1**, our 231 would be written as $\overline{\sigma \lambda \alpha}$, the overscore indicating a number rather than text, or with primes $\sigma' \lambda' \alpha'$. Three separate addition tables are needed, for units, tens and hundreds and the full multiplication table has $27 \times 27 = 729$ entries! Not all products can be represented within this number system (but see later for extensions to larger values).

The Greek digit codes are shown in Table **11.1**, with the entries for 6, 90 and 900 using the three archaic letters *digamma, qoppa* and *sampi*.

Roman numbers are similar, but replicate some symbols and also introduce a confusing subtractive element into the representation. The basic symbol equivalences are

$$I \leftrightarrow 1, \ V \leftrightarrow 5, \ X \leftrightarrow 10, \ L \leftrightarrow 50, \ C \leftrightarrow 100, \ D \leftrightarrow 500, \ M \leftrightarrow 1000$$

Table 11.1: Greek and Roman Digit Codes, with Names of Added Symbols

	Greek	Roman		Greek	Roman		Greek	Roman
1	α	I	10	ι	X	100	ρ	C
2	β	II	20	κ	XX	200	σ	C
3	γ	III	30	λ	XXX	300	τ	CC
4	δ	IV	40	μ	XL	400	υ	CCC
5	ε	V	50	ν	L	500	φ	CD
6	F	VI	60	ξ	LX	600	χ	D
7	ζ	VII	70	ο	LXX	700	ψ	DC
8	η	VIII	80	π	LXXX	800	ω	DCC
9	θ	IX	90	ϙ	XC	900	⸀	CM
	F digamma			ϙ qoppa			⸀ sampi	

One of the larger symbols may be preceded by the immediately smaller "units" symbol (I, X or C) which is then *subtracted* to give values of 4, 9, 40, 90, 400 or 900. The "unit" symbols (I, X, C, M) may be duplicated to give 1 to 3, or possibly 4 of that value. Except that it uses a group of up to 4 symbols for what we would regard as units, tens or hundreds digits, the Roman system is similar to the Greek. Historically, the Roman numbering system is far messier than the conventional form just given; these matters are discussed in more detail in Section **11.8**.

The alphabetic Greek numbers stopped at 999. We describe here what seems to be the dominant extension to larger values, but there do seem to be other alternativess. For values up to 9000, the first 10 digits were preceded by a prime, as shown in Table **11.2**. Values beyond that were based on the *myriad*, (M = 10 000), with the number of myriads written as a count over an M, again shown in Table **11.2**.

Table 11.2: Examples of Large Greek Numbers

ʹA	ʹB	ʹΓ	ʹΔ	ʹE	ʹF	ʹZ	ʹH	ʹΘ
1 000	2 000	3 000	4 000	5 000	6 000	7 000	8 000	9 000

$\overset{α}{M}$	$\overset{β}{M}$	$\overset{γ}{M}$	$\overset{δ}{M}$	$\overset{ε}{M}$	$\overset{F}{M}$	$\overset{ζ}{M}$	$\overset{η}{M}$	$\overset{θ}{M}$

Hybrid representations (Ifrah's term) are an intermediate step between the additive and positional systems. In modern terms, hybrid representations combine the digits 1...9 with auxiliary codes to indicate the significance or weight of the adjoining digit. Thus we might use a following D to represent tens, C hundreds and K thousands, writing out 2356 as 2K3C4D6, and 3004 as 3K4. (Note the absence of any "fill" digits in this last case.)

Computational (Ifrah's *positional*) representations such as "2673" extend the earlier forms in a manner that eventually facilitates computation. The positional notation seems to have developed from the hybrid forms as a shorthand for representing the numbers on an abacus. As each column of the abacus corresponds to a specific weight code, a shorthand form may omit the code, writing the full value 2K3C4D6 as 2356. But the value represented as 3K4 had empty abacus columns; these were conveniently filled by empty, null, filler or cypher symbols as 2 · · 4 or even 2 ∘ ∘ 4 (as a circle is more definite than a dot).

The crucial step in the development of our present number system was the realisation that the null or filler symbol behaved as an extra digit similar to 1...9 and that the rules of addition and multiplication were readily extended to include it. The *null* symbol ∘ was eventually promoted or enlarged to our present 0.

In Hindu/Arabic numbers the digits change their meaning according to their position within the number, so the "4" can mean "4 units" (4), "4 tens" (40), "4 hundreds (400)" and so on. The example value is written as 501, to show the absence of the tens and to place the '5' in the correct "hundreds" position. In contrast to representational systems, larger numbers just need more digits rather than extra symbols (although we may need new words to talk about them).

Many satisfactory *representational* number systems were developed (perhaps for each major written language) and zero was developed by both Babylonians and the Maya; see Ifrah [60]. But it seems that *positional* numbers developed only once, in India in the 5th century AD, appearing first in the Sanskrit document *Lokavibhaga* in 458[1] although the concept was clearly known well before then.

---

[1]From internal astronomical evidence, Ifrah dates this document to Monday 25 August 458.

The Indian number system came to Baghdad in 773[2], and the "Arabic" numbers first appeared in a European document in 976, (arriving actually through North Africa and Spain) although it was several centuries before they found general use. An indication of the subtlety of zero is that when Gerbert of Aurillac took the Hindu/Arabic numbers from Spain to France c970, he took the digits 1...9, but not the digit 0! The importance of *nothing* completely escaped him. It was only from contacts with Moslem scholars during the Crusades and work by Fibonacci, both 2–300 years later, that the Hindu/Arabic system truly came to Europe.

As a final comment we must note that *computational* numbers are really a special case of *positional* numbers; the two are not truly synonymous. Equivalently, *positional* number representations do not necessarily simplify *computation*. Section **2.2** showed that there are many number systems where the digits are undifferentiated and their positions are significant; all are described there by the scalar product $N = \mathbf{d} \cdot \mathbf{w}$. But it is only those where the *weight vector* $\mathbf{w}$ corresponds to a polynomial in an integer base b that facilitate computation. Thus base-1, Zeckendorf and mixed-base representations are all positional but have more-or-less difficult procedures for arithmetic.

Ifrah makes a similar point in discussing the Maya numbers. They had a genuine zero, possibly devised well before the Hindus, and used a mostly base 20 number system, with successive bases of $\{\ldots, 20, 20, 20, 18, 20\}$, or digit weights of $\{\ldots, 144\,000, 7200, 360, 20, 1\}$. The discontinuity at the second digit meant that the Maya never discovered the computational advantages of zero.

The "18" appears to have been inserted so that '100' (their system) is nearly equal to the days in a year. In retrospect, a base-19 system might have been better and even lead to proper use of zero; $19^2 = 361$, which is closer to 365 than 18×20.

11.1.1   History of Fractions

Just as the integers arise naturally from counting, so do fractions arise from measurement and ideas of ratio or division into parts. The ideas of fractions are probably as old as the ideas of measurement, but often restricted to values such as $\frac{1}{2}$, $\frac{1}{3}$, and perhaps $\frac{2}{3}$. Greek mathematics concentrated more on *ratio* in an attempt to retain the natural numbers.

---

[2]It may be no coincidence that first Arab and later European science flowered following the adoption of a flexible numbering system.

The ideas of decimal fractions in the modern sense have been traced to al-Kashi of Samarkand, with his 15th century work "The Key to Arithmetic". The European use of decimals dates from Simon Stevin, with his 1582 (or 1585 or 1586) text "The Tenth". Guedj [48] reproduces a page from a French edition of "The Tenth", showing both his new form $2\ 7\ⓞ8\①4\②7\③$ and the older $27\frac{847}{1000}$.

Duncan [24], describing the development of the calendar, ascribes the invention of the decimal point proper to either G.A. Magnini in 1592 (who used 27.847, as now used in English-speaking countries), or to Clavius in 1593. (Duncan also ascribes the invention of decimal fractions to the Syrian Abdul Hassan al-Uqlidsi in 952 or 953. But decimal fractions seemed to be not transmitted to Europe with decimal integers, (possibly because Europeans at that time barely understood fractions anyway.) Also in 1592 Bürgi [60] would have written the value as $2\overset{\circ}{7}847$. Then in 1608 Snellius suggested 27,847 (as now used in most European countries). Napier in his 1619 work on logarithms suggested either "." (variously known as a stop, full stop, or period) or a "," (comma) as reasonable alternatives.

With the extension of the Hindu/Arabic notation to include fractions, the development of the modern system of number representation was essentially complete; Ifrah asserts that it is "a perfect system ... no further development is possible".

11.1.2   Possible Prehistoric Mathematics

Three recent books make claims for far, far, earlier development of "modern" mathematics and numbers; although these claims will certainly be queried, and queried strongly, it is appropriate to mention them here. Although claims such as these are often the stuff of arcane speculation, all three authors here provide considerable factual supporting evidence, evidence which is arguably as strong as that on which many accepted histories are based.

- Menzies [74] links Atlantis explicitly to the Minoan culture (c2000–1470 BC) and its centre at Thera, now Santorini, which erupted violently around 1450BC, terminating the Minoan civilisation. Emphasising the breadth of Minoan trading, he describes the discovery of Minoan artefacts from India, through the Mediterranean, north into Europe and even across the Atlantic to where the Minoans apparently mined copper at Lake Superior.

He concludes by discussing Minoan mathematics as revealed by hitherto undeciphered "Minoan Linear A" inscriptions, with concepts then to be forgotten for 1000 to 1500 years.

- Temple [100], discussing firstly the chronology of Ancient Egypt, moves on to the "Atlantean" culture (*Atlantic*, rather than *Atlantis*, and probably pre-dating Minoa proper, perhaps 4000–3000BC) which constructed many trilithons and megaliths (of which Stonehenge is the best-known example) around the Mediterranean and the Atlantic coast of Europe.

  He produces evidence that these megalithic circles were precise astronomical observatories whose design required advanced mathematics, as did the Atlantean long distance navigation. [Temple claims that "Atlantis" was misinformation to discourage other mariners from sailing past the Pillars of Hercules (Gibraltar) into the profitable Atlantic trading stations; there could be some truth in this too, as a later post-Minoan development.]

- Freeman [41] compares stone circles in Alberta (c3000BC) with Stonehenge (c3000BC – c2000BC), yet again showing that both can act as precise astronomical observatories. The arrival of this knowledge in the heart of North America remains an open question, as does any possible trans-Atlantic connection.

Thus all three authors independently point to Bronze Age, and even Stone Age, cultures with mathematics sufficiently advanced to construct precise astronomical observatories and, in two cases, perform ocean navigation. Whether all were Minoan, or whether the Minoan culture was the climax of a series of predecessors, is open to discussion (and contention), but it certainly appears that "modern" mathematics existed far earlier than previously suspected, only to be forgotten with the collapse of Minoa and the onset of a Mediterranean "Dark Ages".

11.1.3   A Brief Chronology

An enormous amount of mathematical notation was developed in the period 1450–1650, preparing the ground for later developments. While some of this development has been referred to already, some other important dates are given here, largely taken from Ifrah [60].

458		Decimal numbers, with zero, appear in print in Hindu document.
778		"Hindu" numbers, with zero, conveyed to Baghdad.
970	Gilbert of Aurilac	transfers "Arabic" numbers to Europe (*sans* zero).
c1215	Leonardo of Pisa	publishes Arabic numbers (*including* zero).
1484	Nicholas Chuquet	used 0, − for negative numbers, reasonable notation for powers
1489	Johann Widmann	+ and − for addition and subtraction
1525	Christoph Rudolff	the square root sign $\sqrt{}$
1557	Robert Recorde	= to relate the two sides of an equation
1630	Thomas Harriot	the relational symbols < and >
1632	William Oughtred	× for multiplication
1656	John Wallis	∞ for infinity

11.2 Why Use Bits, 0 or 1

Despite discredited claims that the binary number system was known to ancient Chinese, the first documented use of a binary representation was by Francis Bacon in 1605 [53] for cryptography, with the first credible mathematical description given by Napier in 1617. Binary representation was discussed enthusiastically in 1703 by Liebnitz who ascribed to it mystical properties— properties that would rejected as spurious by most modern mathematicians and theologians.

Binary calculation was seriously proposed in 1936 by Phillips [79] and used by Zuse [113] (1936), and by Atanasoff [5](1939) for their pioneering computers.

Interestingly, Atanasoff selected a binary representation from considering speed rather than storage efficiency. Binary coding was also selected by other workers, such as Rajchman [81] in 1942 for artillery fire control computation. Thus by the time of the Burks, Goldstone and von Neumann report [17] in 1946 the binary number system was so well established that they adopted it seemingly without discussion.

People tend to be most comfortable with decimal numbers, to base 10, whereas computers mostly deal with binary numbers, to base 2. We worked earlier with numbers to bases 2, 8 and 16, and later developed ways of working with numbers represented to *any* base. This raises the important question as to why computers do not use say decimal digits, $0 \ldots 9$, in other words numbers to a base of 10?

The reasons may be summarised as ones of logic, engineering and efficiency.

Logic. Computers are built with devices which use "Boolean logic", or "2-valued logic". The logical values (0 and 1) can be regarded as equivalent to the data values (also 0 and 1), making it easy to use logic devices to perform arithmetic. It is unfortunate that the same symbols are used for both numeric values and logical values, because they really have quite separate meanings, but the usage is now so entrenched that it is unavoidable.

Engineering. It is much easier to make devices which can reliably handle only two values (0, 1) than, say, 10 values $(0 \ldots 9)$. There are two issues here.

- Modern logic circuits are designed to "latch" into one of the two states "0" or "1" and in those states they draw negligible power. Most of the power is consumed in switching between the states, While circuits can be designed, and are designed, to handle more than two states, this inevitably leads to increased power consumption in maintaining intermediate values, or slower operation, or both. With millions of logic circuits in a modern processor, the per-circuit power consumption must be minimised; just 1 μW per logic gate converts to several Watts in the complete chip.

- A 2.50 GHz processor operating for 4 weeks without error corresponds to 6×10^{15} error-free operations. The need for good protection against noise and consequent error is obvious. It is difficult enough to design fast reliable 2-state logic; devices which can discriminate reliably between 3 or more states are much more difficult to handle. They exist, but are used mostly in communications where the need for speed makes it desirable to send several bits in each signal state.

Efficiency. With bits as the data units we are forced to use binary representation (or base-2) for numbers. Two ways of looking at efficiency are given.

1. The first analysis considers the number of "states" needed to represent a value in different number bases. It assumes that a base-N digit has a relative cost of "N", for example as a 1-out-of-N

code. This is a somewhat dubious assumption but, given the relative paucity of true N-valued devices, is perhaps not too bad. The cost with binary coding of digits is considered as the second option.

For example, in decimal numbers, each digit position corresponds to 10 states. 100 values $(0 \ldots 99)$ need 2 digits and 20 states. Values to 1000 need 30 states. Similarly, in binary numbers each digit (bit) has 2 states and an N-bit binary number corresponds to a total of $2N$ states. To represent values to 1024 ($1024 = 2^{10}$, and actually 0 $\ldots 1023$) needs 10 digits and 20 states. Thus binary values to about 1000 need only 20 states and are clearly more efficient than the 30 states needed by decimal values to 1000.

In general, a value V to base b requires $log_b V$ digits, each with b states, or a total of $N = b \times log_b V$ states. To find the "most efficient" base, take $dN/db = 0$, giving the minimum value at $b = e$ $(2.718\,28\ldots)$. For $V = 1000$, the costs (or number of states) of several bases are –

number-base	cost (states)
2	19.93
e	18.78
3	18.86
10	30
BCD	48

A base-3 representation (ternary numbers) is very close to the optimum and base-2 is nearly as good. While a very few base-3 computers have been built (such as the Russian SETUN computer in the early 1950s which used a bit pair with weights +1 and −1 and digit values +1, 0 and −1) the practical advantages of base-2 are such that it is almost universal.

2. Unfortunately, the preceding analysis is somewhat misleading because it assumes that the "cost" of a representation is proportional to the number of states. A proportional cost is true if the digit is represented as a "1-out-of-N" code, but is certainly false if a more compact coding is used.

A better comparison acknowledges that digits in any base will be stored as binary values. A value V represented in base b will require $\lceil log_b V \rceil$ digits, with each digit requiring $\lceil log_2 b \rceil$ bits. The costs under this system are shown in Table **11.3**, representing a value of 1 million in bases up to 20.

The costs are the same, and minimum, for powers of 2. As the base increases above a power of 2 the number of digits usually stays about

Table 11.3: Costs of Representing 1 000 000 in Various Bases

base	bits/digit	digits	cost	base	bits/digit	digits	cost
				11	4	6	24
2	1	20	20	12	4	6	24
3	2	13	26	13	4	6	24
4	2	10	20	14	4	6	24
5	3	9	27	15	4	6	24
6	3	8	24	16	4	5	20
7	3	8	24	17	5	5	25
8	3	7	21	18	5	5	25
9	4	7	28	19	5	5	25
10	4	6	24	20	5	5	25

the same, but the bits to represent each digit increases, leading to an overall increase in the cost. On this model a base of 3 is among the worst values. Although base 10 is definitely worse than the powers of 2, there is no change for bases from 10 to 15, at least for the chosen value of 1 000 000.

11.3 "Good" Number Representations

Having looked in detail at numbers, it is desirable to look at the features of a "good" number system (and conversely, a bad one). By contrast, poorer representations will become more apparent in Section **11.1** (Roman and Greek numbers) and especially Section **11.8** (odd variations on Roman numbers).

As seen later in Section **11.2** it is evident that we should use bits to represent numbers within a computer, although the argument is somewhat circular and intertwined with what follows here. Initially, we want some representation for the integers {0, 1, 2, ...} which satisfies the criteria below. It should also be extensible to signed values and to fractional values.

Uniqueness While it is evident that each code should represent only one value, it is also desirable that each integer should be represented by only one code[3]. This aspect interacts with the next.

---

[3]This requirement may be slightly relaxed for signed zeros, and perhaps some BCD codes

Density All possible codes should be used and each distinct code should represent a separate integral value, as otherwise we waste code space and could, with a better representation, handle more values.

Uniformity Given the representation for any integer N, there should be a simple and uniform method of obtaining the representation of $N + 1$ (and also $N - 1$), assuming that both N and $N + 1$ are within the range of represented values. By extension, addition and subtraction should also be defined by simple and uniform methods, as also for multiplication and division.

Arithmetic As a corollary of the last point, the representation should facilitate arithmetic.

We saw (Section **2.2**) that these criteria are satisfied by representing a value N by a polynomial in a "base" b with digits $\{d_n, d_{n-1}, \ldots, d_2, d_1, d_0\}$ with b an integer and $0 \leq d_i < b$.

$$N = d_n b^n + d_{n-1} b^{n-1} + \cdots + d_2 b^2 + d_1 b + d_0$$

But they are not satisfied by most of the "classical" number systems. In general they represented only a limited range of values, with arithmetic being difficult if not impossible. These matters are discussed separately, in Section **11.1**

11.4 History of "Word", "Byte", and "Bit".

The origins of these terms too often seem to be shrouded in folklore, with many curious and ingenious explanations. Fortunately, some of the history is well documented by people who were present at the invention; as far as possible it is summarised here.

word Historically, the term "word" goes back at least to the 1945 report by Burks, Goldstine and von Neumann [17], where they propose a computer with 40-bit words. They justify the word size of 40 bits (and a memory of 4096 words!), but the use of binary numbers and bits seems to be so obvious that it warrants no discussion at all, even though ENIAC was a decimal machine. There is evidence that Rajchman [81] used "word" as early as 1942.

byte The term was devised in 1956 by Buchholz and originally meant any part of a word, especially a part large enough to hold a digit or character. Buchholz [16] states "The term is coined from from *bite*, but respelled to avoid accidental mutation to *bit*." Bloch, [11] discussing the IBM 7030 (Stretch) in 1959 stated that "*Byte* is a generic term to denote the number of bits to be operated on as a unit by a variable-field-length instruction". Brooks [15] states

> The term "byte" was coined by Dr. Werner Buchholz, System Planning Manager for Project Stretch, in 1956 or '57. I know, because I was there when it happened, and I remember it clearly. Dr. Harwood Kolsky, who was also in the System Planning group with us, has also written recently his recollection, which is the same as mine.

When IBM introduced the System/360 computers in 1964 they adopted an 8-bit byte as the fundamental unit of data addressing. It was well-matched to both the 8-bit EBCDIC character code and to the (7-bit + parity) ASCII code as well as matching other data units of 2^n bits.

The introduction of EBCDIC, and especially ASCII, coincided with the development of "mini-computers" with a 16-bit data unit, superseding some older ones with 12 bits or 18 bits (although computers based on the 6-bit characters never disappeared). These 16-bit computers became widespread and the 8-bit measure combined well with their 16-bit and 32-bit data units. Thus the 8-bit byte became ubiquitous and the earlier general meaning forgotten.

bit The origin of the term "bit" as an abbreviation for "binary digit" is described in a memorandum by MacMillan, quoted by Tropp [103]. The term was suggested by John Tukey, apparently during a lunchtime conversation at Bell Laboratories in late 1946. It is certainly used in a memorandum by Tukey, dated January 9, 1947, in the sense of a *binary digit*.

Very soon afterwards, the same term was adopted by Shannon [90] to mean, not a *binary digit*, but the *binary information unit* (and Shannon could well have been at that lunchtime discussion). Shannon also attributes the name *bit* to Tukey.

This use is sufficiently close to "binary digit" to cause considerable confusion. Under optimal coding, one bit (digit) can on average represent one bit (unit) of information, but it generally represents less. One individual bit-digit can however represent far more than one bit-unit, but only if it represents an improbable event.

This aspect was encountered in Chapter **9**, in connection with text compression. There probabilistic measures are used to estimate the average information content per letter (measured in bit-units) and this measure is compared with the coding density, in bit-digits per letter. Even to somebody working in the field, the distinctions of "bit" are sometimes confusing and extreme care is needed.

11.5   Of kilobytes and Megabytes

It is both convenient and unfortunate that $10^3 \approx 2^{10}$ or, $1000 \approx 1024$. The tradition has grown in computing of speaking of "kilobytes" and "megabytes" as a rough, order of magnitude, expression of size. While in "computerese" itself there is little problem, that is not necessarily the case where computing meets other disciplines.

In particular data communications has a very strong engineering background where 1 MHz means precisely 1 000 000 Hz, and 1 Mbit/s means precisely 1 000 000 bits per second, often accurate to parts in 10^6 or better. Most certainly, 1 MHz *does not* mean 1 048 576 Hz. There is considerable scope for confusion—for example an 800 Mbit/s data link (engineering terminology) cannot send 100 Mbytes in 1 second (computing terminology).[4] Or a cleverly crafted exercise which just overloads a communications link collapses completely when the student assumes that 100 Mbit/s is 104 857 600 bit/s. (Observe too that a disk whose size is quoted in 10^6 units may appear larger than one measured in 2^{20} units!).

In all there are at least *three* meanings for the prefix "Mega-" –

1. The traditional engineering or scientific 10^6 (1 000 000).

2. The computing 2^{20} (1 048 576).

3. A curious hybrid measure used in giving the size of computer disks. Here a megabyte is 1000×1024 or 1 024 000. Stating the capacity in this hybrid measure is much more impressive for marketing. With 1 Tbyte

---

[4]Confusion between units is not confined to computers. NASA has lost a Mars vehicle because of confusion between metric and imperial units. And at least one aircraft is reputed to have run out of fuel for the very same reason.

(TeraByte, 10^{12} bytes), the discrepancy is about 4% and the user will see at best 0.96 Tbyte (less of course space lost "for formatting" *etc.*) [5]

The author has a "640 Gbyte" disk, which the computer reports as "596.17 Gbyte". But $596.17 \times 2^{30} = 640.132 \times 10^9$, so all are correct – it just depends on the units!

Some people have adopted an informal convention where the suffix $K = 2^{10}$, just as $k = 10^3$. While this is a useful convention, it is not widely accepted and provides no solution to the corresponding problem for Mega- and Giga-, *etc.*

Accordingly, one international standardisation body, the International Electrotechnical Commission (IEC), approved in 1998 an IEC International Standard which specified names and prefix symbols for *binary* multiples as used in data processing and data transmission. The prefixes are shown in Table **11.4**

Table 11.4: International Standard Binary Multiples

Factor	Name	Symbol	Origin	Derivation
2^{10}	kibi	Ki	kilobinary $(2^{10})^1$	kilo - $(10^3)^1$
2^{20}	mebi	Mi	megabinary $(2^{10})^2$	mega - $(10^3)^2$
2^{30}	gibi	Gi	gigabinary $(2^{10})^3$	giga - $(10^3)^3$
2^{40}	tebi	Ti	terabinary $(2^{10})^4$	tera - $(10^3)^4$
2^{50}	pebi	Pi	petabinary $(2^{10})^5$	peta - $(10^3)^5$
2^{60}	exbi	Ei	exabinary $(2^{10})^6$	exa - $(10^3)^6$

These values are *not* formal international standards in the sense of the similar decimal prefixes, but follow the spirit of those better-established standards and have been adopted by various regional standards authorities. However much dissension remains.

It is suggested that in English, the first syllable of the name of the binary-multiple prefix should be pronounced in the same way as the first syllable of the name of the corresponding SI prefix, and that the second syllable should be pronounced as "bee". So we have a "kilobee", or a "Gigabee", and so on.

---

[5] Just remember that a disk *always* has more "Marketing Gigabytes" than "Engineering Gigabytes".

11.6   The Development of Character Codes

As stated earlier in Chapter **8**, there were two main streams of character encodings used in computers, one derived from punched card equipment and one from data transmission and communications. We now examine those two streams in more detail.

11.6.1   Card-based Codes

Punched cards had their first major use in data processing when Hermann Hollerith adopted them for the 1886 US census, after being introduced nearly 100 years earlier to control Jacquard looms and used by Babbage as storage and control in his Analytical Engine. Through the early 20th century companies such as IBM and Powers-Samas (later Remington-Rand and then Sperry) developed punched card based equipment to perform often quite complex data processing functions.

Devices included key-punches, sorters, printing tabulators and computing tabulators, many including fixed programming based on plug-boards. When these business equipment manufacturers started to build computers the existing card or "unit-record" devices were ready-made for connection to the new computers to provide input-output facilities.

Both IBM and Remington-Rand used cards $3\frac{1}{4}$ by $7\frac{3}{8}$ inches and 0.007 inches thick[6]. The Remington-Rand cards had 45 columns with round holes and two 6-bit characters per column, with one character towards the top of the card and one towards the bottom.

Overall the two systems offered similar equipment and facilities.

The dominant punched card technology however was that of IBM, using 80-column cards with rectangular holes and 12 rows per column; characters were coded as combinations of the 12 holes, with one character per column. Initially at least, digits were coded as single punches in rows 0 ... 9, with a '+' as a '12' punch (top row) and a '-' as an '11' punch. When letters were added they were coded as multi-punches, using rows 12, 11 and 0 (the three top rows) as "zone" indicators with 1 ... 9 as "digits" or "numerics". Later still, "special" or punctuation codes were also needed; these often used the "8"

---

[6]The size (but not thickness!) was the then size of a US dollar bill, and allowed bill-handling machines to be used for punched cards.

row as a further zone. This led to character encodings as shown in Table **11.5**.

Table 11.5: Representative IBM Punched Card Codes (BCD)

characters		punches	
		zone	digit
0 ... 9			0 ... 9
A ... I		12	1 ... 9
J ... R		11	1 ... 9
S ... Z		0	2 ... 9
/		0	1
.		12, 8	3
$		11, 8	3
,		0, 8	3
*		11, 8	4
−		11	
+	&	12	
=	#	8	3
'	@	8	4
)	%	12, 8	4
(	⌑	0, 8	4
Scientific	Business		

Unfortunately, two parallel character sets developed, a "commercial" set and a "scientific" set (perhaps more accurately a "numerical computing" set). They shared the same punch combinations, with the "scientific" characters shown to the left in Table **11.5**. Thus '+' and '&' shared the same code, as did '=' and '#'.

When IBM rationalized their separate scientific and commercial lines of computers in the early 1960s with the release of the IBM S/360 computers, they also introduced a revised card code, with an accompanying 8-bit internal representation known as EBCDIC (Extended Binary Coded Decimal Interchange Code). The new code was clearly based on the earlier BCD code described above, but introduced many new punctuation or "special" characters and a set of communication control characters.

The notion of "zone" and "digit" punches was retained in the EBCDIC card code, but rows 12, 11, 0, 8 and 9 could be zones (in any combination), with none or one of the rows 1...9 used as the digit. All 256 byte values had a card-punch representation, even though some were seldom used. The zones (12, 11, 0, 8 and 9) could be used as a 5-bit code in conjunction with the 3 bits from encoding no-punch, or 1 ... 7 in binary to give an intermediate 8-bit code before forming the final EBCDIC code, perhaps by table look-up. (The final EBCDIC code was based more or less on the combination of card punches, but with some quite anomalous encodings for rarer characters.)

Table 11.6: EBCDIC Codes for Visible Characters

zones → ↓ rows	4	5	6	7	8	9	A	B	C	D	E	F
0 0000	sp	&	-									0
1 0001				/	a	j			A	J		1
2 0010					b	k	s		B	K	S	2
3 0011					c	l	t		C	L	T	3
4 0100					d	m	u		D	M	U	4
5 0101					e	n	v		E	N	V	5
6 0110					f	o	w		F	O	W	6
7 0111					g	p	x		G	P	X	7
8 1000					h	q	y		H	Q	Y	8
9 1001					i	r	z		I	R	Z	9
A 1010	¢	!		:								
B 1011	.	$	,	#	{	}	[	]				
C 1100	<	*	%	@								
D 1101	(	)	_	'								
E 1110	+	;	>	=								
F 1111			¬	?	"								

The EBCDIC encoding is shown in Table **11.6**, omitting the first four columns which are used for transmission control and similar functions and all non-printing codes. The code for a character is the concatenation of the hexadecimal row and column headings. Thus 'A' is coded as C1 (1100 0001) and '+' as 4E (0100 1110).

In comparison with the ASCII code of the next section –

- The EBCDIC code is quite sparse, spreading the codes over most of the possible code space, but with major breaks. Thus, 'special' characters seldom share columns with letters or digits.

- Just as with ASCII, a 6-bit subset can combine upper-case letters, digits, and most of the punctuation symbols.

- The collation order is quite different; indeed the blocks of digits, upper-case and lower-case letters are in the reverse order, although the orders are of course the same within the blocks.

- The characters sets *almost* coincide. EBCDIC has the characters ¢ and ¬, while ASCII includes ˜ and ˆ. EBCDIC originally omitted braces and brackets { } [and]. Even though they were later included, the actual encoding seemed to depend very much on the actual computer system. These matters pose grave difficulties for systems which must translate between ASCII and EBCDIC (see Section **8.6**).

The EBCDIC code has been used mostly in mainframe computers, especially those made by IBM and Burroughs (now Unisys). Although important, it lacks the widespread acceptance of ASCII and its successors and will not be used in the rest of this section.

11.6.2   Transmission-based Codes

The first of these codes was devised by Emile Baudot in about 1882. It is a rather subtle code, which is fully described by Heath [53] and, in modern terms, used 5 bits to encode each character. It was meant to be encoded on a manual keyboard, using "chords" on the left and right hands, with two fingers on the left and three fingers on the right as shown in Table **11.7**. A single left hand key, and none on the right, switched between the "letters" and "figures" shift.

Table 11.7: Baudot's Original Code

Gauche				Droite		Gauche				Droite
10	11	01	00			10	11	01	00	
lettres		chiffres				lettres		chiffres		
t	K	J	A	100		.	(	6	1	100
Z	L	H	É	110		:	=	h	&	110
X	M	G	E	010		,	)	7	2	010
W	N	F	I	011		?	No	F	o	011
V	P	D	O	111		'	%	0	5	111
T	Q	C	U	101		!	/	9	4	101
S	R	B	Y	001		;	-	8	3	001

A different code now known as the "Baudot" code, (also a 5-bit code but with an English flavour) was invented around 1903 by Murray, a New Zealander working in London. It used a typewriter-like keyboard instead of Baudot's five "piano" keys; the operator did not have to know the symbol codes. The code allocation looks quite arbitrary, but generally encodes frequent characters with fewer bits. It is officially called the International Telecommunications Union International Alphabet 2 (IA-2).

When people first started making computers, those who already made unit-record or punched card equipment tended to use their existing devices for input-output, as described in the previous section. Many of the other computer developers, often smaller and universities or similar organisations, chose to use what was readily available and not too expensive. Often that equipment was teleprinters and paper tape.

Table 11.8: The Murray (IA-2, "Baudot") Code, Extended to 6 Bits

high-order →		0 0	0 1	1 0	1 1
low-order		0	1	2	3
↓ bits		Letters		Figures	
0 0 0 0	0	BLK	T	BLK	5
0 0 0 1	1	E	Z	3	"
0 0 1 0	2	LF	L	LF	$\frac{3}{4}$ or)
0 0 1 1	3	A	W	-	2
0 1 0 0	4	sp	H	sp	◇
0 1 0 1	5	S	Y	BELL	6
0 1 1 0	6	I	P	8	0
0 1 1 1	7	U	Q	7	1
1 0 0 0	8	CR	O	CR	9
1 0 0 1	9	D	B	$	$\frac{5}{8}$ or ?
1 0 1 0	10	R	G	4	&
1 0 1 1	11	J	FIGS	′	FIGS
1 1 0 0	12	N	M	$\frac{7}{8}$ or ,	.
1 1 0 1	13	F	X	$\frac{1}{4}$ or !	/
1 1 1 0	14	C	V	$\frac{1}{8}$ or :	$\frac{3}{8}$ or ;
1 1 1 1	15	K	LTRS	$\frac{1}{2}$ or (	LTRS

Teleprinter equipment had been available since the early 20th century, using the 5-bit IA-2 code. This 5-bit code operates in two modes—'letters shift' and 'figures (or numeric) shift', with explicit codes to force entry to one mode or the other. With the current shift encoded as an extra bit, it immediately leads to a 6-bit computer code capable of handling mono-case letters, digits and some punctuation. This code is shown in Table **11.8**. The two "column" bits are used as a prefix to the four "row" bits in forming the final 6-bit code.

A major problem is the arbitrary order of both letters and digits, which makes comparisons and ordering extremely difficult. This code is not well suited to computers although for simple data transmission the arbitrary encoding is quite irrelevant[7].

The situation was not helped by the multiplicity of internal codes used on various computers in the late 1950s. They were usually 6-bit codes and often based on card code, but incompatible in the details[8]. That did not matter as long as computers were isolated entities, but with communications becoming important there was a clear need for a standard code.

As one example, the Univac 1108 computer was originally designed to to hold six 6-bit characters in each 36-bit word. For ASCII, the word was divided into four 9-bit quarter words, each holding one 8-bit character with one spare bit.

Table 11.9: Table of ASCII-63 Character codes (• may be 0 or 1)

binary	hex	•000	•001	•010	•011	•100	•101	•110	•111
0000	0	NULL	DC0	SP	0	@	P		
0001	1	SOM	DC1	!	1	A	Q		
0010	2	EOA	DC2	"	2	B	R		
0011	3	EOM	DC3	#	3	C	S		
0100	4	EOT	DC4	$	4	D	T		
0101	5	WRU	ERR	%	5	E	U		
0110	6	RU	SYNC	&	6	F	V		
0111	7	BELL	LEM	'	7	G	W		
1000	8	FE0	S0	(	8	H	X		
1001	9	HT/SK	S1	)	9	I	Y		
1010	A	LF	S2	*	:	J	Z		
1011	B	VT	S3	+	;	K	[		
1100	C	FF	S4	,	<	L	\		ACK
1101	D	CR	S5	-	=	M	]		
1110	E	SO	S6	.	>	N	↑		ESC
1111	F	SI	S7	/	?	O	←		DEL

Given the limitations of the 5-bit code and the plethora of 6-bit codes,

---

[7]The author well remembers a code patch sent for a B6700 computer in the 1970s, over a teleprinter link which used 5-bit IA-2. Its Algol language made much use of symbols such as : [ ] ; all of which had to be spelled out, or at least with obvious abbreviations. It provided a graphic illustration of the deficiencies of older transmission alphabets.

[8]It is not surprising that Univac based a code on the Remington-Rand 40 × 2 column card format, whereas IBM used their 80 column card.

the American National Standards Institute issued in 1963 a new code, the "American Standard Code for Information Interchange", generally known as ASCII-63. It was a 7-bit code (8-bit with parity) and provided a rich set of transmission control codes, in addition to the usual letters and digits and a good set of punctuation symbols. ASCII-63 was still upper-case-only, lacked some punctuation symbols, and had some of its control codes aligned more with traditional transmission equipment than with the requirements of computer communication. It is shown in Table **11.9**.

A revised code was issued in 1967. ASCII-67 extended the alphabet to include lower-case letters and an extended set of punctuation symbols, still within the bounds of a 7-bit code, and renamed some of the transmission codes to reflect more general functions. It is this code which is generally known as "the ASCII code". (Strictly the name should be ANSCII, for "American National Standard Code ...", but few people seem to use that term.) The international equivalent is known as the International Alphabet 5 (IA–5). National codes, of which ASCII-67 is an example, differ mainly in the coding of currency symbols.

The 7-bit code fitted well with the advent of the 8-bit byte as a fundamental data unit in computers, and is shown in Table **11.10**. The 8th (most significant) bit may be 0, 1, or parity.

Two subset codes were also defined in the 1963 standard.

- The 'central' four columns (headed '010' to '101') provide a 6-bit subset which was, at that time, suitable for many computers which required 6-bit codes. (But there are no symbols for "end-of-line", *etc.*)

- The first ten digits in the fourth column and the last six symbols in the third column provided a "4-bit" subset suitable for calculators and the like. (The resulting codes 0 ... 9, * + , − . and / are those now provided on the numeric keypads of most keyboards.)

The adoption of the ASCII code was hastened by the widespread use of Teletype[TM] units ASR-33 and ASR-35 (for ASCII 63) and ASR-37 (for ASCII 67) which combined keyboard and printing with paper tape reader and punch, albeit all at 10 characters per second. Possibly supplemented with higher performance paper tape equipment, these and similar devices provided *the* input-output facilities for the first generation of minicomputers and time-sharing computers.

Table 11.10: Table of ASCII-67 Character Codes (• may be 0 or 1)

binary	hex	•000	•001	•010	•011	•100	•101	•110	•111
0000	0	NUL	DLE	SP	0	@	P	'	p
0001	1	SOH	DC1	!	1	A	Q	a	q
0010	2	STX	DC2	"	2	B	R	b	r
0011	3	ETX	DC3	#	3	C	S	c	s
0100	4	EOT	DC4	$	4	D	T	d	t
0101	5	ENQ	NAK	%	5	E	U	e	u
0110	6	ACK	SYN	&	6	F	V	f	v
0111	7	BEL	ETB	'	7	G	W	g	w
1000	8	BS	CAN	(	8	H	X	h	x
1001	9	HT	EM	)	9	I	Y	i	y
1010	A	LF	SUB	*	:	J	Z	j	z
1011	B	VT	ESC	+	;	K	[	k	{
1100	C	FF	FS	,	<	L	\	l	|
1101	D	CR	GS	-	=	M	]	m	}
1110	E	SO	RS	.	>	N	^	n	~
1111	F	SI	US	/	?	O	_	o	DEL

6-bit ASCII subset

11.7   More on Decimal Coding

Although almost all decimal applications now use the simple "BCD" coding in which four bits as { 0000, 0001, ..., 1000, 1001 } represent the digits 0 ...9, with weights {8, 4, 2, 1} there are other representations which have been important and it is appropriate to mention. Some were used for good technical reasons, while others were used to avoid actual or apparent patent protection on the 8421 code. A comprehensive review of early decimal coding is included in Richards [84].

Examples of these codes are shown in Table **11.11** and are explained in the following text. Not all are unique, or even well-defined. There are two columns headed "BCD". The left hand one is the "direct" and obvious BCD code discussed earlier, while the right hand column is derived from the "BCD" card code.

4221 Apart from BCD {8, 4, 2, 1}, the only important decimal code seems to be "4221" with weights of {4, 2, 2, 1} (or often as {2, 4, 2, 1 }). This is a "self-complementing" code, in which inverting the bits gives the 9s complement of the decimal value. There are alternative codings

Table 11.11: Examples of Various Decimal Codings

	BCD	4221		excess 3		2 out of 5		biquinary
N		N	$9-N$	N	$9-N$	IBM 650	BCD	
0	0000	0000	1111	0011	1100	00110	01010	01 00001
1	0001	0001	1110	0100	1011	00011	10001	01 00010
2	0010	0010	1101	0101	1010	00101	10010	01 00100
3	0011	0011	1100	0110	1001	01001	00011	01 01000
4	0100	0110	0111	0111	1000	01010	10100	01 10000
5	0101	1001	1000	1000	0111	01100	00101	10 00001
6	0110	1100	0011	1001	0110	10001	00110	10 00010
7	0111	1101	1000	1010	0101	10010	11000	10 00100
8	1000	1110	0001	1011	0100	10100	01001	10 01000
9	1001	1111	0000	1100	0011	11000	01010	10 10000

for the 4221 code such as {4 → 1000, 5 → 0111}, subject always to the constraint that 9s complements of the digits use 1s complements of the codes.

excess-3 This is another self-complementing code and represents a digit N by the BCD representation of $N + 3$. It has been used in some computers.

2 out of 5 These are examples of "constant-parity" codes, perhaps more correctly "constant weight") where all representations have the same number of "1" bits. The 2 out of 5 codes have 2 1s and 3 0s for each digit, which can represent $^5C_2 = 10$ values. (They use as many bits per digit as a BCD code with conventional parity.)

Two versions of the 2-out-of-5 constant parity code are shown in the table. The "IBM 650" version shown is that used in the IBM 650 computer (Brooks & Iverson, 1963) [14] for data in memory. Except when coding the digit '0', its bits have weights of { 6, 3, 2, 1, 0 }; the '0' bit functions as a parity (which is a interesting example of parity). The column headed "BCD" uses BCD codes with parity as far as possible. Representations with a single 1-bit have a parity bit added, while those with two 1s need no extra parity. Digits 0 and 7 with respectively 0 and 3 bits need special representation.

biquinary This code uses 7 bits per digit, broken into groups of 2 and 5; as each group must have precisely one 1-bit it is another constant parity code. The two bits of the first group have weights of 5 and 0, while the 5 bits of the second group have weights of 4, 3, 2, 1 and 0. (The coding resembles that of an abacus.)

The biquinary code was used in the processing logic of the IBM 650 following its use in the Bell Laboratories Mark V [63] and Harvard Mark II [1] relay computers described in the middle 1940s.

Table 11.12: The Weighted 4-Bit Decimal Codings

c	8	7	-4	-2		7	4	2	1		6	3	2	-1		5	4	-3	2
	8	6	-4	1		7	4	2	-1	czp	6	3	2	-2		5	3	2	1
c	8	6	-4	-1		7	4	-2	1		6	3	1	1	c	5	3	2	-1
	8	5	-4	2		7	4	-2	-1	czp	6	3	1	-1		5	3	1	1
	8	5	-4	-2		7	3	2	1	czp	6	3	-1	1	zp	5	3	1	-1
	8	4	3	-2		7	3	2	-1		6	3	-1	-1	zp	5	3	-1	1
	8	**4**	**2**	**1**	c	7	3	-2	1	czp	6	3	-2	2		5	3	-2	1
	8	4	2	-1	z	7	3	-2	-1		6	3	-2	1		5	2	2	1
	8	4	-2	1	z	7	-3	2	1	z	6	3	-2	-1		5	2	2	-1
c	8	4	-2	-1		7	-3	2	-1		6	2	2	1	c	5	2	1	1
	8	4	-3	2		7	-4	2	1	c	6	2	2	-1	c	4	4	3	-2
	8	4	-3	-2		7	-4	2	-1	zp	6	2	-2	1		4	4	2	1
c	8	-4	3	2	c	7	-6	5	3	zp	6	-2	2	1	c	4	4	2	-1
	8	-4	3	-2		6	5	4	-3	z	6	-3	2	1		4	4	-2	1
	8	-4	2	1	c	6	5	-3	1		6	-4	3	2		4	3	2	1
	8	-4	2	-1		6	5	-4	3		6	-4	2	1		4	3	2	-1
	8	-4	-2	1	c	6	5	-4	2		6	-5	4	3	c	4	3	1	1
c	8	-5	4	2		6	4	3	-2		5	4	3	-2	c	**4**	**2**	**2**	**1**
c	8	-6	4	3		6	4	2	1	czp	5	4	3	-3	c	3	3	2	1
	8	-6	4	1		6	4	2	-1		5	4	2	1		-6	5	4	3
	7	6	-5	3	c	6	4	-2	1		5	4	2	-1		-7	6	5	3
	7	5	-3	1		6	4	-2	-1		5	4	-2	1					
	7	5	-3	-1	c	6	4	-3	2		5	4	-2	-1					
c	7	5	-4	1		6	3	2	1	czp	5	4	-3	3					

Because the conventional BCD coding with weights of $8, 4, 2, 1$ uses only $5/8$ of the available combinations, there are other ways of representing decimal digits with 4 bits. Richards [84] gives a table with 70 weighted codes, but as he comments "the listing is more for the record than any practical value". In similar spirit, Table **11.12** extends his listing and shows 93 possible codes for decimal digits, where each of the four bits has a constant weight. The listing here has been prepared by a search of all possible 4-bit codes and is believed to be complete. The weights are ordered in non-increasing absolute values. The two "boxed" entries are the usual BCD codes. Special codes are flagged as —

c "Self-complementing" codes; inverting all the bits of these codes gives the 9s complement of the original value. [Assume a weight vector **w** where

$\sum w_i = 9$. A digit vector $\mathbf{d}$ represents a value $\sum d_i w_i = N$. To complement the representation, replace each d_i by $1 - d_i$; the changed value is then $\sum(1-d_i)w_i = \sum w_i - \sum d_i w_i = 9-N$, which is the 9s complement.]

p Each of these codes is a permutation of another code; half are redundant.

z These allow 0 to be represented by a non-zero code; the codeword 0000 is legitimate, but with these weights there is always another way of representing a zero value; all codes have some negative weights.

11.8   Roman Numbers, and Oddities

Here we take a further look at Roman numbers. They provide an excellent example of a poorly-designed number system; assuming that is that they were ever really designed at all.

To recap, the "official" Roman number system is based on the symbols I=1, V=5, X=10, L=50, C=100, D=500, M=1000. Numbers are written in *decreasing* significance of the symbols, adding the represented values. The symbols I, X, C and M may be repeated, so that XX represents 20 and CCC 300. However a lesser symbol may be written as a prefix to an immediately greater one, and is then *subtracted*, so that IV represents 4 and XC 90, although 90 can be written as LXXXX and 4 as IIII.

Despite the problems to be discussed, the Roman representation seems now to be well defined and stable, at least for values up to MMMCMXCIX. As the Roman representation is now usually restricted to dates and page numbers, this limit is not important.

That Roman numbers are not uniquely defined is immediately obvious from many clock faces, which use IIII for 4 and VIIII for 9. But these are the least of the variations. Ifrah [61] discusses the extension of Roman numbers to larger values; the extensions are best described as inconsistent and confusing. For example, an overline *could* represent multiplication by 1000, so that $\overline{\text{M}}$ represented 1 000 000. But the overline could also represent letters being used as numerals. To reduce *this* confusion, the overline could be accompanied by side bars giving

$$557\,274 = |\overline{\text{DLVII}}|\ \text{CCLXXIV} = 557 \times 1000 + 274$$

Or, the sidebars could sometimes mean multiplication by 100 000! The Roman number system was conducive to neither accuracy nor arithmetic.

There is doubt about even uniqueness of representation. Within the basic rules of adding most values, but subtracting lesser prefixes, there seems to be precedent for almost anything that worked! Or rather, anything that looked as though it might work!

Should 999 be written as CMXCIX, as IM, or perhaps as XMIX? There is even precedent for writing 18 as IIXX [26], but also for writing 2000 as IIM where the prefix acts as a multiplier! [9]

There is no uniform rule by which the progression from I $\rightarrow$ II implies VIII $\rightarrow$ IX, and so on. While it might be obvious that I + II $\rightarrow$ III, is there *any* obvious reason why MCMXCVIII+II $\rightarrow$ MM?

Variations on the Roman number system were many and inconsistent. From a book on one-letter words [20], we can obtain the codes in Figure **11.1**.

Figure 11.1: Roman Digits—Usual and Unusual

B	300	*C	100	*D	500	E	250	#F	40	G	400
H	200	*I	1	J	1	K	250	*L	50	*M	1000
N	90	O	11	P	400	#Q	500	#R	80	S	70
T	160	V	5	*X	10	#Y	150	#Z	2000		

"Standard" codes are preceded by *; occasional mediæval codes by #

The general level of Roman mathematical ability is well illustrated by their calendar [24, pp 40ff]. When Julius Cæsar introduced the "Julian Calendar" in 46 BCE (having taken advice from Egyptian astronomers, who possibly knew even then that a year of $365\frac{1}{4}$ days was not completely accurate) he had first to decree a year of 445 days to correct for accumulated errors and "adjustments". But before long the priests started having leap years every *three* years instead of four.... And matters were not helped by counting years afresh with each new Emperor's reign.

The problems remained until work by Cassiodorus and Dioysius Exeguus introduced the "*Anno Dominii*" (AD or CE) calendar around 520 [24, pp 96–101], calculating all dates from a calculable historical date.

---

[9]Many of these aberrations may do no more than reflect the incompetence and innumeracy of the workers concerned. The mistakes of stonemasons are especially durable.

11.9   Scaling Invariance

The material of this section is rather philosophical, dealing with the underlying justification for logarithmic representations and, especially, floating-point. While it somewhat removed from most ideas of Computer Data it is a topic which is seldom described. But, and this is the most important, I found it interesting!

In 1881 Simon Newcomb observed that the earlier pages of a book of logarithms showed much greater use than later pages, and in 1938 Frank Benford found that over an enormous variety of naturally occurring values, about 30% had a first digit of 1, 18% started with 2, but only about 5% started with a 9. Empirically, Benford's law states that the probability of the first digit of a value being n varies as $\log(1+1/n)$. It was then shown by Pinkham [80] in 1961 that this distribution follows from combining many independent distributions.

Hamming [51] deals specifically with floating-point numbers in computers, showing that values in base b follow the *reciprocal distribution*

$$r(x) = \frac{1}{x \ln b}$$

In particular he shows that this is a *limiting distribution*, to which others tend under multiplication and division, stating that this fact is "well-known (to comparatively few people)"[10]. He also discusses the distribution of floating-point exponents and conjectures that exponents tend to a normal distribution, with a variance proportional to the number of operations.

Physically, Benford's law follows from the requirement that physical values must maintain their mutual relationships irrespective of any change of units or scaling. Computationally, the principle of scaling invariance has important consequences in the design of number representations for physical quantities. Here, it may be stated as –

> *The results of a computation should be independent of the system of units, after allowing for any necessary scaling to reconcile the units.*

As an adjunct to the principle of scaling invariance, there are good economic reasons to avoid excessive precision in number representation. Excessive precision costs money in hardware and storage because both costs increase at least

---

[10]This phrase, or variants, seem to be a "Hamming trademark".

linearly with precision. It also costs execution time with multiplication and division often increasing as $n \log n$ or n^2 for n-bit precision; "higher" functions often show an even stronger variation of cost *versus* precision. Thus we assume that the *calculation precision* should be commensurate with *data precision* (with a sufficient guard against rounding and truncation errors), but not greatly in excess of that precision.

Real-world problems may be set and solved in any acceptable set of physical units (such as inches or centimetres, kilograms or pounds). After scaling appropriate to the units, results should be the same in any consistent system. Thus, the final answer should not depend on whether the calculation is done in units of metres, centimetres or kilometres (or even nanometres or lightyears!).

In the *large scale* conversion between older cgs (centimetre-gram-second) and newer MKS (metre-kilogram-second) units immediately introduces factors of 100 in length and 1000 in mass, with derived factors of 10^5 for force (1 Newton = 10^5 dyne) and 10^7 for work (1 Joule = 10^7 erg). Further complications arise in the cgs system, where two systems of electrical units, electromagnetic units (emu) and electrostatic units (esu), differ by the velocity of light ($c \approx 3 \times 10^{10}$) as the scaling factor, or even by a ratio of $c^2 \approx 9 \times 10^{20}$). Just changing the measurement units can change numerical values by factors up to 3×10^{10}, placing considerable demands on the number system. Fixed-point integers or fractions are certainly inappropriate.

A length of 500 metres (MKS) corresponds to a length of 50 000 centimetres (cgs); a fixed-point precision adequate for MKS units is quite inadequate for cgs units. MKS values to cgs precision will appear to be much more accurate than cgs values for the corresponding calculation, with correspondingly reduced rounding and truncation. The results will *seem* to be much more accurate than with cgs units, in violation of the principle of scaling invariance. The differences are even more significant when cgs electrostatic and electromagnetic units are compared.

In the *small scale* the need for robustness against scaling by small values (say < 20) implies a small number base in the floating-point representation to avoid significant changes in precision over relatively small changes in value. The IBM S/360 representation is notorious in regard to small-scale invariance because the hexadecimal base makes the precision vary between 21–24 bits as values change over a range of 1:16. Its representation of $\pi/4$ is about one decimal digit more accurate than the representation of 2π.

The ideal representation should have a fixed precision that is quite independent of any multiplicative scaling; this implies a fixed-point logarithm as the "best" representation. But the logarithmic representations, as described above, have their own particular problems and are little used. The usual representation (floating-point) then copies directly the standard scientific representation, with the significant digits normalised to a value of $O(1)$ and an exponential scaling factor (that contains the logarithmic aspect).

Chapter 12

Concluding Comments

It is now nearly two-thirds of a century since the first computers operated. In that time computers have "grown" so that, compared with even 25 years ago, (one human generation) a computer then equivalent to a supercomputer (a "strategic export") is now a pocket-sized consumer item and the computing equipment for a major data centre of similar age corresponds to that now on a domestic desk.

In that time there have been corresponding changes in data representation within computers. Although the main data aggregates (arrays, stacks, queues, lists, hash tables, *etc*) appeared very quickly, it took much longer to stabilise the representation of the individual components; that development has been a major theme of this book. Thus we have seen various ways of representing integers (and fractions), "real" numbers and characters (and text), all as described here. Many of these have been tried and found wanting. It is quite likely (famous last words) that there will be little major development beyond what is given here at this most fundamental level.

While it might be possible to squeeze a bit more speed out of processors and somewhat higher data density on storage devices (more famous last words), there are very real physical limits, many involving the time for communication between physically separated components. The major future developments in computing are likely to involve intensive computing on extensive data, areas which are far beyond this book.

Thus this book attempts to encapsulate the present state of data representation within computers and, hopefully, the situation at this level for some time into the future.

Bibliography

[1] H.Aiken, "The Automatic Sequence Controlled Calculator", 1946 see Randell [82]

[2] G.M.Amdahl, G.A.Blaauw, and F.P.Brooks Jr, "Architecture of the IBM System/360", *IBM Journ of Res and Devel.*, Vol 8, No.2, pp 87 – 101, April 1964

[3] A.Apostolico, A.S.Fraenkel, "Robust transmission of unbounded strings using Fibonacci representations", *IEEE Trans.on Inform.Theory*, Vol IT–33 (1987), pp 238–245.

[4] B.Arazi, *A Commonsense Approach to the Theory of Error Correcting Codes*, MIT Press, Cambridge MA, 1988

[5] J.V.Atanasoff, "Computing machine for the solution of large systems of linear algebraic equations", (unpublished memorandum), Ames, Iowa, Iowa State College, Aug 1940. see Randell [82]

[6] D.E.Atkins, "Higher-Radix Division Using Estimates of the Divisor and Partial Remainders", *IEEE Trans.Comp.*, August 1970, pp 720–733

[7] C.Gordon Bell and Allen Newell, *Computer Structures: Readings and Examples*, McGraw-Hill, 1971

[8] E.L.Bentley, *Bentley's Second Phrase Code*, E.L.Bentley, London and Prentice-Hall New York, 1930

[9] J.L.Bentley, A.C.Yao, "An almost optimal solution for unbounded searching", *Info.Proc.Letters*, Vol 5, No 3, pp 82–87 Aug 1976

[10] R.E.Blahut, *Theory and Practice of Error Control Codes*, Addison-Wesley, 1983.

[11] E.Bloch, *The engineering design of the Stretch computer*, Proc FJCC 1959, pp 48–59 (reprinted in Bell & Newell[7]).

[12] A.D.Booth, "A signed binary multiplication technique", *Quarterly Journal of Mechanics and Applied Mathematics*, Vol 4, No.2, pp 236–240, 1951

[13] N.Borenstein and N.Freed,, "MIME (Multipurpose Internet Mail Extensions) Part One: Mechanisms for Specifying and Describing the Format of Internet Message Bodies", *RFC 1522*, Internet Engineering Task Force, September 1993

[14] F.P.Brooks and K.E.Iverson *Automatic Data Processing*, New York, NY : John Wiley, 1963

[15] F.P.Brooks, Private Communication, 2000

[16] W.Buchholz, "Origin of the Word Byte", *Annals of the History of Computing*, Vol 10, No.4, p 340, 1989.

[17] A.W.Burks, H.Goldstine and J.von Neumann "Preliminary Discussion of the Logical Design of an Electronic Computing Instrument", 1946 see Randell [82]

[18] —,*B7000/B6000 Algol Reference Manual*, Burroughs Corporation, Detroit MI, May 1977.

[19] D.Cohen, "On Holy Wars and a Plea for Peace", *Computer*, Vol 14, No 10, pp 48–54, Oct 1981.
See also `http://www.ietf.org/rfc/ien/ien137.txt`

[20] C.Conley, , *One-Letter Words – A Dictionary* Harper-Collins, 2005

[21] D.Crocker, "Standard for the Format of ARPA Internet Text Messages", *RFC 822*, Internet Engineering Task Force, August 1982

[22] P.Deutsch, J-L.Gailly, "ZLIB Compressed Data Format Specification version 3.3", *RFC 1950*, Internet Engineering Task Force, May 1960

[23] R.W.Doran, "The Gray Code", Report 131, Department of Computer Science, The University of Auckland, March 1996.

[24] D.E.Duncan, "The Calendar", Fourth Estate, London, 1998

[25] P.Elias, "Universal Codeword Sets and Representations of the Integers", *IEEE Trans.Info.Theory*, Vol IT 21, No 2, pp 194–203, Mar 1975

[26] *Encyclopaedia Britannica*, 15th Ed *Mathematics, History of* Vol 11 p 647 1978

[27] S.Even, M.Rodeh, "Economical Encoding of Commas Between Strings", *Comm ACM*, Vol 21, No 4, pp 315–317, April 1978.

[28] P.M.Fenwick, "A Binary Representation for Decimal Numbers", *The Australian Computer Journal*, Vol 4, No 6, pp 146–149, Nov 1972.

[29] Fenwick, P.M., "A Fast-Carry Adder with CMOS Transmission Gates", *Computer Journal*, Vol 30, No 1, pp 7779, 1987.

[30] P.M.Fenwick, "Ziv-Lempel encoding with multi-bit flags", *Proc.Data Compression Conference, DCC-93*, Snowbird, Utah, pp 138–147, Mar 1993

[31] Fenwick, P.M., "High-radix Division with Approximate Quotient-digit Estimation", *Journal for Universal Computer Science (J.UCS)* Vol 1, No 1, pp 2–22 Jan 1995

[32] P.M.Fenwick, "A new data structure for cumulative frequency tables", *Software – Practice and Experience*, Vol 24, No 3, pp 327–336 Mar 1994.

[33] P.M.Fenwick, "Punctured Elias Codes for variable-length coding of the integers", Report 131, Department of Computer Science, The University of Auckland, March 1996.

[34] P.M.Fenwick, "Variable-Length Integer Codes Based on the Goldbach Conjecture, and Other Additive Codes", *IEEE Trans.Inform.Theory*, Vol 48, No 8, pp 2412–2417, Aug 2002.

[35] P.M.Fenwick, "Zeckendorf Integer Arithmetic", *Fibonacci Quarterly*, Vol 415, pp 405–413, Nov 2003. Vol 41.5, Nov 2003, pp 405–413

[36] Fenwick, P.M., Burrows Wheeler Compression with Variable Length Integer Codes, *Software Practice and Experience*, Vol 32, No 13, pp 13071316, Nov 2002

[37] E.R.Fiala, D.H.Greene, "Data Compression with Finite Windows", *Comm ACM*, Vol 32, No 4, pp 490–505 , April 1989

[38] Fletcher, J.G., "An Arithmetic Checksum for Serial Transmissions", *IEEE Trans.on Comm.*, Vol.COM-30, No.1, January 1982, pp 247-252.

[39] A.S.Fraenkel, "Systems of Numeration", *Amer.Math.Monthly*, Vol 92 (1985) pp 105–114.

[40] A.S.Fraenkel and S.T.Klein, "Robust universal complete codes for transmission and compression", *Discrete Applied Mathematics* Vol 64 (1996) pp 31–55.

[41] G.R.Freeman, *Hidden Stonehenge*, Watkins Publishing, 2012

[42] P.Gannon, *"Colossus: Bletchley Park's Greatest Secret"*, Atlantic Books, 2006

[43] D.Goldberg, "What Every Computer Scientist Should Know About Floating-Point Arithmetic"; *ACM Computing Surveys*, Vol 23, No 1, Mar 1991 pp5–47.

[44] D.Goldberg, "Computer Arithmetic"; Appendix A in *Computer Architecture: a Quantitative Approach*, J.L.Hennesey and D.A. Patterson, Morgan Kaufmann, San Mateo, California, 1990 (See Hennesey & Patterson below).

[45] S.W.Golomb, "Run-Length Encodings", *IEEE Trans Info.Theory*, Vol 12 pp 399–401 1966.

[46] D.Goldsmith, M.Davis, "UTF-7 A Mail-Safe Transformation Format of Unicode", *RFC 1642*,Internet Engineering Task Force, July 1994

[47] "Gray Code", Wikipedia 2011. `en.wikipedia.org/wiki/Gray_code`

[48] Denis Guedj, *Numbers – the Universal Language*, Thames and Hudson, London, 1996.

[49] Gumm, H.P. "A new class of check-digit methods for arbitrary number systems", *IEEE Trans Inf. Theory*, Vol 31, No 1, (Jan 1985, pp 102–105.

[50] R.W.Hamming, "Error Detecting and Correcting Codes", *Bell Sys. Tech. Journ.*, Vol 29, pp 147 – 160, 1950.

[51] R.W.Hamming, "On the Distribution of Numbers", *Bell Sys. Tech. Journ*, Vol 49, pp 1609 – 1625, 1970.

[52] R.W.Hamming, *Coding and Information Theory*, 2nd Ed, Prentice-Hall, Englewood Cliffs NJ 1986

[53] F.G.Heath, "Origins of the Binary Code", *Scientific American*, pp 76–83, August 1972

[54] J.L.Hennessy and D.A.Patterson, *Computer Architecture : a Qualitative Approach*, Morgan Kaufmann, San Mateo CA, 1990.

[55] H.Hoeve, T.Timmermans and L.B.Vries, "Error correction and concealment in the Compact Disk system", *Philips Tech Rev.*, Vol 40, pp 166–172, 1982.

[56] D.A.Huffman, "A method for the construction of minimum-redundancy codes", *Proc IRE*, Vol 40, pp 1098–1101, 1952.

[57] J.Ibsen, Private Communication, 2006

[58] "IEEE Standard for Binary Floating-Point Arithmetic", *IEEE*, 1985

[59] ITU-T Recommendation X.224, Annex D, "Checksum Algorithms", November, 1993, pp 144, 145.

[60] G.Ifrah, *Universal History of Numbers – The Computer and Information Revolution*, (English Translation), Harvil, 2000

[61] G.Ifrah, *Numbers– The Universal Language*, (English Translation), Thames and Hudson, 1998

[62] K.E.Iverson, *A Programming Language*, Wiley, 1962

[63] J.Juley, "The Ballistic Computer", see Randell [82]

[64] T.Kilburn, D.B.G.Edwards, D.Aspinall, "A Parallel Arithmetic Unit Using a Saturated-Transistor Fast-Carry Circuit", *Proc IEE*, Vol 107B, p573, Nov 1960

[65] N.G.Kingsbury and P.J.W.Rayner, "Digital filtering using logarithmic arithmetic", *Electron.Lett.* Vol 7, pp 56–58, 1971.

[66] D.E.Knuth, "The Art of Computer Programming", Vol 2 *Seminumerical Algorithms*, Addison Wesley 1969

[67] I.Koren, *Computer Arithmetic Algorithms*, Prentice Hall, Englewood Cliffs, NY, 1993.

[68] M.Lehman and N.Burla, "Skip Techniques for High-Speed Carry Propagation in Binary Arithmetic Units", *IRE Trans Elec Comp.*, Vol EC-10, pp 691–698, Dec 1961.

[69] V.E.Levenstein, "On the redundancy and delay of separable codes for the natural numbers", *Problems of Cybernetics*, Vol 20, pp 173–179, 1968.

[70] H.P.Luhn, U.S.Patent No.2,950,048; filed January 6, 1954, granted August 23, 1960.

[71] O.L.MacSorley, "High Speed Arithmetic in Binary Computers", *Proc IRE*, Vol 49, pp 67–91, Jan 1961.

[72] S.McCartney, *ENIAC*, Walker and Co, New York, 1999

[73] J.C.Majithia and D.Levan, "A note on base-2 logarithm computations", *IEEE Proc*, Vol 61, pp 1519–1520, 1973.

[74] G.Menzies, *The Lost Empire of Atlantis*, Phoenix, 2011

[75] J.N.Mitchell, "Computer Multiplication and division using binary logarithms", *IRE Trans Elec.Comp.*, Vol EC-11, pp 512–517, Aug 1962.

[76] P.Montuschi and L.Ciminiera, "Over-Redundant Digit Sets and the Design of Digit-By-Digit Division Units", *IEEE Trans.Comp.*, Vol 43, No 3, March 1994, pp 269 – 277.

[77] K.Moore, "Representation of Non-Ascii Text in Internet Message Headers", *RFC 1522*, Internet Engineering Task Force, September 1993

[78] A.R.Omondi, *Computer arithmetic systems : algorithms, architecture, and implementation*, Prentice Hall, 1994.

[79] E.W.Phillips, "Binary Calculation", *J.Inst Actuaries*, Vol 67, pp 187–221, 1936, see Randell [82]

[80] R.S.Pinkham, "On the Distribution of First Significant Digits", *Annal.Math.Statistics*, Vol 32, pp 1223 – 1230, 1961

[81] J.A.Rajchman, G.A.Morton, A.W.Vance, *Report on Electronic Predictors for Anti-Aircraft Fire Control.* RCA Manufacturing Company, Camden NJ, April 1942. see Randell [82]

[82] Brian Randell (ed), *The Origins of Digital Computers*, 3rd Edition, Springer-Verlag, 1982.

[83] R.F.Rice, "Some Practical Universal Noiseless Coding Techniques", Jet Propulsion Laboratory, JPL Publication 79-22, Pasadena, California Mar 1979

[84] R.K.Richards, *Arithmetic operations in digital computers*, Van Nostrand, Princeton, N.J.,1955

[85] J.E.Robertson, "A New Class of Digital Division Methods", *IEEE Trans.Comp.*, Vol C-7, No 8, September 1958, pp 218–222

[86] D. Salomon, D. Bryant, G. Motta, *Handbook of Data Compression* , Springer, Englewood Cliffs, N.J., 2010

[87] K.Sayood (ed), *Lossless Compression Handbook*, Academic Press, 2003

[88] J.Challoner (ed) *1001 Inventions that changed the world*, New Burlington Books, 2008 ISBN 978-1-84566-275-2.

[89] C.E.Shannon, "A Symbolic Analysis of Relay and Switching Circuits", *American Institute of Electrical Engineers Trans*, Vol 57 (1938), pp713-723. Reprinted in *Claude Elwood Shannon: Collected Papers*, N.J.A.Sloane and A.D.Wyner (editors), IEEE Press, New York, 1993, 471-495.

[90] C.E.Shannon, "A Mathematical Theory of Communication", *Bell Sys.Tech, Journ.*, Vol 27, pp 379–423 July, and pp 623–656 October 1948.

[91] P.H.Sterbenz, *Floating-point computation*, Prentice-Hall, Englewood Cliffs, N.J., 1973

[92] Nancy Stern, *From ENIAC to UNIVAC*, Digital Press, Bedford MA, 1981

[93] L.Stone, M.Greenwald, C.Partridge and J Hughes, "Performance of Checksums and CRCs over Real Data", *IEEE/ACM Trans.on Networking*, Vol 6, No 5, pp529 – 543 Oct 1998.

[94] A.Svoboda, "An Algorithm for Division", *Information Proc Machines*, Vol 9, pp 25 - 32, 1963.

[95] E.E.Swartzlander (Ed) *Computer Arithmetic*, Dowden, Hutchinson and Ross, 1980.

[96] E.E.Swartzlander and A.G.Alexopoulos "THe Sign/Logarithm Number System", *IEEE Trans.Comput.*, Vol C-24, pp 1238–1242, 1975.

[97] D.W.Sweeney, "An analysis of floating point addition", *IBM Sys Journ.*, Vol 4, pp 31–42, 1965

[98] J.Swift, *Travels into Several Remote Nations of the World*, better known as *Gulliver's Travels*, many modern publishers.

[99] F. J. Taylor, R. Gill, J. Joseph, J. Radke, "A 20-bit logarithmic number system processor", *IEEE Trans Comp*, Vol 37, pp 190–199, Feb 1988.

[100] R.Temple, *Egyptian Dawn*, Arrow Books, 2011

[101] K.D.Tocher, "Techniques of Multiplication and Division for Automatic Binary Computers", *Quart.Journ.Mech.Appl.Math.*, Vol 11 Pt 3 pp 364–384

[102] L.Torres y Quevedo, *Essays on Automatics – Its Definition – Theoretical Extent of its Applications.*see Randell [82]

[103] Henry S.Tropp, "Origin of the Term Bit", *Annals of the History of Computing*, Vol 10, No 4, pp 336–340, 1989.

[104] Turing, A.M."On Computable Numbers, with an Application to the Entscheidungsproblem". *Proceedings of the London Mathematical Society.* Vol 42 No.2: pp230–65.1936.

[105] —, *The Unicode Standard, Version 2.0*, Addison-Wesley, 1996

[106] —, *The Unicode Standard, Version 6.2*, the Unicode Consortium, 2012 (`http://www.unicode.org/versions/Unicode6.2.0`)

[107] Verhoeff, J."Error Detecting Decimal Codes", *Mathematical Centre Tract 29*, The Mathematical Centre, Amsterdam, 1969.

[108] N.R.Wagner and P.S.Putter, "Error Detecting Decimal Digits", *Comm ACM*, Vol 32, No 1, Jan 1989, pp 106–110

[109] C.S.Wallace, "A Suggestion for a Fast Multiplier", *IEEE Trans Elec Comp*, Vol EC-13, pp 14–17, Feb 1964.

[110] D.J.Wheeler Private Communication, 2006

[111] L.K.Yu and D.M.Lewis, "A 30-bit integrated logarithmic number system processor", *IEEE J.of Solid-State Circuits*, Vol 26, pp 1433–1440, Oct 1991.

[112] E.Zeckendorf, "Représentation des nombres naturels par une somme de nombres de Fibonacci ou de nombres de Lucas", *Bull.Soc.Roy.Sci.Liège*, Vol 41 (1972), pp 179–182

[113] K.Zuse "Method for Automatic Execution of Calculations with the aid of computers", German patent Z23624 (11 Apr 1936)

Index

www.ingramcontent.com/pod-product-compliance
Lightning Source LLC
Chambersburg PA
CBHW041428050326

40690CB00002B/468